Wilberforce, Wil
A letter on the abolition of the slave trade

Wilberforce, William

A letter on the abolition of the slave trade

Inktank publishing, 2018

www.inktank-publishing.com

ISBN/EAN: 9783747766576

All rights reserved

This is a reprint of a historical out of copyright text that has been re-manufactured for better reading and printing by our unique software. Inktank publishing retains all rights of this specific copy which is marked with an invisible watermark.

A LETTER

ON

THE ABOLITION

OF THE

SLAVE TRADE;

ADDRESSED TO THE

FREEHOLDERS AND OTHER INHABITANTS

OF

YORKSHIRE.

By W. WILBERFORCE, Esq.

" There is neither Greek nor Jew, circumcision nor uncircumcision, Barbarian, Scythian, bond nor free: but CHRIST is all, and in all. Put on therefore bowels of mercies, kindness," &c.—COL. iii. 11. 12.

" GOD hath made of one blood all nations of men, for to dwell on all the face of the earth."—ACTS xvii. 26.

LONDON:

Printed by Luke Hansard & Sons,

FOR T. CADELL AND W. DAVIES, STRAND; And
J. HATCHARD, PICCADILLY.

1807.

CONTENTS.

	Page
INTRODUCTION	1
Sources of Information	11
Methods by which the Slaves are supplied in Africa	18
Slave Trade's Effects in the Interior and on the Coast	30
Proof of Abolitionists' Facts decisive, and contrary Allegations groundless	47
Plea against Abolition, that Negroes are an inferior Race	53-4
Opponents' description of Negro Character contrasted with other Accounts	57
Argument from Africa's never having been civilized, considered	71
New Phænomenon—Interior of Africa more civilized than Coast	86
Plea of Opponents, that Slaves State in Africa extremely miserable	89
Plea from Cruelty of African Despots	92
Ditto, that refused Slaves would be massacred in case of Abolition	95
Middle Passage	96
Opponents' grand Objection—that Stock of Slaves cannot be kept up in West Indies without Importations	103
Presumptive Arguments against the above Allegation, from universal Experience	104
Positive Proof that the Stock of Slaves might be kept up without Importations—Argument stated	109

I.—Abuses sufficient to account for great Decrease.

The Increase a subordinate Object of Attention	116
insufficient Feeding	119

CONTENTS.

	Page
Defective Clothing and Lodging, and over-working	122
Moral Vices of the System - - - - -	123
Especially Degradation of the Negro Race, and its important Effects - - - - - -	127
Proofs of Degradation—a Negro Sale - -	133
Sale of Negroes for Owners Debts - - -	136
Working under the Whip - - - - -	140
Cruel and indecent Public Punishments - -	144
Inadequate legal Protection - - - -	147
Ditto, considered in its Effect of degrading, and late Barbadoes Incidents - - - - -	153
Three other Vices of the System—Abfenteeship	177
Pressure of the Times - - - - -	186
West Indian Speculations - - - -	190
Admirals and Governors contrary Evidence and Remarks - - - - - - -	192
Decisive Proof that Slaves' State is miserable	205

II.—Yet, though Abuses so great, the Decrease quite inconsiderable - - - - - 211

III.—Hence, Abuses being corrected, Slaves would rapidly increase - - - - - 215

West Indians most plausible Objections, and remaining Pleas against Abolition - - -	216
Grand Plea, that Co-operation of Colonial Legislatures necessary - - - - - -	219
Disproved, both by Reason - - - -	222
And Experience - - - - - -	225
Mr. Burke's supposed Plan - - - - -	238
Efficacy and beneficial Consequences of Abolition	241
Immediate, preferable to gradual, Abolition -	254
Abolitionists vindicated for not emancipating	256
Abolition's Effects on Commerce and Manufactures	261
Present West Indian System ruinous - -	266
West Indian Opposition to Abolition accounted for,	274
Strong Party Spirit, Proofs - - - -	282
No Hopes of West Indian Opposition ceasing	288

CONTENTS.

	Page
Appeal to gradual Abolitionists	288
Objection to Abolition on the ground of Slave Trade's Effects on our Marine	302
Objection, that Foreign Nations would carry on Slave Trade if we relinquished it	305
Objection to Abolition on grounds of Justice	312
Objection on grounds of Religion	318
Abolitionists' further Plea against Slave Trade— Insurrection, extreme danger of	321
Our Population drained to defend the West Indies	330
Summary View of the Miseries produced by the Slave Trade	333
Instance of Individual Misery	340
Conclusion	345

APPENDIX.—A few Specimens in Proof of Effects of the Slave Trade in Africa, and of the natural Dispositions and Commercial Aptitudes - - - - - 353 to 394

English Slave Trade as carried on so late as Henry 2d's Time.

For many years I have ardently wished that it had been possible for me to plead, in your presence, the great cause of the Abolition of the Slave Trade. Conscious that I was accountable to you for the discharge of the important trust which your kindness had committed to me, I have longed for such an opportunity of convincing you, that it was not without reason that this question had occupied so large a share of my parliamentary life. I wished you to know, that the cause of my complaint was no minute grievance, which, from my eyes having been continually fixed on it, had swelled by degrees into a false shew of magnitude; no ordinary question, on which my mind, warming in the pursuit of its object, and animated by repeated contentions, had at length felt emotions altogether disproportionate to their subject. Had I however erred, unintentionally, I have too long experienced your candour not to have hoped for your ready forgiveness. On the contrary,

contrary, if the Slave Trade be indeed the foulest blot that ever stained our National character, you will not deem your Representative to have been unworthily employed, in having been among the foremost in wiping it away.

Besides the desire of justifying myself in the judgment of my Constituents, various other motives prompt me to the present address. Fourteen long years have now elapsed since the period when the question was fully argued in Parliament; and the large share of national attention which it then engaged, has since been occupied successively by the various public topics of the day. During the intervening period, also, such strange and interesting spectacles have been exhibited at our very doors, as to banish from the minds of most men all recollection of distant wrongs and sufferings. Thus it is not only by the ordinary effects of the lapse of time, that the impression, first produced by laying open the horrors of the Slave Trade, has been considerably effaced, but by the prodigious events of that fearful interval.

It should also be remembered, that, within the last fourteen or fifteen years, a great change has taken place in the component parts

parts of Parliament, especially in those of the House of Commons; not merely from the ordinary causes, but also from the addition which has been made to the National Legislature by our Union with Ireland. Hence it happens, that, even in the Houses of Parliament themselves, though a distinct impression of the general outlines of the subject may remain, many of its particular features have faded from the recollection. For hence alone surely it can happen, that assertions and arguments formerly driven fairly out of the field, appear once more in array against us. Old concessions are retracted; exploded errors are revived; and we find we have the greater part of our work to do over again. But if in Parliament, nay even in the House of Commons itself, where the subject was once so well known in all its parts, the question is but imperfectly understood, much more is it natural, that great misconceptions should prevail respecting it in the minds of the people at large. Among them, accordingly, great misapprehensions are very general. To myself, as well as to other Abolitionists, opinions are often imputed which we never held, declarations which we never made, designs which we never entertained. These I desire to rectify; and now that the question is once more about to come under the consideration of the legislature,

ture, it may not be useless thus publicly to record the facts and principles on which the Abolitionists rest their cause, and for which, in the face of my country, I am willing to stand responsible.

But farther I hesitate not to avow to you; on the contrary, it would be criminal to withhold the declaration, that of all the motives by which I am prompted to address you, that which operates on me with the greatest force, is, the consideration of the present state and prospects of our country, and of the duty which at so critical a moment presses imperiously on every member of the community, to exert his utmost powers in the public cause.

That the Almighty Creator of the universe governs the world which he has made; that the sufferings of nations are to be regarded as the punishment of national crimes; and their decline and fall, as the execution of His sentence; are truths which I trust are still generally believed among us. Indeed to deny them, would be directly to contradict the express and repeated declarations of the Holy Scriptures. If these truths be admitted, and if it be also true, that fraud, oppression, and cruelty, are crimes of the blackest dye, and that guilt is aggravated in proportion as the
criminal

criminal acts in defiance of clearer light, and of stronger motives to virtue (and these are positions to which we cannot refuse our assent, without rejecting the authority not only of revealed, but even of natural religion); have we not abundant cause for serious apprehension? The course of public events has, for many years, been such as human wisdom and human force have in vain endeavoured to controul or resist. The counsels of the wise have been infatuated; the valour of the brave has been turned to cowardice. Though the storm has been raging for many years, yet, instead of having ceased, it appears to be now increasing in fury; the clouds which have long been gathering around us, have at length almost overspread the whole face of the heavens with blackness. In this very moment of unexampled difficulty and danger, those great political Characters, to the counsels of the one or the other of whom the nation has been used to look in all public exigencies, have both been taken from us. If such be our condition; and if the Slave Trade be a national crime, declared by every wise and respectable man of all parties, without exception, to be a compound of the grossest wickedness and cruelty, a crime to which we cling in defiance of the clearest light, not only in opposition to our own acknowledgments of its guilt, but even of our own declared resolutions to abandon it; is not this then a time in which all who are not perfectly sure that the Providence of God is but a fable, should be strenuous in their endeavours to lighten the vessel of the state, of such a load of guilt and infamy?

Urged by these various considerations, I proceed to lay before you a summary of the principal facts and arguments on which the Abolitionists ground their cause, referring such as may be desirous of more complete information to various original records, * and
for

,* The Report of the Privy Council to the King in 1788, and still more the Reports of the Committee of the House of Commons, to which had been referred the various petitions for and against the abolition, and in the Appendixes to which is contained the Evidence at length of the Witnesses who were examined on that occasion. For the convenience of those who might not have leisure to peruse so voluminous a mass of evidence, an abridged abstract of it was made. This occupies two small octavo volumes, and is entitled "An Abridgement of the Minutes of the Evidence on the Slave Trade. 1790." It is to be purchased at Phillips's, George-yard, Lombard-street.—Various Papers and Accounts, tending to give useful information, have also been laid before the House of Commons from time to time. The titles of these will be found in the House of Commons Journals. See especially a voluminous mass of Papers respecting the Slave Trade, ordered
to

for a more detailed exposition of the reasonings of the two parties, to the printed Report of the Debates in Parliament, * and to various excellent publications which have from time to time been sent into the world. †

The

to be printed 8th June 1804; and another very important set of Communications from the West Indies, ordered for printing 25th February 1805. See also two very interesting Reports of the House of Assembly of Jamaica.

* Vide, especially, an Abstract of the Debate on Mr. Wilberforce's Motion for the Abolition of the Slave Trade in 1791, and of the Debate on a similar Motion in 1792; both printed for Phillips, George-yard, Lombard-street.

† Mr. Clarkson's publications well deserve this epithet, particularly his " Essay on the Impolicy of the " African Slave Trade." See also Remarks on the Decision of the House of Commons concerning the Slave Trade, on April 2d, 1792, by the Rev. J. Gisborne.— Much valuable information likewise concerning Africa is contained in Lord Muncaster's Historical Sketches of the Slave Trade. Again, almost all the principal arguments involved in the discussion concerning the abolition are to be found in Mr. Brougham's Colonial Policy, stated with that author's usual ability.—Once more, a valuable Summary of the Arguments in favour of Abolition, and of the answers to the chief allegations of it's Opponents (by a writer, whose name, if subjoined to it, would have added great weight to the publication) was published two years ago, printed for Hatchard, and Longman and Rees, entitled, a " *Con-* " *cise Statement of the Question, regarding the Abolition* " *of the Slave Trade.*" An Appendix, containing much valuable matter, soon after followed. A valuable publication

The advocates for abolition court inquiry, and are solicitous that their facts should be thoroughly canvassed, and their arguments maturely weighed.

I fear I may have occasion to request your accustomed candour, not to call it partiality, for submitting to you a more defective statement than you might reasonably require from me. But when I inform you that I had just entered on my present task when I was surprized by the dissolution of Parliament, I need scarcely add, that I have been of necessity compelled to employ in a very different manner the time which was to have been allotted to this service. Under my present circumstances, I had almost resolved to delay addressing you till I could look forward to a longer interval of leisure, than the speedily approaching meeting of Parliament will now allow me; but I hope that this address, though it may be defective, will not be erroneous. It may not contain all which I might otherwise lay before you; but what it

cation appeared also some years ago, by a Member of the University of Oxford, now become a dignitary of the church. I might specify several others on particular parts of the case. In short, were it as easy to prevail on mankind to read publications which have been some time before the world, as to peruse a new one, my present task might well be spared.

it does contain will be found, I trust, correct; and if my address should bear the marks of haste, I can truly assure you that the statements and principles which I may hastily communicate to you, have been most deliberately formed, and have been often reviewed with the most serious attention. But I already foresee that my chief difficulty will consist in comprising within any moderate limits, the statements which my undertaking requires, and the arguments to be deduced from them; to select from the immense mass of materials which lies before me, such specimens of more ample details, as, without exhausting the patience of my readers, may convey to their minds some faint ideas, faint indeed in colouring but just in feature and expression, of the objects which it is my office to delineate. If my readers should at any time begin to think me prolix, let them but call to mind the almost unspeakable amount of the interests which are in question, and they will more readily bear with me.

It might almost preclude the necessity of inquiring into the actual effects of the Slave Trade, to consider, arguing from the acknowledged and never failing operation of certain given causes, what must necessarily be

Probable Effects of the Slave Trade.

be its consequences. How surely does a demand for any commodities produce a supply. How certainly should we anticipate the multiplication of thefts, from any increase in number of the receivers of stolen goods. In the present instance, the demand is for men, women, and children. And, can we doubt that illicit methods will be resorted to for supplying them? especially in a country like Africa, imperfectly civilized, and divided in general into petty communities? We might almost anticipate with certainty, the specific modes by which the supply of Slaves is in fact furnished, and foretel the sure effects on the laws, usages, and state of society of the African continent. But any doubts we might be willing to entertain on this head are but too decisively removed, when we proceed in the next place to examine, what are the actual means by which Slaves are commonly supplied, and what are the Slave Trade's known and ascertained consequences? To this part of my subject I intreat peculiar attention; the rather, because I have often found an idea to prevail, that it is the state of the Slaves in the West Indies, the improvement of which is the great object of the Abolitionists. On the contrary, from first to last, I desire it may be borne in mind, that Africa is the

primary

primary subject of our regard. It is the effects of the Slave Trade on Africa, against which chiefly we raise our voices, as constituting a sum of guilt and misery, hitherto, unequalled in the annals of the world.

But, before I proceed to state the facts themselves, which are to be laid before you, it may be useful to make a few remarks on the nature of the evidence by which they are supported; and more especially on the difficulties which it was reasonable to suppose would be experienced in establishing, by positive proof, the existence of practices discreditable to the Slave Trade, notwithstanding the great numbers of British ships which for a very long period have annually visited Africa, and the ample information which on the first view might therefore appear to lie open to our inquiries.

<small>Evidence against the Slave Trade difficult to be procured.</small>

Africa, it must be remembered, is a country which has been very little visited from motives of curiosity. It has been frequented, almost exclusively, by those who have had a direct interest in it's peculiar traffic; as, the agents and factors of the African Company, or of individual Slave merchants, or by the Captains and Officers of slave ships. The situation of captain of an African ship is an employment,

employment, the unpleasant and even dangerous nature of which must be compensated by extraordinary profits. The same remark extends in a degree to all the other officers of slave ships; who, it should also be remarked, may reasonably entertain hopes, if they recommend themselves to their employers, of rising to be Captains. They all naturally look forward, therefore, to the command of a ship, as the prize which is to repay them for all their previous sacrifices and sufferings, and some even of the Surgeons appear, in fact, to have been promoted to it. Could these men be supposed likely to give evidence against the Slave Trade? nay, must not habit, especially when thus combined with interest, be presumed to have had it's usual effect, in so familiarizing them to scenes of injustice and cruelty, as to prevent their being regarded with any proportion of that disgust and abhorrence which they would excite in any mind not accustomed to them? In truth, were the secrets of the prison-house ever so bad, these men could not well be expected to reveal them. But let it also be remembered, that when the call for witnesses was made by Parliament, the question of the Abolition of the Slave Trade had become a party question; and that all the West Indian as well as the African property and influence

were

were combined together in it's defence. The supporters of the trade were the rich and the powerful, the men of authority, influence and connection. They had ships and factories and counting houses, both at home and abroad. Theirs it was, to employ shopkeepers and artizans; theirs to give places of emolument, and the means of rising in life. On the other hand, it was but too obvious (I am sorry to say my own knowledge fully justifies the remark) that, in the great towns especially, in which the African, or West Indian Trade, or both, were principally carried on, any man who was not in an independent situation, and who should come forward to give evidence against the Slave Trade, would expose himself and his family to obloquy and persecution, perhaps to utter ruin. He would become a marked man, and be excluded from all opportunities of improving his condition, or even of acquiring a maintenance among his own natural connections, and in his accustomed mode of life. Any one who will duly weigh the combined effect of all these circumstances, will rather be surprized to hear that any of those who had been actually engaged in carrying on the Slave Trade, were found to give evidence of it's enormities, than that this description of persons was not more numerous.

For,

Evidence actually obtained.

For, notwithstanding all the obstacles to which I have been alluding, much oral testimony of the most valuable kind was obtained from persons who had been engaged in the actual conduct of the Slave Trade. And of by far the greatest part of those witnesses it may be truly said, that the more closely they were examined, and the more strongly their evidence was illustrated by light from other quarters, the more was it's truth decisively established. So much I have thought it the more necessary to observe; because insinuations, to use the softest term, have been not seldom cast against some of the witnesses who gave evidence unfavourable to the Slave Trade, before the House of Commons.—Happily, however, some other sources of information were discovered; and the exact conformity of the intelligence derived from these, with that which has been already mentioned, gave to both indubitable confirmation. A very few men of science were found, who from motives of liberal curiosity had visited those parts of the coast of Africa where the Slave Trade was carried on. Some few also of His Majesty's naval and military officers, who, while on service in Africa, had opportunities of obtaining useful information concerning the Slave Trade, consented to be examined. They were indeed little

on

on shore, and they went to no great distance within the country; but still the facts they stated, were of the utmost importance; the more so, because of the credit which they reflect on the testimony of others, who, on account of their inferior rank in life, might in the judgment of some persons be more exceptionable witnesses.

Lastly, there lay open to the Abolitionists another source of information, to which great attention was due; the acknowledged publications of several persons who at different periods had resided in Africa, some of them for many years, and in high stations, in the employ of the chief Slave trading Companies of the various European nations, and whose accounts had been given to the world long before the Slave Trade had become a subject of public discussion.

Other sources of information:— Old Authors.

It might indeed be presumed, that though no attack had yet been made on the Slave Trade, such persons would be disposed to regard it with a partial and indulgent eye. To it they had owed their fortunes; and, even independently of all pecuniary interest, no man likes to own that he is engaged in a way of life which is hateful and dishonourable. Still, if it be not the express purpose of a narrative to deceive, the truth is apt to

break

break out at intervals, and the Advocates for Abolition might therefore expect to find some indirect proofs, some occasional and incidental notices of the real nature and effects of the Slave Trade. They were at least entitled to claim the full benefit of any facts to the disparagement of the Slave Trade, which should be found in this class of writings; and where these earlier publications, of writers so naturally biassed in favour of the Slave Trade, should exactly accord, in what they might state to it's disparagement, with other living witnesses, several of them, men most respectable in rank and character, and utterly uninterested either way in the decision of the question concerning it's abolition; men too, whose testimony was the result of their own personal knowledge; the facts which should be thus proved, would be established by a force of evidence, little short of absolute demonstration.

Modern valuable information. Lastly, there are several other printed accounts of Travels in Africa, which contain much valuable information. The authors of the publications here referred to, having visited Africa of late years, can scarcely indeed be said to be so unexceptionably free, as those who wrote before the Slave Trade had become a subject of public discussion, from all bias,

bias, either from their connections, their interest, or their preconceived opinions. No imputation, however, is hereby intended to be thrown out against them. With the character of one of them, Dr. Winterbottom, I have long been well acquainted, and it is such as must alone entitle him to the full credit which he has universally obtained. But Mr. Parke justly stands at the head of all African travellers. There prevails throughout his work a remarkable air of authenticity, and to all the facts which it contains, entire credit is due. At the same time, I have heard, from persons who saw his original minutes, that they contained several statements favourable to the views of the Abolitionists, which are not inserted in the publication. His work, however, must ever be read with avidity, from its containing that which perhaps of all human spectacles is the most interesting, the exhibition of superior energies, called into action by extraordinary difficulties and dangers. Other publications concerning Africa have since appeared. That of Golberry, was drawn up and published under the patronage of Bonaparte, about the very time when the latter entered on his crusade against the Blacks in St. Domingo; the Abolitionists may therefore claim the benefit of any facts to the discredit of the

c   Slave

Slave Trade which it contains. Barrow's highly interesting account of the Cape of Good Hope, and his late work, containing the account of the expedition to the Booshuanna country, reflect also much light on the African character, and indirectly on the effects of the Slave Trade.

Methods by which Slaves are supplied. Let us now proceed to examine what are the principal sources from which the Slave market is furnished with its supplies. The result of that Inquiry will enable us to judge what effect that traffic produces on the happiness of Africa. A very large proportion of Wars. the Slaves consists of prisoners of war. But here it becomes advisable to rectify some misconceptions, which have prevailed on this head. The Abolitionists have been represented as maintaining, that in Africa, wars never arise from the various causes whence wars have so commonly originated in the other quarters of the globe; but that they are undertaken solely for the purpose of obtaining captives, who may be afterwards sold for Slaves. In contradiction to this position, various African wars have been cited, which historians state to have arisen from other causes; and it has been denied that wars furnish any considerable supply to the Slave market. Can it be necessary to declare,

clare, that the advocates for abolition never made so foolish, as well as so false an assertion, as that which has been thus imputed to them? Africans are men—The same bad passions therefore which have produced wars among other communities of human beings, produce the same wasteful effects in Africa likewise. But it will greatly elucidate this point to state, that, as we are informed by Mr. Parke, who has travelled farther into the interior of Africa than any modern traveller, there are two kinds of war in Africa. The one bears a resemblance to our European contests, is openly avowed, and previously declared. " This class however, we are assured, is
" generally terminated in a single campaign.
" A battle is fought; the vanquished seldom
" think of rallying; the whole inhabitants
" become panick struck; and the conquerors
" have only to *bind their slaves*,* and
" carry off their plunder and their victims."
These are taken into the country of the in-

---

* In reading accounts of African wars, the attentive reader will continually meet with expressions such as those here used, which incidentally and undesignedly, and therefore the more strongly prove, that the persons of the natives are regarded as the great booty; and we may therefore not unreasonably infer, that they often constitute the chief inducement for commencing hostilities.

c 2   vader,

vader, whence, as opportunities offer, they are sent to the Slave market.

<small>Predatory expeditions.</small> But the second kind of warfare, called Tegria, which means, we are told, plundering or stealing, and which appears to be no other than the practice of predatory expeditions, is that to which the Slave market is indebted for its chief supplies, and which most clearly explains the nature and effect of the Slave Trade. Mr. Parke indeed tells us, that this species of warfare arises from a sort of hereditary feud, which subsists between the inhabitants of neighbouring nations or districts. If we take into the account that the avowed compiler of Mr. Parke's work, the patron to whose good will he looked for the recompense of all his labours, was one of the warmest and most active opposers of the abolition of the Slave Trade, we shall not wonder that the fact alone is stated, without being traced to it's original cause. This however is a case, if such a case ever existed, in which the features of the offspring might alone enable us to recognise the rightful parent. But in truth we know from positive testimony, that though hereditary feuds of the deadliest malignity are but too surely generated by these predatory expeditions, and consequently that hatred and revenge may sometimes

times have a share in producing a continued course of them, yet that, speaking generally, the grand operating motive from which they are undertaken, and to which therefore, as their primary cause, they may be referred, is the desire of obtaining Slaves. " These predatory expeditions," Mr. Parke tells us, " are of all dimensions, from
" 500 horsemen, headed by the son of the
" king of the country; to a single individual,
" armed with his bow and arrow, who con-
" ceals himself among the bushes, until
" some young or unarmed person passes by.
" He then, tyger-like, springs upon his
" prey, drags his victim into the thicket,
" and at night *carries him off as a slave.*"
(Vide note, p. 19). " These incursions," Mr. Parke goes on to inform us, " are generally
" conducted with great secresy; a few re-
" solute individuals, led by some person of
" enterprize and courage, march quietly
" through the woods, surprize in the night
" some unprotected village, and *carry off the*
" *inhabitants*, (vide note, p.19) and their ef-
" fects, before their neighbours can come to
" their assistance."—" One morning," says Mr. Parke, " during my residence at Ka-
" malia, we were all much alarmed by a
" party of this kind. The prince of Foc-
" ladoo's son, with a strong party of horse,

c 3 " passed

"passed secretly through the woods, a little to the southward, and the next morning plundered three towns belonging to a powerful chief of Jollonkadoo. The success of this expedition encouraged the governor of another town to make a second inroad on a part of the same country. Having assembled about 200 of his people, he passed the river in the night, and *carried off a great number of prisoners.* (Vide note, p. 19). *Several of the inhabitants who had escaped these attacks, were afterwards seized* by the Mandingoes *(another people,* let it be observed) *as they wandered about in the woods, or concealed themselves in the glens and strong places in the mountains.*"

Predatory expeditions very common.

" These plundering excursions are very common, and the inhabitants of different communities watch every opportunity of undertaking them."—" They always," as Mr. Parke adds, " produce speedy retaliation; and when large parties cannot be collected for this purpose, a few friends will combine together, and advance into the enemy's country, with a view to plunder, *or carry off the inhabitants."* (Note, vide. pa. 19). Thus hereditary feuds are excited and perpetuated between different nations,

nations, tribes, villages, and even families, each waiting but for the favourable occasion of accomplishing it's revenge. Such is the picture of the Interior of Africa, as it is given by one who penetrated much further inland than any other modern traveller, and of whom it must be at least confessed, that he was not disposed to exaggerate the evils produced by the Slave Trade.

In another part of the country, we learn from the most respectable testimony, a practice prevails called Village-breaking. It is precisely the Tegria of Mr. Parke, with this difference, that though often termed making war, it is acknowledged to be practised for the express purpose of obtaining victims for the Slave market. It is carried on, sometimes by armed parties of individuals; sometimes by the soldiers of the petty kings and chieftains, who, perhaps in a season of drunkenness, the consequences of which when recovered from the madness of intoxication they have themselves often most deeply deplored, are instigated to become the plunderers and destroyers of those very subjects whom they were bound to protect. The village is attacked in the night; if deemed needful, to increase the confusion, it is set on fire, and the wretched inhabitants, as they are

[marginal note: Sources of supply continued. Village-breaking.]

are flying naked from the flames, are seized and carried into slavery. This practice, especially when conducted on a smaller scale, is called *panyaring*; for the practice has long been too general not to have created the necessity of an appropriate term. It is sometimes practised by Europeans, especially when the ships are passing along the coast, or when their boats, in going up the rivers, can seize their prey without observation; in short, whenever there is a convenient opportunity of carrying off the victims, and concealing the crime: and the unwillingness which the natives universally shew to venture into a ship of war, until they are convinced it is not a Slave ship, contrasted with the freedom and confidence with which they then come on board, is thus easily accounted for [*]. But these depredations are far more commonly perpetrated by the natives on each other; and on a larger or a smaller scale, according to the power and number of the assailants, and the resort of ships to the coast, it prevails so generally, as, throughout

<small>Panyaring, or kidnapping.</small>

---

[*] Vide evidence of Naval Officers, &c. taken before the House of Commons.—Smith also, who visited the coast in the service of the African Company in 1726, says "The Natives who came off to trade with us "were mighty timorous of coming aboard, for fear of "being panyard."

the

the whole extent of Africa, to render person and property utterly insecure.

And here, before we proceed to other sources of supply, let us for a moment recur to the assertions formerly mentioned, on which our opponents lay very considerable stress,—that but a small proportion of the whole supply of the market consists of prisoners of war, and that African wars do not often originate from the desire of obtaining Slaves. Should we even concede these points, we are now abundantly qualified to estimate the force of the concession; for though we should grant, that declared and national wars are not often undertaken for the purpose of obtaining Slaves, yet it is at least equally undeniable, that those predatory expeditions which are so common, and of which it is the express object to acquire Slaves, are often productive of national wars on the largest scale, and of the most destructive consequences; while they also are the sure and abundant cause of those incessant quarrels and hereditary feuds, which are said to be universal in Africa, and which acts of mutual outrage cannot fail to generate, in countries where the artificial modes of controlling and terminating the disputes and hostilities of adverse tribes and nations are unknown.

Allegation, " that a small proportion of Slaves are prisoners of war," considered.

unknown. It appears also, that wars are in Africa rendered singularly cruel and wasteful, by the peculiar manner in which they are carried on. So that though we cannot fairly lay to the charge of the Slave Trade all the wars of Africa, we yet may allege that to the causes which produce wars elsewhere, the Slave Trade superadds one entirely new and constant source of great copiousness and efficiency, while it gives to the wars, which arise from every other cause, a character of peculiar malignity and desolation. But happy even, from what has been already stated, happy would it be for Africa, if her greatest miseries were those of avowed and open warfare. War, though the greatest scourge of other countries, is a light evil in the African estimate of suffering. Direct and avowed wars will happen but occasionally, as the circumstances which produce them may arise. Wars, besides, between uncivilized nations, scarcely ever last long; those of Africa, Mr. Parke tells us, seldom beyond a single campaign; and the very consciousness that an evil will be of short duration, mitigates the pain which it occasions. But it is not of accidental or temporary injuries that Africa complains. Her miseries, severe in degree, are also permanent; they know neither intervals or remissions.

But

27.

<small>Sources of supply continued.
Administration of justice.</small>

But the Slave Trade is not sustained exclusively by acts of hostile outrage. The administration of justice is turned into another engine for its supply. The punishments, as we are told by some of the old writers,* were formerly remarkable for their lenity; but by degrees, they have been moulded, especially on the coast, into a more productive form. The most trifling offences are punished by the fine of one or more Slaves, which if the culprit be unable to pay, he himself is to be sold into slavery, often for the benefit of the very judges by whom he is condemned.† When the necessity for obtaining Slaves becomes more pressing, new crimes are fabricated, accusations and convictions are multiplied; the unwary are artfully seduced into the commission of crimes. The imaginary offence of witchcraft becomes often a copious source of supply, a conviction being punished by the sale of the whole family.

* Vide Nyendael and Artus of Dantzic, in De Bry's India Orientalis, &c.—Bosman,—Barbot.

† Moore, many years factor to the African Company, about 1730, says, 'Since this trade has been used, all punishments are changed into slavery, there being an advantage in such condemnations. They strain for crimes very hard, in order to get the benefit of selling the criminal. Not only murder, theft, and adultery, but every trifling crime is punished by selling the criminal for a Slave.'

Indeed,

Native superstitions: Witchcraft.

Indeed, on some parts of the country bordering on the coast, this charge furnishes the ready means of obtaining, especially for a chieftain, the supply of European articles. A person accused of this crime is required to purge himself by the ordeal of drinking what is called 'red water'. If the accused drinks it with impunity, he is declared innocent, but if, as more commonly happens, the red water being generally medicated for the purpose, the party is taken sick, or dies, in general the whole, or at the least a certain number of his family, are immediately sold into slavery. An eye witness, who stated the effects of this system, mentioned his having seen king Sherbro, the chief of the river of that name, kill six persons in that way in a single morning. In some extensive districts near the windward coast of Africa, almost every death is believed by the natives to be occasioned by magical influence; and the belief, it is difficult to say, whether real or pretended, in this superstition, is carried to such an extent as to break every tie of natural affection. In these districts it is estimated that two thirds of the whole export of Slaves were sold for witchcraft. Every man who has acquired any considerable property, or who has a large family, the sale of which will produce a considerable profit, excites

cites in the Chieftain near whom he resides, the same longings which are called forth in the wild beast, by the exhibition of his proper prey, and he himself lives in a continual state of suspicion and terror.

To this long catalogue are to be added two other sources, famines, and insolvency. In times of extreme scarcity, persons sometimes sell themselves for subsistence; and still more frequently, it is said, children are sold by their parents to procure provisions for the rest of the family. These famines, Mr. Parke, who mentions this source of slavery, observes, are often produced by wars. But while on the one hand we must remark, that this effect arises chiefly out of that peculiarly wasteful manner of carrying on war in Africa, which we have already noticed; so may we not fairly presume that to the Slave Trade also, and to the habits of mind which it generates, it is to be ascribed, that in such seasons of general distress, he who possesses food refuses to part with so much as will suffice for the bare maintenance of his neighbours and fellow sufferers, at any price except that of selling themselves or their children into perpetual slavery? With respect to debt or insolvency, the laws respecting debtor and creditor which prevail in Africa, furnish a
striking

Famine and Insolvency.

striking illustration of the effect of the Slave Trade, in gradually moulding to it's own purpose all the institutions and habits of the country in which it prevails, and rendering them instrumental in forwarding the grand object of furnishing a supply for the Slave market. Creditors, in compensation of their claims on the debtor, have not only a right to seize his own person, and sell him for a Slave, but also any of his family; and if he or they cannot be taken, any inhabitants of the same village, or, as Mr. Parke says, any native of the same kingdom. Indeed it is very rarely that the debtor himself is molested, it is his neighbours or townsmen who are the sufferers. Hence persons become debtors more freely, because, while they gratify their appetites by obtaining the European goods they want, they are not likely to pay for their rashness in their own persons. The Captains of Slave ships are in their turn less backward in advancing goods on credit to the Black factors, and they again to other native dealers, knowing that from some quarter or another the Slaves will surely be supplied.

Distinctions between the Interior countries, and those on the Coast.

In giving this general account of the manner of procuring Slaves, it ought to be observed, that the number and extent of the countries

countries whence the Slaves are furnished, and their varying circumstances, will doubtless occasion some variations in the manner of carrying on the traffic: still we might presume that the same causes, operating for a long course of years, on human beings, in something like the same rude state of society, would produce nearly similar effects. In fact we find, from positive testimony, that there is this general similarity in the consequences of the Slave Trade wherever it exists. But there is one distinction which ought to be noticed, that between the inland countries and those on the coast: The proportion furnished by them respectively varies in different parts of Africa; but every where the greater number is supplied from the interior. Many of them come from great distances inland, and the sufferings of these unhappy beings during their journey are such as would alone, if the voice of humanity were to be heard, prompt us to abandon at once so horrid a traffic. Mr. Parke travelled down with a small party of them; and hard indeed must be the heart of that man who can read his account without shuddering.

The difference between the circumstances of the inland districts and those adjacent to the coast, will of course create some corresponding

ponding difference in the effects produced on them by the Slave Trade. In the interior of the country, the kingdoms, though even they are often split into a number of independent states, are generally of greater extent than on the coast, which is often, especially on the Windward and Gold coast, separated into numberless petty communities, under their respective Chieftains or Aristocracies. It should likewise be remarked, that on one extensive part of the coast of Africa which is divided into a number of different states, every black or white factor who has acquired a little property, forms a settlement or village, and becomes a petty chieftain, and carries on against his neighbours a predatory warfare, by which they are of course excited to reciprocal acts of hostility. In the interior, acts of depredation on members of another community, though, as we are told, very common, are not near so frequent as on the coast; except, perhaps, on the boundaries of kingdoms: and it is remarkable, that Mr. Parke informs us, that the boundaries even of the most populous and powerful kingdoms are commonly very ill peopled. On members of the same community also, these depredations, though undoubtedly frequent, are for many reasons much less common than in the countries

tries bordering on the shore. The concealment of any such act of rapine would be obviously much more difficult; neither might it be easy for private traders to secrete their victims, during the long interval which might elapse, before an opportunity might offer of disposing of them. Again, the chieftains or kings of these large communities, while on the one hand, their more abundant revenues place them above the necessity of resorting to such ruinous means of supplying their wants, as the pillage of their own villages, so on the other, not coming into immediate contact with the Slave Traders, they are not so liable to be suddenly instigated, in the madness of intoxication, to the commission of such outrages. The same difference in the circumstances of the interior, prevents the administration of justice, or the native superstitions, being resorted to in the same degree as on the coast. And it is remarkable, that though Mr. Parke speaks of crimes as one source of supply to the Slave Trade, we do not find in his narrative, one single instance specified of a Slave having been so furnished. But, above all, let it be remembered, on the coast the grand repository of temptations is palpable, and on the spot; of temptations commonly of that precise kind, which, by the gratifications they hold out to the depraved appetites,

Evils of Slave Trade aggravated on the Coast.

appetites, and bad passions of man, spirituous liquors, gunpowder, and fire-arms, the incentives to acts of violence, and the means of committing them, are apt to operate most powerfully on uncivilized men. The love of spirituous liquors, is a passion also, which becomes from indulgence, more craving, and difficult to be resisted. The Captains of Slave ships, who are sound practical philosophers, thoroughly conversant, at least, with all the bad parts of human nature, are well aware of these propensities, and of the advantages which may be derived from them; and hence, they often begin by giving to the petty king or chieftain a present of brandy or rum, anticipating the large returns for this liberality, which future acts of depredation will supply. It is almost a happy circumstance when the chieftain, by possessing the implements of war, is tempted to revenge some old injury, or to ravage and carry off the inhabitants of some neighbouring district, instead of preying on his own miserable subjects. Meanwhile the Slave factor himself takes no part in the quarrels between contending chieftains, but which party soever is victorious, he finds his advantage in the war. He supplies all the contending parties with fire-arms and ammunition, and receives all the Slaves which are made on both sides with perfect impartiality.

impartiality. Under such circumstances, might we not anticipate, what we know from positive evidence, that the factor stirs up and inflames dissensions, from which, whoever else may be the loser, he is sure to gain. It has been even imputed to neighbouring chiefs, who, assisted by their respective allies, have carried on with each other a long protracted war, that by a mutual understanding, they have abstained from wasting each other's territories, while each carried on his ravages against the allies of his enemy with great activity and success. But it is not to kings or chieftains only, that the Slave Trade holds out strong temptations. The appetite for spirituous liquors is universal. European commodities are coveted by all. Whether for attack or defence, fire-arms and gunpowder are most desirable. In such a loose state of society, almost every one has some malice to wreak, some injury to retaliate. Thus sensuality, avarice, hostility, revenge, every bad passion is called into action; while there lies the Slave ship, ready to receive old and young, males and females, all in short who are brought to it, and, without question or exception, to furnish the desired gratification in return. The Captains of Slave ships themselves, who gave evidence before the House of Commons, frankly and invariably acknowledged,

ledged, that it is the universal practice, if the price can be agreed on, to purchase all who are brought to them, without examination as to the manner in which the Slave has been obtained, as to his former condition, or the vendor's right to sell. So well did they seem ~~to be~~ aware how much the success of their traffic might depend on this mode of conducting it, that they even resented it as an insult on their understandings, when they were asked whether any questions of this kind were put by the purchaser. Thus, whenever a Slave ship is on the coast, a large and general premium is immediately held out for the perpetration of acts of fraud, violence, and rapine. Every child, every unprotected female that can be seized on, can be immediately turned to account. No wonder that, as Captain Wilson informs us, the inhabitants are afraid of venturing out of their own doors without being armed; a practice of which one of themselves gave him the explanation, by significantly pointing to a Slave ship which then lay in sight, completing her cargo.

But it is not only without doors that the Slave ship holds out its lure; it is not only by open violence that it operates. When the Slave ships arrive, unjust convictions are multiplied. Accusations for witchcraft become

come frequent. And it is well worthy of remark, that these native superstitions, being thus maintained in continued life and action, have continued in full force in those very districts, where the intercourse of the natives with the Europeans has been the longest, and the most intimate; while in the interior, the same barbarous practices have either gone into decay of themselves, or seem to have faded away before the feeble light of Mahometanism. Even among private families the seeds of insecurity and cruelty are copiously sown; and from the pressure of present temptation, a husband or a master is often induced, in a fit of temporary anger or jealousy, to sell his wife or his domestics, whom afterwards he often in vain wishes he could recover.

But besides these general and powerfully operating causes of evil, which have been already noticed, there is one circumstance in the manner of conducting the trade on the coast, which so naturally tends to the production of frequent acts of violence, as to deserve a distinct specification. It affords another striking instance of the way in which the Slave Trade has in a long course of years gradually imparted a taint to all the institutions and customs of Africa. It is the ge- neral

Practice of receiving relations as pawns, and consequences of it.

neral custom for Captains of Slave ships, in exchange for the goods which they advance on credit, and of which the value, as has been stated, is to be repaid to them in Slaves, to receive the children or some other near relations of the Black Factor as pledges, or as they are termed in Africa *pawns*, whom the Slave captains are to return when the stipulated number of Slaves has been delivered. With the goods which have been intrusted to him he commonly goes up the country; and, knowing that by some means or other the requisite number of Slaves must be furnished, or that his own nearest relatives, and he himself too if he can be taken, will be carried off into slavery, it is obvious, that when the day for the sailing of the ship draws nigh, he will not be very scrupulous in the means to which he resorts for completing his assortment. Thus even parental instinct and the domestic and social affections are rendered by the Slave Trade the incentives to acts of cruelty and rapine. But it would be endless were I to attempt to lay before you in detail all the various forms and modes of wickedness, and misery, of which, directly and indirectly, the Slave Trade is productive. It's general and leading features have been now exhibited to you.

Such

Such are the methods by which from eighty to one hundred thousand of our fellow creatures, a race of people too, declared by Mr. Parke himself, to be perhaps beyond all others, passionately attached to their native soil, are annually torn from their country, their homes, their friends, and from whatever is most dear to them. All the ties of nature, and habit, and feeling, are burst asunder; and, by a long voyage, the horrors of which were acknowledged to constitute of themselves an almost incalculable sum of misery, these victims of our injustice are carried to a distant land, to wear away the whole remainder of their lives in a state of hopeless slavery and degradation, with the same melancholy prospect for their descendants after them, for ever.

Recapitulation of effects of SlaveTrade.

Yet even this is not all. There is one consequence of the Slave Trade, a consequence too, most important to Africa, which still remains to be pointed out. It were much to foment and aggravate, not seldom to produce, long and bloody wars—to incite to incessant acts of the most merciless depredation—to poison and embitter the administration of the laws—and in general, to give a malignant taint to religious and civil institutions; thus, turning into engines of oppression

oppression and misery, that very machinery of the social state, which is naturally conducive to the protection and comfort of mankind. It is much to compel men to live at home amid the alarm, elsewhere only felt, and with the precautions only used in an enemy's country,—to hold out a direct premium to rapine and murder,—in short, to produce the general prevalence of selfishness, and fraud, and violence, and cruelty, and terror, and revenge. And all this, not on a small scale, or within narrow limits, but throughout an immense region, bounded by a line of coast of between three and four thousand miles, and stretching inland to various depths, not seldom to a distance which it requires several months to travel. But there is one triumph still behind; one effect of the Slave Trade: which, if it excite not at first the same lively sympathy, as some others of it's more direct outrages, on the comforts of domestic or the peace of social life, will yet, in the deliberate judgment of a considerate mind, appear on reflection to be of more importance than all the rest. This is, that by keeping in a state of incessant insecurity, of person and property, the whole of the district which is visited by Europeans, we maintain an impassable barrier on that side, through which alone

Another most important consequence of the Slave Trade.

alone any rays of the religious and moral light and social improvements of our happier quarter of the globe might penetrate into the interior, and thus lock up the whole of that vast continent in it's present state of wretchedness and darkness.

It prevents the civilisation of Africa.

Here, then, we see the bitter cup of Africa filled to the very brim. For the above consideration shews but too clearly, that she cannot expect any natural termination of her sufferings from the gradual progress of civilization and knowledge, which have, in some other instances, put a period to a less extended traffic for Slaves in countries differently situated. The very channels through which alone, according to all human calculation, Africa might have hoped to receive the blessings of religious and moral light, and social improvement, are precisely those through which her miseries flow in upon her with so full a tide. Thus the African Slave Trade provides for it's own indefinite continuance. Here also, as in other instances which have been already pointed out, it turns into poison what has been elsewhere most salutary, and renders that very intercourse, which has been ordinarily the grand means of civilization, the most sure and operative instrument in the perpetuation of barbarism.

No natural death of the Slave Trade.

At

Our aggravated guilt.

At length, then, we are prepared to form some judgment of the effects of European intercourse on the state and happiness of Africa. The darkness of Paganism were a very insufficient palliation of such a tissue of cruelty and crimes. But surely it is no small aggravation of our guilt, that We, who are the prime agents in this traffic of wickedness and blood, are ourselves the most free, enlightened, and happy people that ever existed upon earth. We profess a religion which inculcates truth and love, peace and good-will, among men—We are foremost in a commerce which exists but by war, treachery, and devastation. We enjoy a political constitution of government, eminent above all others for securing to the very meanest and weakest the blessings of civil liberty, of personal security, and equal laws—yet We take the lead in maintaining this accursed system, which begins in fraud and violence, and is consummated in bondage and degradation. Blessed ourselves with religious light and knowledge, we prolong in Africa the reign of ignorance and superstition. In short, instead of endeavouring to diffuse among nations, less favoured than ourselves, the blessings we enjoy; after our crime has been indisputably proved to us, in defiance alike of conscience and of reputation, we industriously

ously and perseveringly continue to deprave and darken the Creation of God.

There is scarcely any point of view in which the nature and effects of our intercourse with Africa will appear so peculiarly disgraceful to us as a christian nation, as when we contemplate them in connection with the benefits which the Africans derive from their intercourse with the Mahometans. When we cast our eyes towards the south-west of Europe, and behold extensive countries, once possessed by the most polished nations, the chosen seats of literature and the liberal arts; and now behold one universal waste of ignorance and barbarism, we have always been accustomed to ascribe the fatal change to the conquest of a band of Mahometan invaders, and to regret that such fine countries should remain under the benumbing effects of a Mussulman government. On the other hand, in contemplating the superior state of our northern parts of Europe, we have been used, with reason, to ascribe much of our light and liberty, and many of our various blessings, to the influence of that pure religion which is the friend of freedom, of peace, and goodwill among men. But with what shame must we acknowledge, that in Africa, Christianity and Mahometanism

tanism appear to have mutually interchanged characters.—Smith, the African Company's own agent in 1722, tells us, "the discerning "natives account it their greatest unhap- "piness that they were ever visited by the "Europeans. They say that we Christians "introduced the traffic of Slaves, and that "before our coming they lived in peace. "But, say they, it is observable, that where- "ever Christianity comes, there come with "it, a sword, a gun, powder and ball."*

The same picture may appear to claim still greater attention from the hand of Mr. Parke, whose visit is more recent, and whose knowledge of Africa is more extensive.— Speaking of the Foulah nation, who are many of them professed Mahometans, he says, "religious persecution is not known among "them, nor is it necessary, for the system "of Mahomet is made to extend itself by "means abundantly more efficacious. By "establishing small schools in the different "towns, where many of the Pagan as well "as Mahometan children are taught to read "the Koran, and instructed in the tenets "of the prophet, the Mahometan priests "fix a bias on the minds, and form the cha- "racter of their young disciples, which no

* Vide Smith's Voyage to Guinea, p. 266.

"acci-

" accidents of life can ever afterwards re-
" move or alter. Many of these little schools
" I visited in my progress through the coun-
" try, and observed with pleasure the great
" docility, and submissive deportment of
" the children, and heartily wished they
" had had better instructors, and a purer re-
" ligion." Again, speaking of the Mandin-
goe country, and of other parts of Africa,
and of the eagerness which the natives,
both Pagan and Mahometan, shew to acquire some knowledge of letters, Mr. Parke
speaks out still more intelligibly, and appears
feelingly alive to the humiliation of his own
religion; and, from motives of christian
zeal as well as of humanity, he recommends
our endeavouring to introduce the light of
true religion into that benighted land.* "Al-
" though," says he, " the negroes in general
" have a very great idea of the wealth and
" power of the Europeans, I am afraid that

* Surely Mr. Parke, when he suggested this, forgot that experience as well as reason teach us, that we must first abolish the Slave Trade before we attempt to diffuse among the Africans the lessons of peace and love; lest we are asked the same well-known question, and receive the same reply, as the Spanish priest from the poor dying Peruvian, when the Spaniards in America were acting on the plan which is here advised, of at once ravaging and converting: "Are there to be any Europeans in this "Heaven, where you wish me to secure a place?" Being told yes, "Then it is no place for Peruvians."

" the

"the Mahometan converts among them think but very lightly of our superior attainments in religious knowledge. The white traders in the maritime districts take no pains to counteract this unhappy prejudice."—" To me, therefore, it was not so much the subject of wonder, as matter of regret, to observe, that while the superstition of Mahomet has in this manner scattered a few faint beams of learning among these poor people, the precious light of Christianity is altogether excluded. I could not but lament, that although the coast of Africa has now been known and frequented by the Europeans for more than two hundred years, yet the negroes still remain entire strangers to the doctrines of our holy religion."—" The poor Africans, whom we affect to consider as barbarians, look upon us, I fear, as little better than a race of formidable but ignorant Heathens."

Such was Smith's relation, near a century ago, of the judgment formed by the Africans, of the effects of their intercourse with the Christian nations. Such is the acknowledgment of Mr. Parke, who is certainly disposed to paint the effects of the Slave Trade in the softest colours. Is it possible for any one who calls himself a Christian, and a member

of

of the British Empire, to read the passage without the deepest humiliation and sorrow, and without longing also, not only to stop the guilty commerce we have so long carried on, but to endeavour to repair, in some degree, the wrongs of Africa, and with active but tardy kindness, to impart to her some small share of the overflowings of our superabundant blessings?

"But surely," you will long ere now have been ready to exclaim, "Surely the facts which "you have laid before us, though believed by "the abolitionists, could not have been esta- "blished in the judgment of the majority of "the House of Commons;"—and you may justly require some decisive evidence in proof of them.

To adduce all the specific testimony by which the above allegations were established, would be to fill a volume. I mean, as a specimen of the whole, to extract, and subjoin in an appendix, a few passages from the vast body of evidence with which we are furnished on this subject. But it would be injustice to the great cause I am pleading, not to declare, that the above statements were established beyond all possible dispute; and also, that, with occasional

Evidence by which the above statements are established.

sional variations, resulting from the difference in the forms of government, and in other circumstances, they were found to be applicable not to particular parts only of Africa, but to the whole of that vast district which is visited by the European Slave ships; to be, not the exception, but the rule; not the occasional, but the general and systematic effects of the Slave Trade ships. We have the evidence of several most respectable Officers of the navy, to prove, that wherever they touched, acts of depredation were common. The same practices were found to prevail in the widely distant countries of Senegambia and the Gold coast, by men of Science, one of whom produced a journal, kept at the time, in which he daily entered all that appeared to him worthy of remark; and it was from this record that the Committee read the affecting account which has been mentioned, in which one of the African Kings, with every appearance of sincerity, repeatedly expressed his deep remorse for having been instigated, in a season of intoxication, into which he had been drawn by the Slave merchants, to oppress and pillage his subjects. Much of the Abolitionists' information was also obtained from those who, in different capacities, chiefly as surgeons, more commonly as mates, and in some few

instances

instances as common sailors, had been actually employed in Slave ships; some of these persons had likewise been for many months on shore among the natives; and several of them had witnessed the practice of attacking villages by armed parties in the night, and carrying away, and selling all they could seize.

In opposition to all this testimony, the Slave Traders produced several witnesses, who were either still engaged in the Slave Trade, or who had formerly carried it on, some of whom had resided several years in Slave factories on the coast. By them it was generally declared, that acts of depredation for the purpose of procuring Slaves were never committed; they had never even heard of such practices, nor had they ever heard of the practice, or of the term, of panyaring or kidnapping.* Crimes and witchcraft were said to be the chief sources of supply; a few were furnished

Opponents' contrary evidence.

---

* This is the more astonishing, because it is mentioned by the older writers as well as by more recent travellers, as Captain Sir G. Young and Sir T. B. Thompson, as a term of which the meaning is clear, and the use perfectly familiar. Thus, as a single instance, Smith, after saying "the natives were afraid of being panyard," (p. 104.) subjoins the meaning in a note,—"To panyar is to kidnap or steal men. It is a word used all over the Coast of Guinea."

by

by insolvency. The trials were said to be fair, the convictions just. In short, according to their report, the Africans, of whose natural dispositions and character they at the same time gave a highly unfavourable representation, and whose government was said to be very loose and imperfect, must have been a people of the most extraordinary moral excellency, who had for centuries resisted present and strong temptations, which in every other country had proved too powerful to be successfully opposed. Such, according to these witnesses, was the state of things on the coast. Of the interior, from whence the greater part of the Slaves were brought, they professed to know little or nothing.

Opponents' evidence decisively refuted;

The allegations of these persons, even though they had not been effectually disproved by the concurrent testimony of the various classes of witnesses already noticed, carried their refutation on the very face of them. But if any doubts could have been entertained to which of the two accounts most credit was due, to that of men who were still concerned in carrying on the Slave Trade, or had made their fortunes by it, on the one side; and of witnesses on the other, most of whom, highly respectable, both in point of rank and character, had no interest

at

at stake either way; these doubts would have been completely removed by another branch of evidence. For, happily for the cause of truth and justice, we were able to adduce, in support of our allegations, the testimony of another set of witnesses, against whom our opponents at least could urge no objections, persons in the employ of the African Company or of private merchants, who had been long resident in Africa, for the express purpose of carrying on the Slave Trade, and who, as was formerly mentioned, had published to the world the result of their observations and experience. It might indeed have been feared, that we should be compelled to except against their testimony; and it must be confessed, that for the sake of their own credit, and for that of the occupation by which they had made their fortunes, they would naturally be disposed, even in acknowledging abuses, to touch them with a tender and favourable hand. Yet, however short of the truth we may reasonably suppose their representations to fall, where they are discreditable to the Slave Trade, we find our charges positively and abundantly proved.

especially by accounts of Africa, published by Slave Traders, and before the Slave Trade had been attacked.

But it is due to our opponents themselves in the House of Commons, excepting only such of them as were personally connected with

Slave Trade's cruelty and guilt acknowledged by the parliamen-

*tary oppo-
sers of the
abolition.* with the places whence the Slave Trade is principally carried on, who are allowed a certain license of speaking and reasoning, on the ground of their being understood to utter the language of their constituents rather than their own; to the rest even of our opponents it is due, to declare, that they never for a moment affected to entertain a doubt of the substantial correctness of our statements. Of the injustice and inhumanity of the Slave Trade, there was but one opinion. The chief advocates for gradual abolition, and even the very few who resisted abolition in any form, reprobated the traffic in the plainest and strongest terms; avowing their firm conviction of its incurable wickedness and cruelty. One of them declared, that he knew no language which could add to it's horrors; another, that in the pursuit of the general object he felt equally warm with the Abolitionists themselves; another acknowledged the Slave Trade was the disgrace of Great Britain, and the torment of Africa. Whatever might be thought of the consistency of our opponents, who, after thus admitting our premises, stopped short of the conclusions to which such premises might be thought infallibly to lead, it was no great stretch of candour in them to speak in such terms of the Slave Trade, when, so clearly indisputable were

were it's nature and effects, that Mr. Bryan Edwards, one of the ablest, and most determined enemies of abolition, while avowedly opposing the measure in an eloquent speech (which was afterwards published by authority) made the following memorable declaration. After having confessed he had not the smallest doubt that " in Africa the effects of " the Slave Trade were precisely such as I " had represented them to be ;" he added, " the whole or the greatest part of that im-" mense continent, is a field of warfare and " desolation ; a wilderness, in which the in-" habitants are wolves towards each other; " a scene of oppression, fraud, treachery, and " blood."—" The assertion, that a great " many of the slaves are criminals and con-" victs, is mockery and insult." *Mr. Bryan Edwards's declaration to the same effect.*

But if the charges which the Abolitionists brought against the Slave Trade were thus clearly proved, you may now be much more disposed to wonder, what arguments could be found sufficiently strong to induce the House of Commons of Great Britain to hesitate, even for a moment, to wipe away so foul a blot from our national character. *Pleas against abolition.*

The grand operating consideration, which, from the very first discussion of the question in in 1791 to the present moment, has prevented the actual abolition of the Slave Trade, though so long a period has elapsed since Mr. Pitt congratulated the House of Commons, the Country, and the World, that " its sentence was sealed, that it had received " it's condemnation," has undoubtedly been, the persuasion that it's continuance is necessary to the well-being of our West Indian colonies. We will, therefore, inquire into that necessity. But as several other allegations were set up, and various arguments urged, on the part of the Slave Traders, it may be best to consider, previously, such of them as are included in the African division of the subject, in order to clear the way for what may be termed, the West Indian branch of the subject.

The Negroes an inferior race. The advocates for the Slave Trade originally took very high ground; contending, that the Negroes were an inferior race of beings. It is obvious, that, if this were once acknowledged, they might be supposed, no less than their fellow brutes, to have been comprised within the original grant of all inferior creatures to the use and service of man. A position so shameless, and so expressly contradicted by the Holy Scriptures, could not long be maintained in plain terms. But many others,

others, which may not improperly be supposed, from their features, to belong to the same family, were afterwards brought forward. To this class belong the assertions, that, though it might scarcely be justifiable to withhold from the Africans the name of men, yet that they were manifestly inferior to the rest of the human species, both in their intellectual and moral powers. Hence, doubtless, it was, that they never had attained to any height of civilization; whence it was also inferred, that they never could be civilized; that therefore they might be reasonably regarded, as intended by Providence to be the hewers of wood and drawers of water of the species; as a race originally destined to servile offices, and fairly applicable to any purpose by which they might be rendered most subservient to the interest and comfort of the Lords of the Creation. This, indeed, was high ground, as has been already remarked; but it was not injudiciously selected, had it been but tenable; for our opponents well knew, that could they but obtain credit for their representations of the incorrigible stupidity and depravity of the Negro race, our commiseration of them would be proportionably lessened, and then all, except perhaps a few stubborn advocates for justice in the abstract, would be content to leave them to their fate.

It therefore becomes highly interesting, in a practical point of view, to ascertain the real character and qualities, both intellectual and moral, of the natives of Africa; and, remembering the advantages we derived in a former instance, from publications which had appeared before the Slave Trade became a subject of public discussion, we might be disposed to congratulate ourselves in having access, on the present occasion, to a work which was published many years before any proposition had been brought forward for abolishing the Slave Trade. The publication to which I allude is Mr. Long's elaborate History of Jamaica, a work which has been long regarded as of the highest authority on all West Indian topics. We may consider it as containing a more fair representation of the opinion entertained of the Negroes, and of the estimation in which they were held by the well-informed colonists, than any statements which, having been subsequently made, may be supposed to have received a tincture from that discussion. Mr. Long's work appeared long before the necessity of vindicating the Slave Trade, and the difficulty of finding arguments for that purpose

Mr. Long's account of the Negro race.

purpose had driven the enemies of abolition to the unworthy expedient of calumniating the African character. Yet we find this commonly respectable author speaking of the race of Negroes in such terms, as they who have read the more recent accounts of Africa will peruse with astonishment, as well as with disgust. Far be it from me to quote them with any design of injuring the reputation of a work of established credit. But the passages are in several points of view highly important, and well deserving of your most serious consideration.

"For my own part (says Mr. Long) I think "there are extremely potent reasons for believ- "ing that the white and the negro are two dis- "tinct species." "In general (he goes on) the "African negroes are void of genius, and seem "almost incapable of making any progress in "civility or science. They have no plan or "system of morality among them. Their bar- "barity to their children debases their nature "even below that of brutes. They have no "moral sensations; no taste, but for women, "gormandizing and drinking to excess; no "wish but to be idle. Their children, from "their tenderest years, are suffered to deliver "themselves up to all that nature suggests to "them. Their houses are miserable cabins.
"They

Extracts from Long's History of Jamaica.

" They conceive no pleasure from the most
" beautiful parts of their country, preferring
" the most sterile. Their roads, as they call
" them, are mere sheep paths, twice as long
" as they need be, and almost impassable.
" Their country in most parts is one continued
" wilderness, beset with briars and thorns.

" They use neither carriages nor beasts
" of burthen. They are represented *by all
" authors* as the vilest of the human kind, to
" which they have little more pretension of
" resemblance than what arises from their
" exterior form.

" In so vast a continent as that of Africa,
" and in so great a variety of climates and
" provinces, we might expect to find a pro-
" portionable diversity among the inhabi-
" tants, in regard to their qualifications of
" body and mind; strength, agility, indus-
" try, and dexterity, on the one hand;
" ingenuity, learning, arts and sciences, on
" the other. But on the contrary, a gene-
" ral uniformity runs through all these va-
" rious regions of people; so that if any dif-
" ference be found, it is only in degrees of
" the same qualities; and, what is more
" strange, those of the worst kind; it being
" a common known proverb, that all people
" on

" on the globe have some good as well as
" ill qualities, except the Africans. What-
" ever great personages this country might
" anciently have produced, and concerning
" whom we have no information, they are
" now every where degenerated into a bru-
" tish, ignorant, idle, crafty, bloody, thiev-
" ish, mistrustful, and superstitious people,
" even in those states where we might ex-
" pect to find them more polished, humane,
" docile, and industrious."—" This bruta-
" lity somewhat diminishes when they are
" imported young, after they become habi-
" tuated to clothing, and a regular disci-
" pline of life; but many are never reclaimed,
" and remain savages, in every sense of the
" word, to their latest period. We find
" them marked with the same bestial man-
" ners, stupidity, and vices, which debase
" their brethren on the continent, who seem
" to be distinguished from the rest of man-
" kind, not in person only, but in possess-
" ing in the abstract every species of inhe-
" rent turpitude that is to be found dis-
" persed at large among the rest of the
" human creation, with scarce a single fea-
" ture to extenuate this shade of character,
" differing in this particular from all other
" men; for in other countries, the most
" abandoned villain we ever heard of has
" rarely,

"rarely, if ever, been known unportioned "with some one good quality at least in his "composition."—"Among so great a num- "ber of provinces on this extensive conti- "nent, and among so many millions of peo- "ple, we have heard but of one or two in- "significant tribes, who comprehended any "thing of mechanic arts, or manufacture; "and even these, for the most part, are said "to perform their work in a very bungling "and slovenly manner, perhaps not much "better than an oran-outang might with a "little pains be brought to do."

"Ludicrous as the opinion may seem, I "do not think that an oran-outang husband "would be any dishonour to a Hottentot "female."

"Maize, palm-oil, and a little stinking "fish, make up the general bill of fare of "the prince and the slave."

"They esteem the ape species as scarcely "their inferiors in humanity."

"Their hospitality is the result of self- "love; they entertain strangers only in "hopes of extracting some service or profit "from them."

"Their

" Their corporeal sensations are generally
" of the grossest frame," &c. &c. &c.

Such is Mr. Long's portrait of the negro character; such was the state of contempt into which the whole race had fallen, in the estimation of those who had known them chiefly in that condition of wretchedness and degradation into which a long continued course of slavery had depressed them. Can anything shew more clearly, with what strong prejudices against the negro race, the minds not only of low uneducated men, but of a West Indian, whose authority is great, and whose name stands high among his countrymen, were some years ago at least infected: consequently they prove with what spirit and temper, even well-informed men, among the colonists, entered on the consideration of the various questions involved in the large and complicated discussion concerning the abolition of the Slave Trade.

But the subject is of the very first importance in another view; for it is a truth so clear, that it would be a mere waste of time to prove it in detail—that our estimate of the intellectual and moral qualities, of the natural and acquired tempers and feelings, and habits, of any class of our fellow creatures, will determine our judgment as to what is

The question of highly important practical tendencies.

necessary

necessary to their happiness, and still more as to the treatment they may reasonably claim at our hands. Now let it be remembered, the author, whose account of the Africans has been just laid before you, was the very best informed of those on whose views and feelings, respecting the Negroes, our opponents would have had us entirely rely. Must not the representations of such witnesses against the Negroes be received with large abatement, and ought we not to lend ourselves to their suggestions with considerable diffidence? What judgment would they be likely to form of the consideration to which, whether in Africa, on ship-board, or in the West Indies, the negro Slaves were entitled? By how scanty a measure would their comforts be dispensed to them! And when, in answer to our inquiries, we were assured that in these several situations, their treatment was *sufficiently* mild and humane, and that *due* attention was paid to their wants and feelings, might we not reasonably receive these assurances with some reserve, on calling to mind that they proceeded from persons whose estimate of *sufficiency* was drawn from their calculations of what was *due* to the wants and feelings, the pleasures, and pains of a being little above the brute creation; not, of a Being of talents and passions,

of

of anticipations and recollections, of social and domestic feelings similar to our own?

The account given by the witnesses produced by the Slave Traders, of the natural and moral qualities of the Negroes, was of the same unfavourable kind, though considerably less strong in its colouring. I should detain you too long by stating it in detail. It may suffice to mention, in general, that the Africans were represented, in respect to civilization and knowledge, as but very little advanced beyond the rudest state of savage life. The population was said to be thin; their agriculture in the lowest state, their only manufacture a species of coarse mat or cloth. They very rarely used any beasts for draught or burthen, they had no public roads; no knowledge of letters, or apparent sense of their value. But the account of their personal qualities was still more melancholy; because it was such as to leave but slender hopes of their ever emerging out of this dark and barbarous state. The most respectable witnesses produced by the Slave Traders, some of whom had resided among the Africans many years, and on various parts of the coast, declared, that their stupidity, and still more their indolence, were so firmly rooted in their nature, as to be absolutely invincible; and,

Slave Traders account of the Negro character.

and, what may perhaps be justly regarded as indicative of the worst natural disposition, that they were deficient in domestic and parental affection.

Mr. Bryan Edwards's account. Even Mr. Bryan Edwards, though in common more liberal than other defenders of the Slave Trade, gives in his History of the West Indies a highly unfavourable account of the African character. It ought, however, in all fairness, to be urged in his defence, that his judgment of the Negroes was formed under circumstances highly disadvantageous to them; being grounded on what he had known and heard of them in our West India colonies, where their natural character must necessarily have derived a deep taint from the depraving effects of a long continued state of slavery. To this cause, indeed, he himself very frankly ascribes most of the bad qualities which he enumerates. After exhibiting the different shades of character of the Slaves brought from different parts of Africa, he goes on to state, what may be deemed the general properties of the Negro race, and these are of the most debasing and depraving kind. They are in general distrustful and cowardly; falsehood is one of the most prominent features in their character; they are prone to theft; sullen, selfish,

ish, unrelenting; and while the softer virtues are seldom found among them, they are so sunk in dissoluteness and licentiousness, that the attempt to introduce the ceremony of marriage among them, would be impracticable to any good purpose. One of the few pleasing traits in their character is their high veneration for old age.

After this melancholy picture, it is a relief to the humane mind, to peruse the accounts of the intellectual and moral dispositions and character of the Negroes, which have been given by persons who have had far superior means of information. The chief of them, Mr. Parke, and Mr. Golberry, were also, from their connections, unfriendly to the abolition, and cannot therefore be supposed to be tinctured with any of the prejudices which may be presumed to bias the minds of the avowed advocates of the negro race. It would be a grateful task to lay before you such copious extracts, as would give you a full and minute enumeration of the particulars of the negro character; but my extracts, to do justice to the subject, would almost fill a volume. I must therefore refer you to my appendix for a brief specimen of them, and content myself here with exhibiting the mere outlines of the very different portrait which

Parke's character of the Negroes.

F   has

has been taken of the Negroes, after a more familiar and extended survey of their tempers and conduct.

Mr. Parke represents the Africans of the interior as naturally superior, both in their intellectual and moral endowments, to almost any other uncivilized nation. He speaks in high terms of their powers of ingenuity and invention, of their quickness and cheerfulness; of the value which they set on the learning within their reach, and the price at which they are willing to acquire it for themselves, or their children; of the skill which they display in several arts and manufactures. But the natural character of the Africans rises in our estimation, when, from considering their intellectual, we take a fair survey of their moral qualities; of the reverence for truth in which the children are educated by their mothers, among the Mandingoes, who, let it be observed, constitute the bulk of the inhabitants in all the vast districts of Africa visited by Mr. Parke; of their almost universal benevolence, gentleness, and hospitality; of their courage, and, when they have any adequate motive to prompt them to work, of their industry and perseverance; of their parental and filial tenderness, of their social and domestic affection,

fection, of the conjugal fidelity of the women, combined with great cheerfulness and frankness; of the extraordinary attachment of the Negroes to their country and home; in some cases, of their magnanimity, of which two instances are given, scarcely inferior to any thing which is recorded in Greek or Roman story.

Mr. Golberry's account of the negro character is at least equally favourable. "The " Foulahs, he says, are intelligent and indus- " trious, fine, strong, brave men; but, from " their habitual commerce with the Moors, " they are become savage and cruel. The " Mandingoes are well informed, graceful, " and active, and, in their mercantile cha- " racter, clever and indefatigable. The " Jaloffs are honest, hospitable, generous, " and faithful; their character mild, and " inclined to good order and civilization." Besides this account of particular nations, he observes of the Negroes in general, that they have both taste, ingenuity, and cleverness, and may be reckoned among the most favoured people of nature. They are, perhaps, the most prolific of all the human species, which is probably owing to the moderation they in general observe, in their habits, regimen, and pleasures. He bears,

<small>Golberry's character of the Negroes.</small>

if possible, a still stronger testimony to the benevolence, hospitality, frankness, and generosity of the negro character. The mothers, says he, are passionately fond of their children, and these discover in return great filial tenderness. The women are always kind and attentive.

Mr. Winterbottom's. Concerning Mr. Winterbottom's account, I will here only state, that it corresponds, in the great essentials of character, with the representations already given, though it be perhaps scarcely so favourable to the negro character.

The Hottentots vindicated. Even the poor calumniated Hottentots, who were long regarded as among the lowest in the scale of being, have at length found respectable and able advocates. Among the many good qualities which the Hottentot possesses, there is one, says Mr. Barrow, of which he is master in an eminent degree, a rigid adherence to truth: he may be considered also as exempt from stealing. Sir James Craig, when he commanded at the Cape, attempted to form an African corps, in defiance of the most confident prediction of the colonists, whose prejudices against the Hottentot race were scarcely less strong than those of Mr. Long himself. " We were told," says

says Sir James, " that their propensity to drunkenness was so great, we should never be able to reduce them to order or discipline; and that the habit of roving was so rooted in their disposition, we must expect the whole corps would desert, the moment they had received their clothing." Both these charges were confuted by experience. Sir James goes on to remark, " Never were people more contented or more grateful for the treatment they now receive. We have upwards of three hundred, who have been with us nine months. It is therefore with the opportunity of knowing them well, that I venture to pronounce them an intelligent race of men. All who bear arms exercise well, and understand, immediately and perfectly, whatever they are taught to perform. Many of them speak English tolerably well. Of all the qualities that can be ascribed to a Hottentot, it will little be expected I should expatiate upon their cleanliness; and yet it is certain, that at this moment our Hottentot parade would not suffer in a comparison with that of some of our regular regiments. They are now likewise cleanly in their persons; the practice of smearing themselves with grease being entirely left off. I have frequently observed them washing themselves in a "rivulet, where they could have in view no "other object but cleanliness." The poor Bosjesman Hottentots are also stated as a docile, tractable people, of innocent manners, and beyond expression grateful to their benefactors.

Character of Booshuanna and Bacoloo natives.

Some later travellers from the Cape of Good Hope, and in the service of Government, have penetrated into the heart of Africa to a great depth, but short of the region in which the Slave Trade prevails, and the account which, both from their own knowledge and from the representations of others, they give of the natives, is still of the same encouraging kind.

Character given of the Negroes by the Abolitionists witnesses.

After these accounts, you will not be surprized to hear, that the representations given of the Africans by the naval officers, and the men of science before alluded to, were highly favourable. One witness spoke of the acuteness of their perceptions; another, of the extent of their memory; a third, of their genius for commerce; others, of their good workmanship in gold, iron, and leather; the peculiarly excellent texture of their cloth, and the beautiful and indelible tincture of their dyes. It was acknowledged that they supplied the ships with many articles of provision, with wood, and water, and other necessaries.

cessaries. Some spoke in high terms of their peaceable disposition; all of their cheerfulness and eminent hospitality.

I have been the more diffuse on this topic, because, though our commercial connection with Africa be of so old a date, we have scarcely, till of late years, had any authentic account of the interior. In a region so vast, there must be a great variety of nations, and very different accounts may be adduced of particular countries; accounts not always, however, of a very authentic kind. But it is highly encouraging, and it is more than enough to rescue the African race from the unjust and general stigma which has been cast on it, to know, that later travellers who have visited the interior, in parts widely distant from each other, have made such pleasing reports of the intelligence, tempers and dispositions, habits, and manners of the natives of this vast continent.

But, notwithstanding all which has been here adduced in favour of the negro character, I am aware that there exists, not uncommonly, in the minds even of men of understanding and candour, a strong prejudice against the African Negroes, on the ground of their never having advanced to any considerable

Yet Africa never was civilized.— Argument resulting from that fact considered.

derable state of civilization and knowledge, in any period of the world. Let me be permitted, in the first place, to consider that position more particularly. They were always, it is alleged, to a considerable degree barbarous. Still more, in the remotest times to which our accounts extend, slavery, and even a Slave Trade, have been found to prevail in Africa. Hence a presumption arises, that her inhabitants are incapable of civilization, and that Africa cannot much complain of a practice which has become so congenial to her, and which seems to arise, not from European avarice, or cruelty, but rather from the genius and dispositions of her people, or from some incorrigible vice in her system of laws, institutions, and manners.

That Africa, which contains nearly a third of the habitable globe, should never at any period have been reclaimed from a state of comparative barbarism, is, indeed, on the first view, a strange phenomenon. But without stopping to comment on the precision of that reasoning, which, on this ground, should argue that it is justifiable for the European nations to make Africa the scene, and her sons the objects of the Slave Trade, we may confidently affirm, that a considerate review of the history, origin, and progress of civilization

zation and the arts, in all ages and countries, will not only explain the difficulty, but will give us good grounds for believing, that, reasoning from experience, the interior of Africa is full as much civilized as any other race of men would have been, if placed in the same situation.

How is it that civilization and the arts grow up in any country? The reign of law and of civil order must be first established. From law, says a writer of acute discernment and great historical research, from law arises security; from security, curiosity; from curiosity, knowledge. As property is accumulated, industry is excited, a taste for new gratifications is formed, comforts of all kinds multiply, and the arts and sciences naturally spring up and flourish in a soil and climate thus prepared for their reception. Yet, even under these circumstances, the progress of the arts and sciences would probably be extremely slow, if a nation were not to import the improvements of former times and other countries. And we are well warranted, by the experience of all ages, in laying it down as an incontrovertible position—that the arts and sciences, knowledge, and civilization, have never yet been found to be the native growth of any country; but that they have ever been
communicated

communicated from one nation to another, from the more to the less civilized. Now, whence was Africa to receive these valuable presents?

Let us summarily and briefly trace the actual progress of human civilization from the very earliest times. We learn from the Holy Scriptures, and the researches of the ablest antiquaries strongly confirm the supposition, that Mesopotamia was the original seat of the human race. We know not to what extent the globe had been civilized before the Flood; but the single family which survived that event, inhabited the same or an adjacent part of Asia. About a century afterwards, happened the dispersion of nations, and confusion of tongues; when different races of men, like streams from one common fountain, diverged in various directions to people the whole earth. Without going into minute, and therefore difficult, inquiries, we know that Assyria and Egypt were the first nations which attained to any great heights of social improvement. Babylon, the capital of Assyria, was built about 150 years after the flood, and the Assyrian empire is supposed to have soon after risen to a high degree of splendour. The neighbouring province of Egypt, from the mildness of its climate, and its singular fertility,

fertility, naturally attracted inhabitants, who, of course, brought along with them the arts of their native land. It is represented by the Mosaic writings to have been, about 450 years after the flood, a flourishing and well regulated kingdom; and all history testifies that it was one of the earliest seats of the arts and sciences.

Next to these come the Phœnicians, a colony from Egypt, situated on the coasts of Syria, whose advances towards refinement appear to have been great, and commercial opulence considerable. They gradually made settlements in the islands and on the shores of the Mediterranean. By them, the first rudiments of civilization, above all, the art of alphabetical writing, were conveyed to Greece, the various inhabitants of which were then in a far ruder state than most of the African nations in the present day. They are said to have been cannibals, and to have been ignorant even of the use of fire. Indeed, their barbarous state, had it not been proved by positive testimony, might have been almost inferred, from the single circumstance, of their assigning divine honours to him who reclaimed them from living on acorns and other spontaneous fruits of the earth, and taught them to cultivate the
ground

ground for corn. Greece, as is justly observed by Mr. Hume, was in a situation the most favourable of all others to improvements of every kind, especially in the arts and sciences. It was divided into a number of little independent communities, connected by commerce and policy, and exciting each other by mutual competition to those heights of excellence to which they at length attained, and which, in the arts of painting, sculpture, architecture, poetry, and oratory, have perhaps never since been reached by any other nation. About 150 years before Christ, Greece was subdued by the Romans, who thence derived their civilization and knowledge. By the extension of the Roman arms over almost the whole of Europe, the seeds of civilization were first sown in our northern regions, till then immersed in darkness and barbarism; and they sprung up and flourished during the order and security which, previous to the irruption of the northern swarms, prevailed for some centuries throughout the Roman empire. Such was the state of Europe.

In Asia also, the progress of the Roman arms was considerable, and their empire extensive: there were, besides, other great and populous nations, which, from their connection with the earliest seats of civilization, had
attained

attained to various degrees of social refinement. But of Africa, those parts alone which border on the Mediterranean Sea had been settled by colonies from any civilized nation. This will not appear extraordinary, if we consider the geographical circumstances of that quarter of the globe, and, still more, the low state of navigation among the ancients. Their knowledge of navigation was so imperfect, that they scarcely ever ventured out of sight of land; and the account of the Phœnicians having penetrated into the ocean, and having found a way into the East Indies by the Cape of Good Hope, although there now seems reason to believe its truth, was in general regarded as bearing on it's very face it's own contradiction. The Romans had therefore no access by the ocean to the interior of Africa; and it was separated from the provinces bordering on the Mediterranean by an immense sea of sandy desert, near nine hundred miles from north to south, and twice that extent from east to west, beyond which, though a few adventurous parties might venture to penetrate, there was nothing of the established regularity and order of a Roman province. The very tales which were told of the inhabitants of these districts, sufficiently denote the imperfect acquaintance and limited intercourse which subsisted with them.

Hitherto,

Hitherto, then, how or whence was civilization to find its way into the interior of Africa?

Next, the Northern nations, who, seeking for a more genial climate and a more fertile soil, in the finest provinces of both the eastern and western empire, overran the civilized world in the fifth century after Christ, were under no temptations to extend their settlements beyond those natural barriers which had formed the boundaries of the Roman conquests. While the coasts of the Mediterranean therefore were throughout ravaged and colonized, the interior of Africa was still neglected.

At length the all-conquering followers of Mahomet issued forth, and, after desolating the fine African provinces which were subject to Rome, some of their adventurous bands seem to have penetrated in various quarters into the interior, and, occupying the banks of one of the finest rivers, to have planted themselves, in greater or less numbers, beyond the immense desert which forms the northern boundary of interior Africa. But it should be remembered, that while the Mahometans, who overran the various provinces of both the eastern and western

western empires, became civilized by the nations they subdued, as Rome had been before by her conquest of Greece, so that they soon attained to a great degree of knowledge and refinement; the tribes which planted themselves in Africa, finding only nations as illiterate and as unpolished as themselves, retained all their original barbarism; while their ferocious tempers and habits, and their intolerant tenets, led them to keep down their negro subjects in a state of grievous subjection, and prevented that secure enjoyment of person and property which prompts men to industry, by securing to them the enjoyment and use of what they have acquired, and is indispensably necessary for enabling the mind to exercise its powers with freedom. Here, perhaps however, the first faint beams of knowledge and civilization shot into the darkness of the negro nations; and it is remarkable, that, barbarous as were the first Mahometan settlers of interior Africa, and hostile to all improvement as is the genius of Mahometanism, yet such is the effect of any regular government, that in those districts in which the Mahometans either possess the entire government, or a very considerable influence over it, there were many centuries ago great and populous cities, provinces not ill cultivated, and

and a considerable degree of social order and civilization.

It may therefore be boldly affirmed, that the interior, to which may be added the western coast of Africa to the south of the great desert, never enjoyed any of that intercourse with more polished nations, without which no nation on earth is known ever to have attained to any high degree of civilization; and that, contemptuously as we and the other civilized nations of Europe now speak of the Africans, had we been left in their situation, we should probably have been not more civilized than themselves.

Let the case be put, that the interior of Africa had been made by the Almighty the cradle of the world—that issuing thence, instead of from the north-western part of Asia, the several streams of nations had pervaded and settled the whole of that extensive continent—that the banks of the Niger, not less fertile than those of the Euphrates or the Nile, had been the seat of the first great empire—that the kingdoms of Tombuctoo and Houssa had been the Assyria and Egypt of Africa, and that the arts and sciences had been communicated to a cluster of little independent states, and, under the same favourable

able circumstances, had been carried to the same heights of excellence as that which they attained in European Greece—that these had been however in their turn swallowed up, together with the whole of that vast continent, by the arms of a single nation, the Romans of Africa, under the shelter of whose established dominion the various nations throughout that spacious extent, enjoying the blessings of civil order and security, the natural consequence had followed, that in every quarter the arts and sciences had sprung up and flourished—Might not our northern countries have been then in the same state of comparative barbarism in which Africa now lies? Might not some African philosopher, proud of his superior accomplishments, have made it a question, whether those wretched whites, the very outcasts of nature, who were banished to the cold regions of the north, were capable of civilization? And thus, might not a Slave Trade in Europeans, aye, in Britons, have then been justified by those sable reasoners, on precisely the same grounds as those on which the African Slave Trade is now supported?

However the last supposition may mortify our pride, it will appear less monstrous to those who recollect, that not only in
ancient

ancient times the wisest among the Greeks considered the barbarians, including all the inhabitants of our quarter of the earth, as expressly intended by nature to be their slaves; not only that the Romans regularly sold into slavery all the captives whom they took in the wars, by which on all sides they gradually extended their empire till it was almost commensurate with the then known world; but that our own island long furnished it's share towards the supply of the Roman market. Even at a later period of our history, we Englishmen have been the subjects of a Slave Trade, for which it is remarkable that the city of Bristol* was the grand emporium. That ancient city has now, I trust for the last time, retired from that guilty commerce.

In fact we know from history, that the great principle, of the demand producing the supply, has been amply verified in this instance, and that when countries in which slavery has been tolerated, have been sufficiently affluent to purchase Slaves, the Slaves have been caught and brought, like other wild animals, from the less civilized regions of the earth, where the inhabitants were less secure against fo-

---

* The account given of this Slave-trade by an almost contemporary historian, will be found in the Appendix.

reign

reign invaders, or against internal violence. Had not our island therefore been conquered by the Romans, who lodged in the soil the seeds of civilization which sprung up afterwards, when circumstances favoured their growth; and had the neighbouring provinces on the continent, from which otherwise the rays of knowledge might have enlightened us, remained also unsubdued; what reason is there to suppose that we, any more than the inhabitants of any other savage country, should now be a civilized nation? than, for instance, the whole continent of America before it was settled by Europeans? than the islands in the Pacific Ocean to this day?

But it may be even affirmed, that the Africans, without the advantages to be derived from an intercourse with polished nations, have made greater advancements towards civilization than perhaps any other uncivilized people on earth. Nor is this the state of those nations only, which, from their having received some tincture of the Mussulman tenets, may be supposed to have owed their improvement to their Mahometan invaders, but in a considerable degree in those countries also where there are no traces whatever of any such connection.

Let

Let us appeal to experience. In what state was Britain herself, when first visited by the Romans? More barbarous than many of the African kingdoms in the present day. Look to the aboriginal inhabitants of both the northern and southern continents of the new world, both when America was first discovered, and at the present day, with the exception, perhaps, of only the kingdom of Mexico. Look to New Holland, a tract of country as great as all Europe; look to Madagascar, to Borneo, to Sumatra, to the other islands in the Indian seas, or to those of the Pacific Ocean. Are not the Africans far more civilized than any of these? The fact is undeniable. Instead of a miserable race of wretched savages, thinly scattered over countries of immense extent; destitute almost of every art and manufacture (this is the condition of the greater part of the nations above specified), we find the Africans, in the interior, in the state of society which has been found, from history, next to precede the full enjoyment of all civil and social blessings; the inhabitants of cities and of the country mutually contributing towards each others' support; political and civil rights recognized both by law and practice; natural advantages discerned, and turned to account; both agriculture, and, still more, manufactures, carried to a tolerable a tolerable state of improvement; the population in some countries very considerable; and a strong sense of the value of knowledge, and an earnest desire of obtaining it. How great is the progress which the Africans have made, compared with the scanty advantages they could derive from their barbarous Mahometan invaders!

But it has been the peculiar misery of Africa, that nations, already the most civilized, finding her in the state which has been described, instead of producing any such effects as might be hoped for from a commercial connection between a less and a more civilized people; instead of imparting to the former the superior knowledge and improvements of the latter; instead of awakening the dormant powers of the human mind, of calling forth new exertions of industry, and thus leading to a constant progression of new wants, desires, and tastes; to the acquisition of property, to the acquisition of capital, to the multiplication of comforts, and, by the more firm establishment of law and order, to that security and quiet, in which knowledge and the arts naturally grow up and flourish: instead of all these effects; it has been the sad fate of Africa, that when she did enter into an intercourse with polished nations, it was an intercourse of such a nature, as, instead of

polishing

polishing and improving, has tended not merely to retard her natural progress, but to deprave and darken, and, if such a new term might be used where unhappily the novelty of the occurrence compels us to resort to one, to barbarize her wretched inhabitants.

<small>New phænomenon: interior of Africa more civilized than the coast.</small>

And now we are prepared both to admit and to understand a fact, which, though found to take place universally in Africa, is contrary to all former experience. In reviewing the moral history of man, and contemplating his progress from ignorance and barbarism, to the knowledge and comforts of a state of social refinement, it has been almost invariably found, that the sea coasts and the banks of navigable rivers, those districts which from their situation had most intercourse with more polished nations, have been the earliest civilized. In them, civil order, and social improvement, agriculture, industry, and at length the arts and sciences, have first flourished, and they have by degrees extended themselves into more inland regions. But the very reverse is the case in Africa. There, the countries on the coast are in a state of utter ignorance and barbarism, which also are always found to be the greatest where the intercourse with the Europeans has been the longest and most intimate;

intimate;—while the interior countries, where not the face of a white man was ever seen, are far more advanced in the comforts and improvements of social life.

This is so extraordinary a phenomenon, and it points out so clearly the pernicious effects of the Slave Trade on the prosperity of Africa, that it deserves the most serious attention. However extraordinary the statement may appear, it is confirmed by the unvarying testimony of all African travellers. Such is the result of the experience of Mr. Parke, who penetrated deep into Africa in one part; such is that of Mr. Winterbottom, who travelled about 200 miles inland in another: and the same extraordinary fact has since received a most striking confirmation, in the accounts, before recited, of the Booshuana and Baroloo nations.

Surely more than enough has been stated, to shew how far the present state of Africa is from furnishing any just grounds for believing that the Africans are incapable of civilization. Our only cause for wonder is, not that on the coast, where all is anarchy and insecurity, the inhabitants should have gradually declined from the state of civilization to which they had attained, and should have

have at length sunk into a state of profound ignorance and barbarism; for they have long been in circumstances which have been ever found utterly incompatible with the rise and progress of civilization and knowledge; the more just subject of astonishment is, that the kingdoms in the interior should still be found in a condition of so much civil order and improvement, in spite of the pernicious effects of the Slave Trade on their moral and social state. But, through the gracious ordination of Heaven, the political, like the natural body, can exist under severe and harrassing disorders. They may materially injure its health and comfort, and yet not utterly destroy it. Thus the evils which the interior countries suffer from the Slave Trade, are great and many; but their effects are not, as they commonly are on the coast, such as to break up the very foundations of society, and destroy the cohesion of its elementary parts. In the interior, the Slave Trade exercises powers of destruction which justly entitle it to the character of one of the greatest scourges of the human race. But it is on the coast, that it reaches its full dimensions, and attains to the highest point of its detestable pre-eminence.

But if the foregoing remarks prove plainly
that

that our Slave dealers have no just grounds for arguing, from the present uncivilized state of the coast, that it is incapable of civilization; surely we cannot but be astonished at the finished assurance, as well as the consummate injustice and cruelty, with which they would charge on the natural constitution and character of the natives of Africa, that very barbarism of which they themselves are the authors; and not only so, but which, after having produced it, they urge on us as a plea for continuing that wretched land under the same dreadful interdict, not only from all the comforts of the civilized state, but from all the charities of life; from all virtue and all happiness; sealing her up for ever in bondage, ignorance, and blood.

You have been detained, I fear, far too long before this melancholy picture; and yet I am almost ashamed of apologizing for prolixity, when I consider what " a world of woes" it is which I have been exhibiting to your view.

When men began to question the soundness of that logic, which grounded the right to carry off the natives of Africa into slavery, on their state of barbarism and ignorance; and still more, when it was retorted, that, even

<small>Slave Traders' argument that the Negroes were at home in a worse state of slavery.</small>

even granting the premises, that the Africans were thus dark and savage; the conclusion of a Christian reasoner ought naturally to be, that it was the duty of more favoured nations to civilize and enlighten, not to oppress and enslave, them; another set of arguments was brought forth; that two-thirds, or perhaps three-fourths, of the Africans were Slaves in their own country; and not only so, but that partly from the cruel and bloody superstitions, partly from the political despotism common in Africa, their state was so wretched at home, (the very worst West Indian slavery, as Mr. Edwards affirms, being infinitely preferable to the very best in Africa) that, independently on any motives of interest, humanity alone would prompt us to transport them from such a condition of misery and degradation, to the comparative Paradise of West Indian servitude. To all this the reply was obvious, that we had no right to make men happy against their will; and that whatever effect such an argument might have had on us, if urged from African lips, yet that it came before us in a very suspicious shape, when proceeding from those of a West Indian. But since all the above allegations, however unsatisfactory on grounds of justice, must be acknowledged to have some place in determining the practical effect

The assertion answered and refuted.

effect of the Slave Trade, on the happiness of the Africans themselves; it may not be improper to observe, that these assertions also are utterly disproved by Mr. Parke, and by other recent travellers, no less than by the witnesses produced by the Abolitionists.

The slavery of Africa appeared, in truth, to be a species of feudal or rather of patriarchal vassalage. The Slaves could not be sold by their masters but for crimes; not without the form of a trial, nor, in several parts, even without the verdict of a jury. They were described as sitting with their masters, like members of the same family, in primitive simplicity and comfort. "In all the laborious "occupations which Mr. Parke describes, both "agricultural and manufacturing, the Master "and the Slave work together without any "distinction of superiority." It appears also, from a passage in Parke, that Master and Slave stand towards each other in a parental and filial relation: "Have I not served "you—" said an African, who had served Parke in the capacity of a domestic Slave, "Have I not served you as if you had been "to me a father and a master?" Indeed it was the more ill-advised to make any comparison between the slavery of Africa and of the West Indies, because even the witnesses of

African Slaves real state.

our

our opponents give much the same account of the condition of the African Slaves.

These remarks ought ever to be borne in mind in all our considerations and reasonings concerning the state of society in Africa. They are sometimes, however, forgotten by the very writers themselves by whom they have been made. Our opponents have availed themselves of the ambiguities of language; and the state of these domestic Slaves, who are styled the bulk of the African population, is spoken of in terms applicable only to the condition of those wretched beings who are destined for the Slave-market, and who are waiting in fetters for a purchaser. The existence of this milder species of vassalage may even facilitate the complete civilization of the negro nations, by having familiarized their minds to the gradations of rank, and by having accustomed them to submit to the restraints of social life, and to be controlled by the authority of law and custom.

Opponents argument from the cruelty of the African despots, and particularly from those of the King of Dahomy.

Much use was likewise attempted to be made of the cruelties of some of the African monarchs, and especially of a certain king of Dahomy. " It was mercy to the poor Negroes to rescue them from such barbarities."

ties." But the argument was only a proof of the wretched straits to which our opponents must be reduced, when they called in the aid of such an auxiliary. Yet was this argument urged with a grave face by men of education and intelligence; and it may therefore deserve a serious, though a brief answer. It is probably true that the kingdom of Dahomy had the misfortune to be governed by a cruel tyrant. His invasion of the neighbouring kingdom of Whidah, was attended with a dreadful slaughter; and it may be fact, that, like a celebrated oriental conqueror, Nadir Shah, he thatched his palace with the heads of his prisoners. His cruelties, and still more those of the Dahoman monarchs in general, must however have been excessively exaggerated, since Mr. Devaynes, whose personal knowledge of Dahomy was greater than that of any other person, and who, though not favourably inclined to our cause, delivered his evidence with great frankness and candour, declared that the Dahomans were a very happy people. But, not to insist on the unfairness of attempting to justify the Slave Trade in general, by the cruelties said to be practised in one particular district, which constitutes not perhaps a fiftieth part of the region from which the Slaves are supplied; not to urge, moreover,

moreover, that, but for the Slave Trade, this whole system of superstition would probably have been ere now at an end; the cruelties of the Dahoman court are the effect of the native superstitions, and it therefore seems very doubtful, whether or not the Slave Trade lessens the number of the victims: while, as the very witness, who dwelt most strongly on this argument, himself allowed; it leaves their place, by having taken off the convicts who would otherwise have been sacrificed, to be supplied by innocent individuals. But, what will you say, when you hear that, as Atkins [*] informs us, the cruelties practised in the invasion of Whidah were committed by him in a war undertaken with a view of punishing the adjacent nation, for having stolen away some of his subjects, for the purpose of selling them for Slaves? Thus, it appears, that to the Slave Trade itself is fairly to be imputed this greatest of all recorded instances of the cruelties of an African warfare, that very instance on which our opponents have relied.

[*] Atkins was a surgeon in the Royal Navy, who visited all the British Settlements in Africa, with the Swallow and Weymouth men of war, in 1721; and whose account is the more to be credited, from his being a disinterested witness, whose testimony also was given before the justice or humanity of the Slave Trade had been called in question.

But

But an argument for the continuance of the Slave Trade has been grounded on the massacre, which would otherwise take place, of the Slaves which had been brought down to the coast for sale. This slaughter, however, even granting it to be well founded, ought, in all fairness, to be charged to the account of the Slave Trade, which had created the demand for these wretched victims. At any rate it would only happen once; for the Slave hunters would cease to catch and bring down for sale this species of game, when it was known there could no longer be any demand for it. But in truth, as the supposition is utterly contrary to common sense, so it is abundantly contradicted by experience; for it clearly appears from Mr. Parke, as well as from the testimony of other witnesses, that Slaves, when brought down to the coast for sale, are set to work for their own maintenance, or for their master's emolument, either when there is no demand for them, or when the price offered for them is deemed inadequate to their value. It further appears that, even at this time, " It sometimes hap-
" pens, when no ships are on the coast, that
" a humane and considerate master incorpo-
" rates his purchased Slaves among his dome-
" stics; and their offspring, at least, if not
" the

The Slaves brought to the coast for sale would be massacred in case of abolition.

The assertion positively contradicted by opponents partisans.

"the parents, become entitled to all the pri-
"vileges of the native class."*

Middle passage.

On the middle passage but little shall be said; but we must not pass from Africa to the West Indies, without some few observations.

When the public attention was first called to this branch of the subject, it was alleged, and with considerable plausibility, that self-interest alone would be a sufficient security against abuses; for not only was the owner of the Slave ship interested in having the Slaves brought to the port of sale in the best possible condition; but the master, officers, and surgeons of the ships had all a similar interest, their profits being made to depend, in a considerable degree, on the average value of the cargo. To this argument from self-interest, it must be confessed, that more weight was justly due in this part of the case, than in any other; because the interest was nearer, and more direct, and was not counteracted

* See Parke, p. 26. 290. 356.——So Lieutenant Matthews (an Opponents' witness, Privy Council Report p. 27.) says, "The Slaves that are purchased be-
"fore the rainy season commences are employed upon
"their plantations, and are sold to the Europeans, and
"sometimes among themselves, from one master to
"another, after the rice is planted."

by

by any interest of an opposite nature; yet even here it was proved but too decisively, that, as in other cases, nature was too hard for reason, the passions too powerful for interest. The habit of viewing, and treating these wretched beings as mere articles of merchandize, had so blinded the judgment, and hardened the heart, as to produce a course of treatment highly injurious to the interest of the owners and officers of Slave ships, and at the same time abounding in almost every circumstance that could aggravate the miseries of the Slaves. When the condition therefore and treatment of the Negroes on shipboard were first laid open, the indignation of the House of Commons was excited so strongly, that though the Session of Parliament had nearly closed, a Bill was immediately brought in and passed, with a view to mitigate their sufferings, during even the short period for which, it was then conceived, the existence of the Slave Trade could be tolerated. Human ingenuity had almost been exhausted in contriving expedients for crowding the greatest possible number of bodies into a given space; and when the smallpox, the flux, or any other epidemic, broke out among them, the scene was horrible beyond description. Even where there was no such peculiar aggravation, the sufferings of the poor wretches were such as exhausted all powers

powers of description. Accordingly, the average mortality on board the Slave ships was very considerable. Often, during a voyage of a few weeks, so many perished, that if in any country the same rate of mortality should prevail, the whole population would be swept away in a single year. The survivors also were landed in such a diseased state, that four and a half per cent. of the whole number imported were estimated to die in the short interval between the arrival of the ship and the sale of the cargo, probably not more than a fortnight; and, after the Slaves had passed into the hands of the planters, the numbers which perished from the effects of the voyage were allowed to be very considerable*.

A Bill for mitigating these evils was proposed by that justly respected member of the House of Commons, Sir William Dolben, and, after great opposition, was passed into a law. That law has since been from time to time renewed and amended, prescribing certain conditions and regulations, with a view to the health and comfort of the Slaves. For want of some effectual means of enforcing this law, many of its provisions have not, it is supposed,

* Vide Report of the Committee of the House of Assembly of Jamaica, in the Privy Council Report.—Vide also Long's History of Jamaica.

been

been carried into strict execution. Still its primary object has been attained, and the evils, arising from crowding great numbers into too small a space, have been considerably mitigated. Much good has likewise been done by turning the attention of the Slave dealers to the subject, and by convincing them that parsimony is not always œconomy.

But many of the sufferings of these wretched beings are of a sort, for which no legislative regulations can provide a remedy. Several of them, indeed, arise necessarily out of their peculiar circumstances, as connected with their condition on shipboard. It is necessary to the safety of the vessel, to secure the men by chains and fetters. It is necessary to confine them below during the night, and, in very stormy weather, during the day also. Often it happens that, even with the numbers still allowed to be taken, especially when some of those epidemic diseases prevail, which, though less frequent than formerly, will yet occasionally happen; and when men of different countries and languages, or of opposite tempers, are linked together; such scenes of misery take place as are too nauseous for description.* Still,

* Vide evidence of Mr. Newton, Mr. Claxton, and others.

in rough weather, their limbs must often be excoriated by lying on the boards; still they will often be wounded by the fetters:* still food and exercise will be deemed necessary to present the animal in good condition at the place of sale: still some of them will loath their food, and be averse to exercise, from the joint effect perhaps of sea-sickness and mental uneasiness; and still while in this state they will probably be charged with sulkiness; and eating, and dancing in their fetters will be enforced by stripes: still the high netting will be necessary, that standing precaution of an African ship against acts of suicide: but, more than all, still must the diseases of the mind remain entire, nay, they may perhaps increase in force, from the attention being less called off by the urgency of bodily suffering; the anguish of husbands torn from their wives, wives from their husbands, and parents from their

* I cannot vouch for the following fact, but it was related at the time with every appearance of authenticity. A few years ago the male convicts suffered very severely during their passage to New South Wales, and if I mistake not, for I speak from memory, several of them at length died from the hardships which they endured. On inquiring into the cause, it was stated to be, that the person whose province it was to provide necessaries for the voyage, had, by mistake, purchased such fetters as were used on board Slave ships, instead of the common fetters for convicts.

children;

children; the pangs arising from the consideration, that they are separated for ever from their country, their friends, their relatives, and connections, remain the same. In short, they have the same painful recollection of the past, and the same dreadful forebodings of the future; while they are still among strangers, whose appearance, language, and manners are new to them, and every surrounding object is such as must naturally inspire terror. In short, till we can legislate for the mind; till by an Act of Parliament we can regulate the affections of the heart, or, rather, till we can extinguish the feelings of nature; till we can completely unman and brutalize these wretched beings, in order to qualify them for being treated like brutes; the sufferings of the Slaves, during the middle passage, must still remain extreme. The stings of a wounded conscience man cannot inflict; but nearly all which man can do to make his fellow creatures miserable, without defeating his purpose by putting a speedy end to their existence, will still be here effected; and it will still continue true, that never can so much misery be found condensed into so small a space, as in a Slave ship during the middle passage.

But this part of the subject should not be quitted without the mention of one circumstance,

cumstance, which justly leads to a very important inference as to other parts of the case. When Parliament entered into the investigation of the situation and treatment of the Slaves, during the middle passage; notwithstanding the decisive proofs, adduced, and fatally confirmed by the dreadful mortality, of the miseries which the Slaves endured on shipboard, the Slave Traders themselves gave a directly opposite account; maintained that the Slaves were even luxuriously accommodated, and, above all, that they had abundant room, even when there was not near space sufficient for them to lie on their backs.* They added likewise, that at that very period the trade hung by a thread, and that the proposed limitation as to numbers, if carried into a law, would infallibly and utterly ruin it. The agent for the West Indies joined in their opposition, and predicted the mischief which would follow. The limitation was adopted; and scarcely had a year elapsed, before we heard from the West Indies, from the Assembly of Jamaica itself, of the benefits which the measure was likely to produce, on account of the gross abuses which had before notoriously prevailed, fatal alike to the health of the Slaves and the interest of the planters. Many years have now elapsed, and it is at length universally ac-

* Vide evidence taken before the House of Commons.

knowledged,

knowledged, that the measure has eminently contributed to the interest of every one of the parties concerned.* May we not infer, that probably, in other parts of this question, the parties do not always judge very accurately with respect to their real interests; and that the prospect of immediate advantage may cause them to be insensible to a greater but more distant benefit.

But against all, which justice and humanity could bring forward against the Slave Trade, it was still to be urged, that the continuance of it was necessary to the existence of our West Indian colonies. To put the argument in a more specific form, it was objected, that the stock of Slaves then actually in the West Indies could not be maintained by natural generation, without being recruited from time to time by importations from Africa, and therefore, that the abolition of the Slave Trade would produce the sure, though gradual, ruin of our colonies, with all those effects on the wealth and strength of the mother country which must follow from the loss of so valuable a member of the empire. *[margin: Grand allegation of West Indians, that the stock of Slaves cannot be kept up without importations.]*

To the examination of this objection, let me intreat your most serious attention; for on it, in fact, the whole argument turns, so far as policy is in question. For my own

* Vide the late Publication of a professional Planter.

part

part I hesitate not to say, that, let the apparent temptation of profit be what it may, it never can be the real interest of any nation to be unjust and inhuman; to suppose the contrary, would be almost to arraign the wisdom and goodness of the Almighty, as it would undoubtedly be, to admit a principle directly at war with his revealed will. Nor can I forbear taking occasion to congratulate my country, that in the discussions on this subject, the greatest of her statesmen, both dead and living, even those who have differed almost on every other question, have declared their concurrent assent to that grand and aweful truth, *that the principles of justice are immutable in their nature, and universal in their application; the duty at once, and the interest, of nations, no less than of individuals.*

Fully impressed with the force of these sentiments, I could not believe that the prosperity of the West Indies must necessarily be built on a foundation of injustice and cruelty; neither could I understand why, in the West Indies alone, the Negroes could not even keep up their numbers. The contrary supposition is in truth refuted, not only by its being a contradiction of the great Law of Nature, but by its being contrary to the universal experience of all other countries. For elsewhere, even under the most unfavourable circumstances,

<small>Presumptive arguments to the con-</small>

circumstances, not merely the human species, but specifically the Negro race, had been found to increase; indeed Negroes were said to be by nature peculiarly prolific. The climate of the West Indies is similar to that of Africa. Why then should the same race of beings gradually diminish in the former country, which in the latter have so increased and multiplied, as for two centuries to bear the continual drain of their population to the opposite side of the Atlantic. On examining whether in fact the negro race has kept up its numbers in other foreign countries, we find that it has increased, and sometimes rapidly, even where the influence of the climate might be justly supposed to be highly unfavourable.

trary, furnished by experience.

In Africa.

The climate of the United States of America is far from being well suited to the negro constitution, which, we are assured, is so little patient of cold, as even in the West Indies to suffer from it*. The cold in America is often very severe in the winter, even in

In the United States of America, Negro Slaves increase.

---

* Vide Practical Rules for the Management of Negro Slaves, by a professional Planter. " New Negroes " says he, court the warmest situations they can find, " nothing less intense than actual fire being too hot for " them. Hence we see that when they turn out in " the morning, even in the low lands in the West " Indies, they embrace their bodies closely with their " wrappers to defend them from the cold."

the

the southern states; and the peculiar nature of the employment of great numbers of the Slaves who work on the rice plantations, must operate very unfavourably on their health; yet the Negro Slaves are universally acknowledged to have so rapidly increased in that country, that, according to the last census of the American population, without taking into the account any importations, the Negroes had increased so much in the ten years last preceding the augmentation, that, advancing at the same rate, their numbers would be doubled in about twenty-four years.

Slaves increase, in Bencoolen.

Again, in Bencoolen, which has been accounted one of the most unhealthy climates on earth, the Negro Slaves had increased *.

Slaves increase, in the West Indies themselves.

But, lest the decrease in our Islands should be supposed to arise out of some peculiarity of the West Indian climate, even in the West Indies themselves undoubted instances of negro increase can be adduced. The crew of a Slave ship had been wrecked on the unsettled island of St. Vincent's, about the beginning of the 18th century. They had every difficulty to contend with, were wholly unprovided with necessaries, and were obliged to maintain a constant war with the native

* Vide the evidence of ———— Botham, Esq. in the Minutes of Evidence taken before the Privy Council.

Charaibs;

Charaibs; yet they had soon multiplied exceedingly.

Even in the island of Jamaica itself, the Maroons, the descendants of the Negro Slaves, who, when the island was originally captured, made their escape into the mountains, and ever afterwards lived the life of savages; the Maroons, who were acknowledged by the West Indians themselves to be, under peculiar circumstances, so unfavourable to the maintenance of their numbers, that their decrease would furnish no fair argument for the general impossibility of keeping up the stock, were found by actual enumeration to have nearly doubled their numbers in the period between 1749 and 1782. *The Maroons increase.*

In the same island of Jamaica, the domestic Slaves were said by Long to increase rapidly. The free Blacks and the Mulattoes, it was allowed by Mr. Long, increased. Several particular instances were adduced of gangs of Slaves having been kept up, and even having increased, without importations; and one of the most eminent of the medical men in Jamaica, who had under his care no less than 4,000 Negroes, stated, that there was a very considerable increase of Negroes on the properties of that island, particularly in the parish in which he resided, one of the largest in *The Domestic Negroes increase. The Free Blacks and Mulattoes increase.*

in Jamaica. All these instances certainly afforded a strong presumptive proof, that the stock of Slaves in the islands might be kept up, and might even increase without continual importations.

But the conclusion resulting from so much and such diversified experience was established also by positive and decisive proof. The assertion, that the stock of Slaves actually in the islands could not be maintained without continual importations, received an unanswerable refutation, especially from Mr. Pitt, whose superior powers of reasoning, as well as of eloquence, were never more powerfully displayed than in the debate of that memorable night when this subject was under discussion, and whose positions were clearly deduced from the very documents and accounts which had been supplied by the islands themselves.

Importance of the question, concerning the keeping up of the stock of Slaves without Importations.

Here, undoubtedly, lies the main stress of the case, so far as policy is concerned. On the determination of this question must obviously rest all the assertions which have been so industriously circulated, and all the apprehensions which have so generally prevailed, that the immediate abolition would prove ruinous to our West Indian Colonies. Even in 1792, much less in the present day, scarcely any man will deny, that if the stock of Slaves can be kept up, the abolition will, in various ways, be highly beneficial to the islands.

It was proved then, first, That the abuses and the obstructions to the natural increase, which too generally prevail, were sufficient to account for a rapidly decreasing population, and even to lead us to expect it. *Proof that Slave Trade not needed for maintaining the present stock of Slaves.*

Secondly, That the decrease, which really was considerable a century ago, had been gradually diminishing; till at length there was good reason to believe it had entirely ceased, and that the population fully maintains itself.

Thirdly, That, therefore, if the great and numerous abuses which now prevail should be materially mitigated, we might confidently anticipate a great and rapid increase in future.

These three propositions being made out, it follows of course, that the only substantial objection to the abolition, on the grounds of policy, is completely done away. To the proof, therefore, of these propositions respectively, let me beg your most serious attention. And now, in establishing the first of them, it becomes my duty to point out the various abuses of the colonial system, so *Proof of existing abuses unfavourable to increase.*

far

far as they have any natural tendency to keep down the population below its proper level. I am well aware that I am here about to tread on very tender ground. I know that it is imputed to the Abolitionists, that they have endeavoured to excite an unjust clamour against the Colonists by tales of cruelty, which, if not utterly false, or, at least, grossly exaggerated, were, however, individual and rare instances. They have been represented as the rule, it is said, not as the exception, and as fixing a general stigma on all colonial proprietors.

That on a subject naturally calculated to call forth powerfully the feelings of every humane mind, zeal may have carried some of our advocates too far, and made them not sufficiently discriminate between particular cases of ill-treatment, and the general system of management, I will not deny. Yet I might, perhaps, retort the accusation, and object, in my turn, that our opponents have not in general acknowledged even the particular cases of cruelty, and joined with us in reprobating them; but that the facts themselves have been denied, as if it were really the common cause of the Colonists, in which all were to stand or fall together.

Yet, surely, any one who considers how great, even in men of rank and education,
have

have ever been the abuses of absolute power; who recollects, besides, that in the West Indies, Slaves of inferior value are of very low price, and consequently, that any man who possesses a horse in this country might possess a Slave in that, would be sure that individual instances of cruelty must frequently occur. Let any one who should be inclined to pause on this position, consider how that noble animal, the horse, is too often treated in the face of day, in the very streets of the capital of this civilized country. But for myself I can truly declare, that I cannot be justly charged with having insisted on particular cases of West Indian cruelty. On the contrary, I have uniformly abstained from whatever could provoke or irritate the Colonists, as far as was possibly consistent with justice to the cause. I have sometimes even doubted whether the cause may not have suffered from my abstinence.

But, in justice to my own character, let me declare, that I have observed this line of conduct, not merely from interested motives, that our opponents might not be heated into still stronger opposition, but from feelings of a more generous nature. I have borne in mind, that the present generation of West Indian proprietors are not the first settlers of the colonies, or the first maintainers

tainers of the Slave Trade; excepting, however, the formers of the new settlements, which, alas! have been made to a prodigious extent within the last sixteen years. The older proprietors inherited their estates as we in Britain inherited ours; and must we not expect them to be naturally tinctured with the prejudices arising out of their circumstances and situations, since it is almost as difficult to be exempted from the operation of these in the moral world, as for natural productions not to possess the peculiar qualities and flavour of their climate and soil.

But, speaking generally, for the absentees I feel above all other proprietors; many of them born and educated in the mother country, and therefore possessing all the principles, sympathies, and feelings which belong to our state of society. They are most of them ignorant of the real state of things in the colonies; they naturally give credit to the accounts which they receive from their agents and correspondents. They often, I doubt not, in 'some cases I know, they send over orders to their managers to treat their Slaves with the utmost humanity and liberality. There are among them, men who consider the Slaves whom they inherit, as a family of unfortunate men, with whose protection and comfort Providence has charged them, and whose

whose well-being they are therefore bound, by the highest obligations, to promote.

Far therefore be it from me to throw out a general reproach against the whole West Indian body. In this case indeed, as in others of a similar nature, the more the general mass is liable to any taint, the more to be found exempt from it, is honourable. Surely those proprietors whose own consciences acquit them of all inhumanity, nay more, whose general conduct bears testimony to their kind and liberal feelings towards these unfortunate dependants, ought rather to aid our endeavours to reform the existing abuses, than to strive, by interposing their character, to shield them from the view, and, by so doing, to promote their continuance.

Let the West Indians of more enlarged and generous minds join me rather in examining into the vices of the existing system, more especially into those which have hitherto obstructed the increase of the Negro population. But to lay before you the various proofs which could be adduced of those abuses, would require a volume, and that not a small one. Want of time, therefore, will compel me to take a very cursory view of this very important part of my subject. I must content myself with specifying the chief abuses, referring generally for the proofs of them, to authentic, but too often voluminous documents.

It might alone however be sufficient, to establish the positions for which I shall contend, to refer you to a recent and most valuable publication, the work of a professional planter. The author was from the first an active and able opponent of the Abolitionists. But being a man of truth and candour, he has at once furnished a strong argument in support of their cause, and an invaluable service to his brethren, the planters, by not only stating the prevalent vices of the existing system, but by relating the remedies of them, which he himself applied, and the reforms by which, however inadequate, he acquired, in a few years, a large fortune, while at the end of that time, he had the satisfaction to see the number of his Slaves rapidly and greatly increased.

Actuated by motives at once benevolent and patriotic, desirous of mitigating the sufferings of the Negroes, and of directing the planters to those judicious and salutary reforms which would be found in the end to have

have been not more humane than politic, he addressed publicly his West Indian brethren, by whom, both from his general character for understanding and experience, he was naturally much respected, and among whom he was entitled to the more credit for having been among the foremost to repel the attack of the Abolitionists. But it was impossible to address the planters publicly, without his work being at the same time read by the friends of abolition. He must be on his guard therefore, lest he should afford a triumph to the latter by laying open the various evils of the West Indian system in their full extent. He had obviously a most difficult task to perform; and it is no more than justice to say that few men ever performed a difficult task with more ability. It is impossible, however, to peruse his work without perceiving in every page that he felt extremely embarrassed, by wishing to suggest the most salutary remedies without letting the world know too much of the disease. He writes like a man who on the one hand is conscious that he is prescribing to a patient who is very liable to take offence, and who wishes on the other not to disparage the reputation of the system of management which had been pursued by the former practitioner. Hence he rather hints a fault, and hesitates dislike,

dislike, than speaks out plainly. We ought to bear in mind the author's peculiar situation, and it's effects, during our perusal of his work, or we shall form a very inadequate idea of the real strength of the various abuses, from the soft colouring with which he paints them.

The increase a subordinate object of attention. And here I ought to commence with stating, as a grand and universally operative cause why the numbers of the Slaves did not increase more rapidly, that their increase was not made in general a primary object of attention. Here also there were individual instances of a contrary sort, but still the position is generally true. The dependance for keeping up the stock of Slaves was placed not on the increase to be obtained by births, but on the power of purchasing from time to time from the Slave market. This was abundantly proved by positive evidence; nay, even by the express declaration of the managers and overseers themselves; but it was established perhaps still more decisively, by its being almost invariably found that the most intelligent West Indians, who were the most fully acquainted with every other particular of the system, were commonly utterly ignorant of all that related to this important topic. On this head, their minds were a mere

mere blank, wholly unfurnished with any of those particulars with which they must have been familiar, had the increase of their Negroes been any great object of their care. Even medical men, though perfect adepts in all which regarded planting, appeared quite at a loss, when questions were asked of them connected with the breeding and rearing of children.

In some instances, even the colonial statutes have been framed on the same principles, and an annual poll-tax has been laid on Negro Slaves from their earliest infancy.

It is not however, that I impute even to the managers, much less to the proprietors of West Indian estates, that they entered into any grave and minute comparison between the breeding system on the one hand, and the working down and buying system on the other, and that they deliberately gave the preference to the latter as the most economical, in the full view of all its horrid consequences; but the truth is, that under all the circumstances of the West Indian colonies, it was perfectly natural that the buying rather than the breeding system should be pursued; nay, reasoning from experience, I had almost said, it was scarcely possible that the case should be otherwise, for it was a mode of proceeding which resulted from causes of sure and universal operation. Mr. Hume has clearly proved the truth of this position, in his celebrated Essay on the popoulousness of ancient nations; and he himself, after stating why the buying system had been preferred among the ancients, applies the reasoning to our Trans-Atlantic colonies, and speaks of the confirmation which his doctrine receives, from the maxims of our planters, as a known and acknowledged fact.* From the operation of similar causes, buying rather than breeding Slaves became the general policy, among the nations of antiquity; and hence it will infallibly continue the general policy in the West Indies, so long as a Slave market remains open for a purchaser's supply.

Will not they, who might hesitate to adopt this position, be disposed at least to deem it probable, when they hear, that, notwithstanding all the steps which have been taken, for so many years, towards the abolition of the Slave Trade; even yet, the price of women Slaves continues, as it has always been, inferior to that of men. This is the more curious, because our opponents have uniformly

* Vide Hume's Essays, vol. i. page 407. Edinb, 1777. Cadell.

alleged

alleged their not having a due proportion of females, as a primary cause of their not keeping up their numbers. It is obvious, that this is a cause which could, at the utmost, only exist among the imported Africans, and that there would be the usual proportion of males and females among the Slaves born in the islands, which, in all but the new settlements, constitute beyond all comparison the bulk of the Black population. What then can shew more clearly, that the planters do not, even yet, set themselves in earnest to produce an increase by breeding, than that, under an exaggerated impression of the effects of importing a too small proportion of females, and with a probability, at least, of abolition before their eyes, they suffer it to continue the interest of the Slave merchant, in preference to bring over males.

I must begin my enumeration of the abuses of the West Indian system, by mentioning *insufficient feeding*. It must be granted, indeed, that in this particular, the Slaves are very differently circumstanced in different islands. In the larger island of Jamaica, for instance, and in Dominica, wherein the Slaves can be chiefly fed by provisions produced on the estate, their quantity of food is far more ample than in those islands where the land

Vices of the West Indian system:— Insufficient feeding.

is so valuable, that little or none of it can be spared for this service; where also the droughts are so frequent and great, that the Negroes own provision grounds furnish but a very precarious and scanty supply. It might be sufficient to mention, that the allowance of provisions alleged to have been commonly given to the working Slaves, in most of the Leeward Islands, was not above half the quantity which, by an act of Assembly, lately passed in Jamaica, was required to be given to such runaway Slaves as, having been taken up, were lodged in prison till they could be returned to their masters. A prison allowance is not meant to be such as will pamper the body; yet double the food given in the former case to the working Negroes, was prescribed for a Slave in prison, who had nothing to do. I might also mention that acknowledged truth, that during the five or six months of crop time, when the labour is the most severe, the Slaves uniformly become much stouter and fatter, from the nourishment derived from the cane juice.

But as time will not allow me to prove the point completely, let me abstain from an imperfect enumeration of arguments, and satisfy myself with affirming, that I am fully warranted by the very respectable authority just

just now alluded to, in placing insufficient feeding among the general vices of the West Indian system; though in Jamaica, and in some of the other islands, the lands allotted to the Slaves for raising their food is sufficient, had they but time enough for working it. * I will only

* The professional Planter's own words well deserve to be inserted: " For I aver it boldly, melancholy experience having given me occasion to make the remark, that a great number of Negroes have perished annually by diseases produced by inanition. To be convinced of this truth, let us trace the effect of that system, which assigned, for a Negro's weekly allowance, six or seven pints of flour, or grain, with as many salt herrings; and it is in vain to conceal what we all know to be true, that in many of the islands they did not give more. With so scanty a pittance, it is indeed possible for the soul and body to be held together a considerable portion of time, provided a man's only business be to live, and his spirits be husbanded with a frugal hand; but if motion short of labour, much more labour itself, and that too intense, be exacted from him, how is the body to support itself."—" Their attempts to wield the hoe prove abortive, they shrink from their toil, and, being urged to perseverance by stripes, you are soon obliged to receive them into the hospital, whence, unless your plan be speedily corrected, they depart but to the grave. It may possibly be urged in palliation of this practice, that in cases of such short allowance as I have mentioned above, Negroes do not depend upon that solely for their subsistence, but that they derive considerable aid from little vacant spots on the estate, which they are allowed to cultivate on their own account.

only remark farther, that in America, where the Slaves increase so rapidly, the quantity of food allowed to the Negroes was vastly greater than the largest West Indian allowance.

<small>Defects in point of clothing and lodging.</small>

Clothing and lodging are, in the West Indian climate, less important particulars; yet in them too there is room for improvement, as there is also in the point of medical care.

<small>Overworking.</small>

Overworking is a still more important hindrance, in which perhaps the excess in the continuance of the labour, is more injurious than in its intensity. And here I might call in

" count. Though frequently otherwise, this may some-
" times be the case; yet even there it is to be observed,
" that such spots, in the low-land plantations, are ca-
" pable of producing only for a part of the year, either
" through the drought of the season or the sterility of
" the soil, and when that happens, the Negro is again
" at his short allowance; and having no honest means
" of ekeing it out, to make it square with the demands
" of nature, he is compelled to pilfer."—The writer
goes on to state, that the delinquent, extending his
thefts, is detected and apprehended, is severely whipped
and chained, and confined; but as neither chains nor
stripes, nor confinement, can extinguish hunger, he
returns, when released, to the same practices, till, partly
from the discipline, partly from scanty nourishment, and
colds from exposure during his desertion, he, ten to one,
falls into a distempered habit, which soon hurries him
out of the world. The close is very remarkable, " Now
" this was set down as a vicious incorrigible subject,
" and his death is deemed a beneficial release to the
" estate."

in Mr. Long as a witness, from whose experience on this head there ought to be no appeal. The passage is well worthy of attention: " I will not deny that those Negroes breed " the best, whose labour is least, or easiest. " Thus the domestic Negroes have more chil- " dren than those on penns, and the latter " than those who are employed on sugar plan- " tations. If the number of hogsheads, " annually made from any estate, exceeds, or " even equals, the whole aggregate of Ne- " groes employed upon it, but few children " will be brought up on such estate, what- " ever number may be born. But, where " the proportion of the annual produce is " about half a hogshead for every Negro, " there they will, in all likelihood, increase " very rapidly; and not much less so, where " the *ratio* is of two hogsheads to every three " Negroes, which I take to be a good *mesne* " proportion." Does it not then indisputably follow, that where the Slaves diminish, it is owing to the labour being disproportionate to their strength?

But of all the vices of the West Indian system which tend to prevent the increase, those which may be termed the moral vices and preventives, are those on which I must insist most strongly, and on which also I must dwell

Moral defects of the West Indian system.

dwell more particularly, because even by benevolent and liberal minds they have been too generally neglected. These are of all others the most efficient; since, in their consequences, they naturally produce the existence, or at least the aggravation of all the rest. Of these let me first specify the practice of polygamy, and much more the almost universal dissoluteness and debauchery of the Negro Slaves. These are evils which have been almost always assigned by the West Indian gentlemen themselves, as the grand obstacle to the production and rearing of children. And yet, strange as it may seem, no attempts whatever appear to have been made, excepting by three or four enlightened and liberal proprietors, to reform these abuses. Can a more decisive proof be afforded, either that the increase of the Negroes was never any serious object of general attention, or that the prejudices and passions of men often make them act contrary to their clear and known interest? No efforts have been made for the religious instruction and moral improvement of the Negroes, and any plans of that kind, when adopted by others, have been considered as chimerical, if not dangerous. This is the more extraordinary, because an example on a large scale, has been of late years furnished in the little Danish islands, and in one

Neglect of religious instruction.

one settlement, at least, of our own smaller islands, of the happiest effects resulting from such endeavours: so that men of great knowledge and experience in West Indian affairs, in estimating the effects of the labours of the missionaries, who were employed in this benevolent service, by a pecuniary standard, declared, that a Slave, by becoming one of their converts, was worth half as much more than his former value, on account of his superior morality, sobriety, industry, subordination, and general good conduct.*

In the French islands, likewise, the religious instruction of the Slaves was an object of very general care; and the intelligent West Indian Writer before alluded to, frankly declares, "that no person who has visited the French islands can deny, that in consequence of the improvements derived from this source, their Slaves are incomparably better disposed than our own." This is no singular opinion, and the Governor of Dominica stated an undeniable truth, when, in answer to the queries sent out by his Majesty, he declared, that " he was satisfied it was principally from this cause (of religious instruction), that the French Slaves were, in general, better, more

* Vide Privy Council Report—head, Antigua and Barbadoes—and some following articles.

attached,

attached, more contented, more healthy, more cleanly than ours." Their greater attachment and contentment are the more worthy of remark, because it is pretty generally agreed, that they were treated with more severity, and worked harder than our own.

In the Portuguese settlements also, and probably in the Spanish likewise, the religious instruction of the Slaves has ever been regarded as a concern of high importance.

Might we not then have expected that our own West Indian Proprietors would be prompted, not only by considerations of self-interest, but by motives of a still higher order, to pay some attention to the religious instruction of their Negroes? Might not mere humanity have enforced the same important duty? Might we not have hoped, that the Slaves of this Protestant and free nation, might have had some compensation made to them, for the evils of their temporal bondage, by a prospect being opened to them of a happier world hereafter, a world of light and liberty? But, alas! no such cheering prospects are pointed out to them. It is left, alas! to Paganism to administer to them, I had almost said happily, a faint imitation of that more animating hope which Christianity should

should impart; and these poor beings are comforted by the idea, that death will once more restore them to their native land; on which account it is, that, as we learn from most respectable testimony, the negro funerals in the West Indies are seasons of joy and triumph, whereas in Africa, they are accompanied with the usual indications of dejection and sorrow.*

But though this neglect of the religious and moral instruction of the Slaves, so manifestly leading to the master's immediate interest, may surprise on the first view, the problem will be completely solved on a farther insight into the system of management; and the mischief may be traced, if I mistake not, to a sure source of numerous and most malignant evils. For the various moral defects of the negro system appear to me often to be almost entirely caused, and always to be extremely augmented, by the Negroes, as a race, being sunk into the lowest state of degradation. *Degradation of the Negro race.*

That this was to be naturally expected, will be obvious to every reflecting mind, which considers, that, for many succesisve generations, the Negroes have not only been an inferior cast, a race of slaves, the slaves too

* Vide Captain Wilson's evidence.

of

of men enjoying, themselves, political freedom, and therefore elevated above them to a still higher point; but that there is a variety of circumstances, not forgetting that most important particular of colour, all tending powerfully to designate, and stamp them, as a peculiar, and that a base and degraded order of beings.

These are considerations of inexpressible importance; for these are they, which, by extinguishing sympathy, render the yoke of African slavery so peculiarly galling, and make it press on the West Indian Slave with such aggravated weight. Slavery, we know, existed among the ancients; and according to the savage maxims of Pagan warfare, (too strikingly agreeing with the mode of carrying on war which the Slave Trade has produced in Africa), not only the soldiery of an enemy, but the peaceable inhabitants of conquered countries were commonly sold as Slaves. But what an idea does it convey of the abhorred system, which, with coadjutors abler than myself, I have been so long endeavouring to abolish; that, just as in Africa, it has forced Christianity to acknowledge the superior power of Mahometanism, in rooting out the native superstitions, and in instructing and civilizing the inhabitants—so in our possessions in the western hemisphere, it combines

West Indian compared with ancient slavery.

bines the profession of the christian faith with a description of slavery, in many repects more bitter in its sufferings, than that which the very darkness of Paganism itself could scarcely tolerate.

This is the more grievous to those who duly venerate and love our most pure and excellent form of christian faith, because to have first mitigated the evils of slavery, and at length in a great degree to have abolished the institution itself, have been numbered among the peculiar glories of Christianity;* and because, what we deem a corrupted system of Christianity, has produced highly beneficial effects on the negro Slaves of our Roman Catholic neighbours in the same quarter. I cannot now enlarge on this topic; but thus much I must state, that the single particular, that the Slaves among the ancients were in general of the same complexion, features, and form, with their masters, was of itself a consideration of extreme importance. These masters were aware their situation was one, into which they themselves might be re-

* Vide a late publication on the beneficial effects of Christianity, by the venerable Bishop of London, a prélate in whom, whether in the closet, the pulpit, or the senate, the poor and the oppressed have ever found a zealous, and eloquent advocate.

duced by the fortune of war: this circumstance, together with the frequent elevation of Slaves to occupations of the highest confidence and importance, with a prospect, frequently realized, of emerging by emancipation into a state of liberty and comfort, was sufficient to render their condition infinitely preferable to that of our West Indian Slaves.* In the case of ancient slavery, instead of there being no place for sympathy, it was often in lively exercise; but even still more, hope was not extinguished; hope, the cordial drop of life, that on which, perhaps, more than on all which rank, and wealth, and power, and prosperity can give, depends the happiness of

---

* "*Are they Slaves?* No, they are men; they are comrades; they are humble friends. Are they Slaves? Nay, rather fellow servants; if you reflect on the equal power of fortune over both you and them."

"Were you to consider, that he, whom you call your Slave, is sprung from the same origin, enjoys the same climate, breathes the same air, and is subject to the same condition of life and death, you might as well think it possible for you to see *him* a Gentleman, as he to see *you* a Slave. In the fall of Varus, how many born of the most splendid parentage, and not unjustly expecting, for their exploits in war, a senatorial degree, hath fortune cast down! She hath made of one a shepherd, of another a cottager. And can you now despise the man, whose fortune is such, into which, while you despise it, you may chance to fall?"—Seneca, Epistle 47, p. 158.

man.

man. But to the West Indian Slave, on the contrary, his colour, his features, his form, his language, his employment, all tend on the one hand to extinguish sympathy, and on the other to shut him up as it were close and bound in his dreary dungeon, without a ray of light, without a chance of escape, the victim at once of degradation and despair.

Can it be necessary for me, in order to justify myself for dilating on so invidious a topic as that of the degradation of the negro race, to insist on the important effects which this degradation must necessarily produce in all the various particulars of negro treatment? Let me not here be misunderstood. The degradation of which I shall speak, and of which, while it continues, I must ever speak in terms of indignation, as of a gross infraction on the just claims of our common species, is not to be regarded as important, only, or chiefly, in the view of its being an outrage on the feelings of the Negroes themselves. If that were all, I might perhaps be charged with over-refining, and with measuring the opinions and feelings of the Slaves by a standard justly applicable only to men of far more enlightened and elevated minds. Though, even in this view, what an idea does it convey to us of their wretched state! How scanty must

Important effects of Negro degradation.

be

be their stock of comforts, when their very happiness is to arise from their being insensible to circumstances of humiliation, which all but a brute must understand and feel.

Hitherto it has been deemed one of the moſt debasing effects of slavery, to render men insensible to the extremity of their own degradation; and it is a new way of considering things to regard this insensibility as an alleviation of their wretchedness. But, alas! this degradation makes itself but too intelligible to the meaneſt capacity, and the most unfeeling heart. Its effects are such as come home at every turn to the Negroes' " business and bosoms."

Surely it would be a waste of time to prove to you in detail, that, throughout all nature, but especially in the human species, in proportion as any being is considered as possessing a higher or a lower place in the scale of existence, in that same proportion shall we be disposed to consider him as entitled to a larger share of our kind consideration; in short, in the same proportion will sympathy be awakened in his behalf, and sympathy is the great author and cherisher of every benevolent emotion. In that same proportion shall we be inclined to reflect on his situation, to spare his

his feelings, to multiply his comforts; in short, to pour, even though with a cautious hand, some drops of comfort into a cup, which, at best, must be but bitter, and of which, wherever sympathy is in exercise, we feel that we ourselves might have been fated to drink. Whatever, therefore, tends to depress that wretched class of our fellow creatures, beneath that low level which in any case they are doomed to occupy, tends compendiously and infallibly to the counteraction of every thing good, and the aggravation of every thing evil, in their unhappy lot.

Let it not then be thought, that in the odious recital which will follow, I am influenced by any invidious or ungenerous feelings towards the colonial Proprietors. I have a solemn duty to discharge, and however painful the task, however invidious, however liable to misconstruction, I must not shrink from it. It may be enough, I hope, to touch on the chief humiliating particulars.

And, first, comes in that most degrading spectacle of a negro sale. *Instances of degradation.*

Mr. Edwards himself acknowledges with *A negro sale.* frankness and liberality, that "there is something extremely shocking to a humane and cultivated

cultivated mind, in the idea of beholding a numerous body of our unfortunate fellow creatures in captivity and exile, exposed naked to public view, and sold like a herd of cattle." * But the account given of one of those sales by a late traveller, in his highly instructive and interesting work,† will convey a more precise idea of the scene:—" The poor Africans, says he, who were to be sold, were exposed naked, in a large empty building like an open barn. Those who came with intention to purchase, minutely inspected them; handled them, made them jump, and stamp with their feet, and throw out their arms and their legs; turned them about; looked into their mouths; and, according to the usual rules of traffic with respect to cattle, examined them; and made them shew themselves in a variety of ways, to try if they were sound and healthy. All this was distressful and humiliating; but a wound still more severe was inflicted on the feelings, by some of the purchasers selecting only such as their

* Edwards's History of the West Indies, 4to. vol. ii. page 124.

† Dr. Pinkard's Notes on the West Indies, printed for Longman. It ought, perhaps, in fairness to be mentioned, that the Author appears originally to have had no prejudices against the West Indian system.

judgment

judgment led them to prefer, regardless of the bonds of nature and affection."

"The husband was taken from the wife, children separated from their parents, and the lover torn from his mistress."

"In one part of the building was seen a wife clinging to her husband. Here was a sister hanging upon the neck of her brother. There stood two brothers enfolded in each others arms, mutually bewailing their threatened separation. In other parts were friends, relatives, and companions, praying to be sold to the same master, using signs to signify that they would be content with slavery, might they but toil together."

"Silent tears, deep sighs, and heavy lamentations, bespoke the universal suffering of these poor Blacks. Never was scene more distressful. Among these unhappy, degraded Africans, scarcely was there an unclouded countenance."

To the honour of the Legislature of Jamaica, the consolidated Slave Act, which passed in 1788, contained a proviso, which Mr. Edwards himself subsequently endeavoured to carry into more complete effect, that,

that, as far as possible, there should be no separation of the different branches of the same family. I might remark that such a law, from the very nature of the case, would be very imperfectly executed. But even where no such humane condition has been prescribed, let me observe, that it is not so much to my present purpose to notice the violence done to the domestic and social feelings of the Slaves, as to point out the tendency which the whole scene must have, to degrade and vilify the wretched beings in the eyes of the spectators.

Sales of Negroes for Owners debts.

It is another particular in the situation of these poor creatures, which should here be noticed; that they are personal estate, or moveable property, and that hence they are liable to be seized and sold for their Owner's debts. This operates the more unfavourably towards them, because, in the West Indies, there is always a more rapid change of property than in any other country; and never has there been more speculation, never more general difficulty and distress, consequently never more seizures and sales, than during the last twenty or thirty years.

These continual sales, often commonly by auction, not only of recently imported, but of

of homeborn and long-settled Negroes, are productive of the most acute sufferings to the Slaves, by tearing open, in the Africans, the old wounds, which might after many years have closed, and by forcing them once more from their homes, their families, and connections, when they had perhaps taken root in their West Indian soil, and multiplied their domestic and social holdings. These transplantations, besides, greatly tend to lessen the little disposition which the Slaves, circumstanced as they are, naturally feel, to endeavour to gain a good character, and obtain a master's confidence, in the hope that they and their families may possess a place in his esteem. There is an object which it is obvious will operate most severely in the case of the most industrious and best-conditioned Slaves. In proportion as they are of this character, they are likely to have multiplied their domestic and friendly relations, and in and about their dwelling-places to have collected such little comforts as have been within their reach, and as have tended to cause home to present, even to them, an idea of consolation and refreshment. But all of them have some home, all have some relatives and acquaintances. From all these they are hurried away, often necessarily separated from the closest of all connections. They are sent,
probably,

probably, to form new settlements, when, perhaps, past the prime of life, and to encounter hardships, and endure labours, to which their bodily strength is scarcely equal.* At least they have to form a new home, new connections, new attachments; and, when the best of their days have now been spent in vain, how must the spirits, even of the well disposed, sink within them, under the consciousness that they have to recommend themselves to a new master, when, from the mere decay of their bodily powers, they cannot hope, by the alacrity and vigour of their services, to obtain any considerable share of notice or esteem; or when, if at an earlier period of life, they are discouraged from attempting it, by the probability, that ere long they may again be transferred to a new owner.

But I wish you not so much to keep in view the deep wounds which the happiness of the

* Even before Mr. Long wrote, between thirty and forty years ago, this was a great evil. "And it is inconceivable," says Mr. Long, "what numbers have perished in consequence of the law for recovery of debts, which permits Negroes to be levied on and sold at vendue. By this means they are frequently torn from their native spot, their dearest connections, and transferred into a situation unadapted to their health, labouring under discontent, which co-operates with change of place and circumstance to shorten their lives." Long's Jamaica, vol. ii. p. 435.

Slaves must sustain from these frequent sales. It is to my present purpose to consider their effect in accustoming men to disregard their comforts and feelings. It is impossible but that such incidents must tend powerfully, and in various ways, to vilify and degrade the Blacks in the general estimation, and hence to produce an habitual disregard to their comforts and feelings.

It may be proper to state, that it was urged by our West Indian opponents, that the grievance we have been now considering, may fairly be laid to the charge of the British Parliament, having been sanctioned by a statute passed in the time of George the Second, for the security of the creditor in the mother country. The West Indian legislatures, it was added, were bound not to enact any provision contrary to the laws of England, and were therefore forced to endure this cruel and pernicious law.

It would not be difficult to shew that this charge is not well founded; but it may suffice, for the present, to remark, that, even granting that the effect of the 5th of Geo. 2d was such as is here supposed, yet that Slaves were not for the first time rendered by that law personal property, and liable to be sold separate from

from the land for the payment of the simple contract debts of the Master. They have always been in that wretched state. Still more it might truly be alleged, that the Legislature of this country was utterly ignorant of the effect of the law on the happiness of the Negroes, and not even a hint was dropped on that subject by any one of the many West Indian Gentlemen in Parliament; and, when the mischievous effects of the statute were explained, Parliament immediately and unanimously consented to the very first proposal which was made for repealing it. We do not find however, that the West Indian legislatures have availed themselves of the acknowledged right of rescinding it, which they now enjoy. Supposing therefore, what is not however the fact, that, in this instance only, the British Parliament and the Colonial legislatures, the former utterly ignorant of all the practical evils resulting to the Slaves from the law in question, the latter having them daily before their eyes, to have been both parties to the wrong; we have at least done our part towards redressing the injury; they have not done theirs.

The universal practice of working under the whip. The next particular which must be mentioned, is, like all the rest, at once an evidence and an effect of the degraded state of the Negroes.

Negroes. It is that universal and established practice of working them under the whip like cattle.* And here is it possible for any one

* But a nearer and more particular view of the manner of working may be necessary to those who have never seen a gang of Negroes at their work:

" When employed in the labour of the field, as for
" example, in *holeing a cane piece*, i. e. in turning up the
" ground with hoes into parallel trenches, for the recep-
" tion of the cane plants, the Slaves of both sexes, from
" twenty perhaps to four score in number, are drawn out
" in a line, like troops on a parade, each with a hoe in
" his hand; and close to them in the rear is stationed a
" driver, or several drivers, in numbers duly proportioned
" to that of the gang. Each of these drivers, who are
" always the most active and vigorous Negroes on the
" estate, has in his hand, or coiled round his neck, from
" which by extending the handle it can be disengaged
" in a moment, a long, thick, and strongly platted whip,
" called a *cart whip*, the report of which is as loud, and
" the lash as severe, as those of the whips in common
" use with our waggoners, and which he has authority
" to apply, at the instant when his eye perceives an
" occasion, without any previous warning. Thus dis-
" posed, their work begins, and continues without inter-
" ruption for a certain number of hours, during which, at
" the peril of the drivers, an adequate portion of land
" must be holed.

" As the trenches (continues our Author) are generally
" rectilinear, and the whole line of holers advance toge-
" ther, it is necessary that every hole or section of the
" trench should be finished in equal time with the rest;
" and if any one or more Negroes were allowed to throw
" in

one not to feel peculiarly shocked at the idea of working females in this method; the consequence of which must unavoidably be, that notwithstanding the immunities which may be allowed in more advanced stages of pregnancy, or even as soon as a woman is known to be in that state, yet that females will in fact be often worked in this mode, at times, and under circumstances, when Nature peculiarly calls for forbearance, tenderness, and support. Let me repeat, that it is not civilization merely, and politeness, as sometimes happens in the case of artificial wants; it is Nature herself, which, in such circumstances, claims some sympathy and indulgence.

" in the hoe with less rapidity or energy than their companions in other parts of the line, it is obvious that the work of the latter must be suspended; or else, such part of the trench as is passed over by the former, will be more imperfectly formed than the rest. It is therefore the business of the drivers not only to urge forward the whole gang with sufficient speed, but sedulously to watch that all in the line, whether male or female, old or young, strong or feeble, work as nearly as possible in equal time, and with equal effect. The tardy stroke must be quickened, and the languid invigorated, and the whole line made to *dress*, in the military phrase, as it advances. No breathing time, no resting on the hoe, no pause of languor, to be repaid by brisker exertion on return to work, can be allowed to individuals: all must work, or pause together."

dulgence. And is this a time, are these circumstances, in which a female should be urged to her labour by the stroke, or even the crack of the whip? To view the practice in a mere mercenary view, surely if the West Indian Gentlemen had been seriously and earnestly intent on superseding the necessity of purchasing from the Slave market, by rearing Negroes on their own estates, the younger women at least, if employed in field-work at all, would not be worked in this rude and undistinguishing manner, when a single inconsiderate lash of the driver's whip, intended not as a punishment, but as a quickener, or a memento, may in its consequences, prevent the birth of a future infant. Surely I need not enlarge on this disgusting topic, or enumerate in detail the various evils which must result from so hateful a practice; it's tendency greatly to lessen, if not almost utterly to extinguish in the Slaves, all honest, I had almost said, all mercenary emulation or competition, all the hopes of obtaining a master's approbation and confidence; it's admitting no occasional remissions of labour, afterwards to be compensated by increased exertions; it's making no allowance for different states of mind or body; but, without inquiry as to these, as the post-horse is to go through his stage, so the Slave under the same impulse is to keep up with his fellows: In short,

short, it's utter forgetfulness of *mind* in the human subject, who is thus considered and treated as of an inferior species, as not capable of being worked upon by the ordinary motives of the hope of reward, or even the fear of punishment; as one who, like the vilest of the brute species, has no foresight or recollection, and must therefore be subjected to the same humiliating regimen.

Cruel and indecent public punishments of Slaves. Another particular, concerning which I am doubtful whether it ought to be noticed chiefly as a cause of the degradation of the Negro race, or as an evidence and effect of that degradation, is the cruel, and, in the case of the female sex, still more the highly indecent punishments inflicted in places of public resort, and in the face of day. Unless the feelings of sympathy towards Blacks, as fellow-creatures, or of decency respecting them as of our own species, were not, to so great a degree, extinct, such exhibitions would not be continued, if from no better motive, yet because they would counteract their own effect, when they were the execution of a public sentence, by interesting all beholders in favour of the criminal, and bringing, to use the phrase of our law, the Government into hatred and contempt; or because, when they were punishments ordered by a master or mistress, besides probably producing a riot, they would render
those

those who ordered them the subject of general obloquy. But, regarded as Blacks now are by the bulk of the population, there seems to have been no fear lest public executions, by the most cruel and protracted tortures, should be matter of public scandal. As for the punishments of Owners, when General T. saw the shameless and cruel flogging, on the public parade, of two very decent women, who, while waiting at table where he was visiting, had been ordered by their mistress, in spite of his expostulations, to go with the Jumper (or public Flogger), to receive a dozen, each stroke of which brought flesh from them, we do not find that the incident excited any surprize or attention in any one but the General himself.* If such could be the treatment sanctioned by public opinion, and general feeling, of decent young women, publicly and in the face of day, what consideration would be likely to be paid to the comforts and feelings of the field Negroes, who are regarded as a far inferior race to the domestics, especially when there are no officious bystanders to witness what may take place.

Let me but ask, what must be the effect necessarily produced on the mind from having been habituated to such scenes as these from

* Vide Evidence taken before the Committee of the House of Commons.

early

early infancy? Can we be surprized to hear that, too often, even the delicacy and tenderness of the female sex is not proof against the natural consequences of daily beholding such spectacles?* Should we not be almost prepared to find, the particular which I confess has ever most deeply affected my mind as being of all others the most decisive proof of the utter vileness and degradation of the Negro race, that utter contempt which too generally prevails of their social and domestic feelings; that they are too commonly regarded as below instruction, below the range of moral precepts and prohibitions, below the sphere of the obligations, duties, restraints, and comforts of conjugal, domestic, and social life.

<small>Other signs of degradation.</small>

Hence, doubtless, proceeds their being in some degree regarded, like their fellow brutes, as below the necessity of observing towards others the proper decencies of life, or of having these decencies observed by others towards them. Hence, while Mr. Parke assures us, that in Africa, adultery is not more frequent than in this country, we hear the most respectable Colonists treat the very idea of introducing marriage among the Slaves, in

* Dr. Pinckard's late publication adds some painful instances of this sort to others contained in the evidence of very respectable men.

their

their present state, as perfectly hopeless or ridiculous.

Do we not here find the explanation of that strange phenomenon, formerly mentioned, that while the prevalence and evils of dissoluteness are universally acknowledged, scarcely any one thinks of applying that which has already appeared from experience so safe, so appropriate, and so beneficial a remedy?

But it is time to pass to another most important particular, which, like those already mentioned, is at once both cause and effect, both an evidence and a consequence of degradation—the inadequate protection afforded to the Slaves by the laws. Inadequate legal protection.

Here again let me not be misunderstood. It is not the matter of my present complaint, that, from the inadequate penalties annexed to the ill-treatment of Negro Slaves, and that still more from the evidence of black and coloured men not being admissible, they are subject to the restraints of civilized society, without being partakers of its benefits. Much might be said, much has been said, to prove how insufficiently they are secured by the laws against injuries and insults. On the other hand, considerable stress, too has sometimes been

been laid on the mildness of the penalties where the offences of Slaves were to be punished, and still more on the laws which have from time to time been passed for the protection of Slaves. The former assertion might be but too effectually disproved, by appealing to various passages in the Colonial statute book; and, where admitted, the lenity might be traced to a cause less generous than disinterested humanity. It might have been suggested to one of the most powerful of our colonial opponents, who urged that capital executions of Slaves had taken place in very few instances, that they might naturally be expected to be more rare, and punishments in general more lenient, where men's own property would suffer from severity.

Concerning all laws for the protection of the Slaves, it might be justly remarked, that so far as the protection of Slaves is concerned against ill usage from all but their Masters, it was natural that the Slaves of any man should be protected equally with his cattle, or any other articles of his property; nor did the Slaves, any more than the cattle, owe this protection to the humanity of the legislature. They were protected merely like the rest of his substance.

But

But as to the far more important consideration, concerning legal protection from the Owner's ill usage, it is unquestionably true, that be the laws what they may, " so long as the evidence of black or coloured men against whites continues inadmissible," the latter, in all that respects the treatment of Negroes, are " in a manner put beyond the reach of the law." Such were the very words in which a much respected Colonial Proprietor, though called as one of our opponents witnesses, acknowledged the important truth.

His testimony on this head was the more worthy of attention, because, besides his long residence in the West Indies, and his known intelligence and habits of observation, he was for some time Chief Justice of one of our islands. He also acknowledged, that till black evidence should be admissible, he knew no possible mode of preventing the most gross infractions of any laws against the ill treatment of Negroes. The subsequent death of this valuable man is deeply to be regretted; because, with several of his immediate connections, he was exempt from many of the prejudices which, in colonial proprietors, too often obstruct the reform of West Indian abuses.

A remarkable

A remarkable proof was afforded how little the Slaves were regarded as under the protection of law, against their Masters ill usage, by a transaction which took place a few years ago, in one of our oldest sugar colonies, and of which an account is contained in the Privy Council report:

A man, named Herbert, in low circumstances, and of very indifferent character, had been guilty of an act of the most wanton cruelty, which was rendered still more atrocious by being committed against the helplessness of infancy. He had most wantonly and cruelly lacerated the mouth and face of a child six years old, his own Slave, in a shocking manner, and bruised various parts of its little body. The crime happened to be committed under circumstances which admitted of legal proof, and, owing to the benevolent and spirited exertions of a man of legal eminence, who then resided in the neighbourhood, and who himself was able to give decisive evidence, a prosecution was carried on against the perpetrator. The facts were clearly established, and most horrible they were; yet so strange and novel a doctrine did it appear to the jury, that a Master was liable to punishment for any act of cruelty exercised on his own Slave, that, after long consultation, they brought in a conditional

conditional verdict, " Guilty, subject to the "opinion of the Court, if immoderate correc-"tion of a Slave, by his Master, be a crime "indictable." The Court determined in the affirmative; and what was the punishment of this abominable act of barbarity? A fine of forty shillings currency, equivalent to about thirty shillings of our money! This was the more extraordinary, because only two years before, in consequence of some recent acts of abominable cruelty, an Act of Assembly had been passed for the express purpose of preventing barbarities of a similar nature, and a fine of £.500 currency, together with six months imprisonment, had been annexed as the punishment of such offences. But so little were the enactments of law in unison with the general' feelings of the bulk of the people, that even after this statute had been passed, not only did a jury doubt whether the most wanton barbarity towards an infant, by its owner, was liable to any punishment; but the idea of calling a Master to account for this ill-treatment of one of his own Slaves created a popular ferment, and a violent cry against the prosecutors of the delinquent, and was resented as a gross and novel infraction of the rights and privileges of ownership. This very Herbert afterwards brought his action against the Provost Marshal, for having taken

taken the poor unoffending boy into his custody, partly that the child might be forth-coming, partly to save him from the violence of his brutal Master. The Provost Marshal, after a long course of judicial proceeding, would have had heavy penalties to pay, had he not got off on a point of law. Herbert was considered as a persecuted man, and became a highly popular character in the community.

But that which renders this incident most of all worthy of remark, is, that unsatisfactory as the issue might appear to us to have been, a detailed account of it, with some other instances too much in the same spirit, was sent over to the Privy Council, by the Council and Assembly of the island, with some apparent satisfaction, as a proof of the protection enjoyed by the Slaves against immoderate punishment or cruelty on the part of their Masters.

Not to insist in this place on the impossibility of enforcing any laws which may be enacted for the protection and comfort of Slaves, a topic on which I may have occasion to say more hereafter, law and slavery are, in their own nature, absolutely and universally incompatible. The Slave's best protection must ever be found in his Master's kindness, especially where kindness is combined with affluence;

affluence; and, by giving to the Slaves a nominal right to definite legal privileges, you only infuse a spirit of discontent into them, and a spirit of suspicion and resentment into their Masters; at least, until the absolute nullity of the law be clearly manifest to both parties. The Master has not the same motives for tenderness, (motives ever powerful in a generous mind) as when all right, all rivalship are excluded, and he knows that his Slaves are given up completely into his power; that they are entirely dependent on his will, and that they must receive every favour as flowing altogether from his spontaneous beneficence. It is not therefore going too far, to affirm, that by destroying, or at least impairing, the force of these feelings, you do the Slave more harm, than can be compensated by any benefit he can derive from the laws.

But to quit this view of the subject, it is the effect, in another direction, of this inadequate protection of the laws, to which I wish to point your particular attention. I wish you to observe the proofs which it affords of the low estimate of the Negro race; as well as the tendency which it must have to keep them in their present abject and depressed condition. *Considered in the view of its degrading effects.*

But

But here, instead of quoting passages from the statute books and judicial records of the several islands, which might be objected to, as an unfair test of the opinions and feelings of the present generation, I will extract from a set of papers, laid not long ago before the House of Commons by Government, the account, given from the most respectable authority, of some transactions which have recently taken place, and which shew the degraded state of the Negro race in, excepting Jamaica, the largest and oldest settled of all our West Indian colonies.

The Governor of Barbadoes, Lord Seaforth himself, I understand, an old West Indian proprietor, in consonance with the wishes of many respectable inhabitants, endeavoured lately, from the most honourable motives, to procure the repeal of a law which had long been the disgrace of the Barbadoes statute book, and for the rescinding of which an effort had been in vain made a few years before; a law, by which the wilful murder of a Slave was punishable only by a fine of £.15. currency, or about £.11. 4 *s*. sterling*. His Lordship therefore sent a message in the common form to the House of Assembly, re-

* Vide House of Commons papers.

commending

commending that an act should be passed to make the murder of a Slave a capital felony. There seems every reason to believe that the Council, or Colonial House of Lords, would gladly have assented to the proposition. But, strange as it may appear to those who are unacquainted with the West Indian prejudices, notwithstanding the time and manner in which the proposition was brought forward, the House of Assembly absolutely refused to make the alteration. But if the bare statement of this fact must shock every liberal mind, how much will the shock be increased, when it is known under what circumstances it was that this refusal took place.

For it happened, that, very recently, several of the most wanton and atrocious murders had been committed. Some of these were accompanied with circumstances of such horrid and disgusting barbarity, as to be too shocking for recital; and yet it scarcely seems justifiable to allow such horrid deeds, from their very atrociousness, to derive impunity. But one of the accounts you must submit to hear, because the narrative contains circumstances which strikingly illustrate the condition and estimation of the Negro race. To myself, to say the truth, it tells me, in the view in which I shall here regard it, nothing more'
than

than I already knew; but it was scarcely to be expected that Providence would furnish such undeniable and glaring proofs, of the assertions we had before established by the most respectable testimony.

Extract of a Letter from the Right Hon. Lord Seaforth, to Earl Camden, one of His Majesty's principal Secretaries of State, dated Barbadoes, 7th Jan. 1805.

" I inclose the Attorney General's letter
" to me on the subject of the Negroes so
" most wantonly murdered. I am sorry to
" say, *several other instances of the same bar-*
" *barity* have occurred, with which I have
" not troubled your Lordship, as I only
" wished to make you acquainted with the
" subject in general."

It will be enough for me to quote that part of the Attorney General's letter in which he gives the account of the single murder which I wish to lay before you:

Extract of a Letter from the Attorney General of Barbadoes, to the Governor of the Island.

" A Mr. ———, the manager of a plan-
" tation in the neighbourhood, had some
" months before purchased an African lad,
" who

" who was much attached to his person, and
" slept in a passage contiguous to his chamber.
" On Sunday night there was an alarm of
" fire in the plantation, which induced
" Mr. ——— to go out hastily, and the next
" morning he missed the lad, who he supposed
" intended to follow him in the night, and had
" mistaken his way. He sent to his neigh-
" bours, and to Mr. C—— among the rest,
" to inform them that his African lad had
" accidently strayed from him; that he
" could not speak a word of English, and
" that possibly he might be found breaking
" canes, or taking something else for his
" support; in which case he requested that
" they would not injure him, but return him,
" and he would pay any damage he might
" have committed. A day or two after,
" the Owner of the boy was informed, that
" Mr. C. and H. had killed a Negro in a
" neighbouring gully, and buried him there.
" He went to Mr. C—— to inquire into the
" truth of the report, and intended to have
" the grave opened, to see whether it was
" his African lad. *Mr. C—— told him,*
" *a Negro had been killed and buried there;*
" *but assured him it was not his, for he knew*
" *him very well, and he need not be at the trou-*
" *ble of opening the grave.* Upon this the
" Owner went away satisfied. But receiving
" further

" further information, which left no doubt
" upon his mind that it was his Negro, he
" returned and opened the grave, and found
" it to be so. I was his leading counsel, and
" the facts stated in my brief were as follow:
" That C. and H. being informed that there
" was a Negro lurking in the gully, went
" armed with muskets,. and took several
" negro men with them. The poor African
" seeing a parcel of men coming to attack
" him, was frightened; he took up a stone
" to defend himself, and retreated into a
" cleft rock, where they could not easily
" come at him; they then went for some
" trash, put it into the crevice of the rock
" behind him, and set it on fire; after it
" had burnt so as to scorch the poor fellow,
" he ran into a pool of water near by; they
" sent a Negro to bring him out, and he
" threw the stone at the Negro; upon
" which the two white men fired several
" times at him with the guns loaded with
" shot, and the Negroes pelted him with
" stones. He was at length dragged out of
" the pool in a dying condition, for he had
" not only received several bruises from the
" stones, but his breast was so pierced with
" the shot, that it was like a cullender. *The*
" *white savages ordered the Negroes to dig a*
" *grave, and whilst they were digging it, the*
" *poor*

" *poor creature made signs of begging for water;*
" *which was not given to him, but as soon as*
" *the grave was dug, he was thrown into it,*
" *and covered over; and there seems to be some*
" *doubt whether he was then quite dead.—*
" C. and H. deny this; but the Owner
" assured me that he could prove it by more
" than one witness; and I have reason to be-
" lieve it to be true, because on the day of
" trial, C. and H. did not suffer the cause
" to come to a hearing, but paid the penal-
" ties and the costs of suit, which it is not
" supposed they would have done had they
" been innocent.

" I have the honour to be, &c."

The same transaction, with another far more dreadful murder, in which there was a deliberate ingenuity of cruelty which almost exceeds belief, is related, with scarcely any variation as to circumstances, by the Advocate General, who, as well as the gentleman of whose estate the criminal was the manager, and who was at the time absent, expressed their most lively indignation against such horrid cruelty. After so shocking a recital, lest you should be instinctively urged to be chiefly affected by the barbarity of this horrid transaction, let me once more remind you, that it is not in the view of its cruelty that
I wish

I wish you to regard the foregoing narrative; but in that of the decisive evidence which it affords of the utter degradation of the negro race.

How striking a proof is afforded of this, in the conduct even of the Owner of the boy, the prosecutor of the delinquent, a man too, as the beginning of the story indicates, "of kind and liberal feelings." Can any thing suggest more strongly, that the protection which the Negro Slave receives from the laws, is too often to be ascribed rather to a Master's care of his property, than to any more generous motive. When he had only reason to believe that *a* Negro had been killed, and buried out of the way, and not that it was his own Slave, he goes away satisfied. Again, it is a suggestion which the circumstances of the story enforce on us, that the crowd, which was now collected, instead of being shocked at such barbarity, were rather abettors of it; and then we hear, the White Savages, as the Attorney General justly styles them, order the Negroes who were present to dig a grave for their wretched countryman; they knew their state too well to refuse, and accordingly we see them immediately obey the order; yet I confess, that with all my ideas of their sunk and prostrate spirit, I was myself surprized, under

under all the circumstances, by this promptitude of obedience.

But I have not leisure to deduce half of the important lessons which we are taught by the above horrid recital. Let us pass to the circumstance which is most of all important; because it proves how little we can expect an identity of sympathies and feelings between the Colonists and ourselves: that this and several other murders, some of them attended with circumstances far more shocking, instead of exciting any just commiseration for the Negro race, had actually worked in a contrary direction, and that not merely among the populace, but in a majority of the House of Assembly itself. This is a problem by no means of difficult solution. It is not that the Barbadian (I say it seriously and with sincerity) is less humane, in general, than the inhabitants of other countries; but Negro Slaves are not comprised within the scale of his humanity; or, to be more accurate, they do not assume, in his estimate of things, the rate and value of human beings. Hence, the proposition for punishing a white man capitally for murdering a Slave, appeared to him a punishment as much disproportionate to the crime, as if, in compliance with the opinion of some speculator on the rights of the

the brute creation, or, of some lover of domestic animals, we were to propose to execute a man in this country for killing a favourite pointer.

One of the other murders supplies so striking an illustration of the nature of this feeling, and of its almost necessary effects in producing a disposition to injury and insult, that, contrary to my original intention, I will lay before you a very brief and summary view of the chief particulars of it.

As a private militiaman was returning home from his duty upon an alarm, with his musket, and bayonet fixed, over his shoulder, he overtook several Negroes returning from their daily labour on the road, and among them, a woman big with child. He began abusing, and threatening to kill them, if they would not get out of the way. Most of them escaped him; but he made after the woman, and, without the least provocation on her part, plunged his bayonet into her, and, as one of the accounts states, very coolly and deliberately stabbed her several times in the breast. Providentially it happened, that a very respectable Gentleman, who was also returning from town, was a witness of the whole transaction. And now comes the curious

ous part of the story; for, when Mr. H. went to him, " spoke harshly to him, and said, he " ought to be hanged, for he never saw a " more wicked unprovoked murder, and that " he would certainly carry him before a ma- " gistrate, and that he should be sent to gaol ;" the man replied, "*for what? killing a Ne-* " *gro!*"—Some of the accounts state, that the man was in liquor; but it is clear from the circumstances, that it was in no such degree as to affect his reason; for neither is this circumstance mentioned by Mr. H. the eyewitness, nor by the magistrate before whom Mr. H., having got assistance, immediately brought him, nor by the President of the Island, before whom, from having no right to commit him, they next carried him. On the contrary, they state distinctly, that the murder was committed in the most wanton, malicious manner, and that he seemed afterwards to be very indifferent about the crime.

It may seem only candid to state the sequel. The President did commit him, though aware that it was a stretch of power; the man's person was thereby secured, and he remained answerable to the amount both of the King's fine, £.11. 4.*s.* sterling, and of the Negro's value, for which he was afterwards arrested by the Owner's representative, and which,

which, as she is stated to have been a valuable Slave, who had five or six children, would be a still larger sum. The man was not worth a shilling, in possession or expectancy, and therefore, as the President adds, may possibly be in confinement for life. It is only due to the President, to add, that in the conclusion of his letter, he expresses himself in terms of the warmest and most indignant feeling, that the Assembly should look on such things with cool indifference, and not provide " that just remedy which has been " found productive of no evil in the still " larger island of Jamaica, and which, in every " other civilized community, is provided by " the law, both of God and man."

Let me subjoin one additional remark, that, but for the circumstance of Mr. H.'s happening to have been at the same time returning from town, this barbarous murder must have remained unpunished for want of evidence. It is fair, also, to acknowledge, that the murder above stated, however horrid, appears (very different, indeed, in that respect, from another shocking incident, which I suppress) to have been an act of wanton insult and contempt, rather than of deliberate cruelty; and to have been precisely such in nature, (though I doubt not, above the ordinary

rate

rate of insults in measure) as I have supposed to proceed from a low estimate of Negroes, as such. Hence the criminal's exclamation, when he was told he deserved to be hanged, and was further threatened with being committed to gaol. *For what?* he replied; *killing a Negro!*—Surely I need not add a word—the fact supplies its own inference.

Shall we allege, in behalf of this poor militiaman, that he was, probably, half drunk; that he was a low uneducated man; that it was the exclamation of passion; or that it was suggested by self-preservation or self-defence? But what shall we say, then, for the Assembly of the Island? They consist of men of liberal education, and liberal manners; yet it is grievous to reflect, that their conduct is but too much in the same spirit as that of this militiaman. Their estimation of a Negro is much the same. Hence, on its being proposed to inflict a capital punishment, not on themselves, but on others, for the murder, though attended with the most horrid circumstances, of a *Negro*, they resent the suggestion, not by a transient and passionate exclamation, but by a deliberate and continued opposition of some years; not unguardedly, not privately, when a man will sometimes hint

hint an opinion he would not avow; but publicly; in opposition to clear explanation; to powerful influence; to eloquent enforcement of the principles of justice and humanity; in opposition, one should have thought, to the natural suggestion of self-interest, and of regard to their own property, when gravely sitting in their capacity of Legislators.

Let me again, however, declare most seriously, that it is not so much of defective, as of misplaced humanity, that I here complain. They had not been used to think and feel concerning Negroes, as concerning their fellow creatures; and to consider that their rights, and comforts, and feelings, were to be protected by the same powerful sanctions. Hence, when it was proposed to inflict a capital punishment for the murder of a Black, their sympathy was excited on the wrong side. They felt, but it was for the offended dignity of a White Man, not for the murdered Negro. The truth is, a certain *esprit de corps* was now called into action, and all the barbarities of which the wretched Negroes might be the victims, would, in such a temper, and such circumstances (taken, I mean, in connection with such a proposed punishment) serve rather to inflame than to mitigate the general fury.

Hence,

Hence, Lord Seaforth, in another letter, declares, " that though he had received no con-
" tradiction of the horrible facts, yet that
" nothing had given him so much trouble as
" to get to the bottom of these affairs, so
" horribly absurd were the prejudices of the
" people."

There are no persons, I am persuaded, who will be more shocked by the above transactions than the West Indian Proprietors themselves, and none especially more than those of the very island of Barbadoes, in which these tragedies were acted. They, like other absentee Proprietors, are most of them, I doubt not, almost utterly ignorant of the real state of things in the West Indies; and they will read with equal astonishment and concern, Lord Seaforth's horrid communication. Let them however remember, these cannot be styled, as some former relations have unjustly been, exaggerations of Abolitionists; but, like Governor Parry's famous charge against the African Captains, they are the official communication of the Executive Government laid before the House of Commons.

Let them, therefore, join with me, in seriously considering the practical conclusions to be drawn from these shocking incidents, and the remedy which should be applied to such crying evils. Let them not retort, as has been sometimes done, that instances of monstrous cruelty have taken place in this country also. It is true, that even in this land of liberty and humanity, we heard some years ago of an apprentice being starved to death. We heard more recently of a British Governor of an African possession, causing the death of a soldier by excessive punishment. But let us complete the parallel; not only were these crimes punished by the death of the criminals; but here, in Lord Bacon's phrase, "mark the diversity;" it was difficult to prevent the indignation even of the populace, from anticipating the sentence of the law. In the West Indies, on the contrary, when you begin to talk of punishing capitally far more horrible murders, the sympathy, among the majority of the community, the highest classes excepted, is for the criminal, not for the wretched and innocent sufferer; and that, not merely among low illiterate men, in whom such prejudices might be somewhat less astonishing, but in the House of Assembly of the Island, the body to which it especially belongs to watch over the rights, and which naturally gives the tone, and fixes the standard

standard for the opinions and feelings of the whole community.*

Let the absentee Proprietors attend, above all, to this, because it leads to the most important practical conclusions. I have been assured privately, (though the information has not yet been laid before Parliament, and therefore I cannot speak with certainty) that Lord Seaforth has at length been able to carry his point, and to prevail on the Assembly as well as the Council, to make the murder of a Slave a capital offence. In my view of the above transactions, this is a matter of small importance. It will not, I trust, appear uncandid; but I must frankly declare, that had

* The very words which I am now writing suggest to my mind another possible explanation of the conduct of the Assembly of Barbadoes. Possibly the majority, in rejecting the Governor's proposition, acted not so much from their own judgment and feelings, as from deference to those of the bulk of the community. Considering that, as is stated above, it must be regarded as a part of their duty to set the tone of public judgment and feelings, this would not be a very creditable plea; nor have I found any hint of it in the papers laid before the House of Commons; but, on the contrary, an expression of resentment against the Governor, with an intimation of the danger of interfering between Master and Slave. But as the idea in question has occurred to me, I think I should scarcely be acting candidly in suppressing it.

the

the Assembly originally consented to Lord Seaforth's recommendation, and made the murder of a Slave a capital crime, I should not have admitted it as any proof of their feeling for the Negroes with any tenderness of sensibility. It would only have shewn that there was no apparent want of common humanity, and therefore have belonged to that class of actions, from the performance of which no man arrogates to himself praise, though to be defective in them we consider as blameworthy. For, might we not fairly have questioned whether the members might not be influenced, not so much by motives of benevolence, as by deference for their Governor, by a regard for their character, by a respect for the feelings, call them, if you will, the prejudices, of the more liberal few among their own community; or even by the apprehensions of the effects which their refusal might produce in forwarding the abolition of the Slave Trade ? Surely, however, the rejection of the proposition shews, that they not only do not themselves regard the Negroes as entitled to the consideration and treatment due to a *human being*, considered as such, but that they cannot even persuade themselves that he will be regarded as entitled to them by the world in general.

Supposing,

Supposing, therefore, that Lord Seaforth's law has passed, and even supposing, (what it is far too much to suppose, considering the extreme difficulty, or rather impossibility of obtaining legal proof, if a murderer would be tolerably cautious) that it does prevent absolute murders; yet how wide a range is still left for the exercise of the worst of passions? To this case surely we may justly apply the maxim, and the important lesson which it inculcates may well excuse a trite quotation, " *Quid leges sine moribus ?*" Will such a law, passed contrary to the real wishes, feelings, and judgment, deliberately entertained and repeatedly avowed for many years, change the real estimation of a Black man in the Barbadian scale of being ? Or will not rather the contrariety between the law and the feelings of men, be likely to stir up a spirit of indignation and hatred towards the Blacks, which must be productive of innumerable injuries and insults towards the Negro race; while, Black evidence not being admissible, they may be almost always injured and insulted with impunity ?

This *esprit de corps* naturally results from the relative circumstances of Blacks and Whites in a West Indian community; and it is the more operative and pernicious, because with pride, itself a passion sufficiently regardless

less of the claims and comforts of others, another principle still more pernicious associates itself but too naturally; a principle of fear, arising out of the consciousness of the immense disproportion in number between the Blacks and the Whites. This fear again but too surely gives rise to hatred; and what may not be expected from the effects of an *esprit de corps* made up of such powerful ingredients? It is not that they who are actuated by it are conscious of these several feelings; but they are not on that account less real or less efficient. This *esprit de corps* which has long prevailed, was many years ago nearly proving fatal to the life of a most honourable, upright, and resolute Judge, who, in the discharge of his public function, dared to act as duty and conscience prescribed to him. But among the inferior orders of Whites especially, this spirit has been naturally called forth of late years into more lively exercise, by the very efforts which have been made to ameliorate the condition of the Negro race.

I have detained you very long on this topic: but I have dwelt the more largely on the vileness and degradation of the Negro race, because it appears to me to be the grand master vice of the colonial system. If duly considered, and traced into its almost infallible
operations,

operations, it will establish the prevalence of all the other evils which have been specified; for it is of a nature so subtle and powerful, as to extend its effects into every branch of negro management; and wherever its influence does extend, it has a natural and sure tendency to lessen the enjoyments of the Slaves, and to aggravate their sufferings. If all the various other causes which operate unfavourably on the condition and treatment of the Slaves could be done away, it contains within itself the pregnant source of numerous, most important, and, so long as it continues, incurable mischiefs.

Let me, therefore, once more conjure the West Indian Proprietors to give their due weight to all the foregoing facts and considerations; to observe how low a point in the scale of being is now allotted to the Negro race; and to estimate duly the effects on their treatment, and comforts, and feelings, which must necessarily result from such vileness and degradation. I cannot quit this head without once more assuring them, that it is unspeakably painful to me to appear to be charging the bulk of the resident White population of the West Indies with having too low an estimate of the Negroes as a race, and of the consideration and comforts which are due to them.

them. But the nature of my undertaking renders it my duty to state facts, such as I really believe them to be. If I have fallen into any error, I shall be most willing to correct it, and shall be sincerely thankful to any one who will set me right. But I will frankly own, also, to the resident West Indians, that, judged at the bar of equity and candour, we in this country are more in fault than they in that. Of them it can only be said, that causes of powerful, and, where great numbers of human beings are concerned, of almost infallible operation, have produced their natural effects. We have no such excuse to allege. We have not been familiarized by habit, or misled by interest, or prejudice, or party spirit, into contemplating without pain, a system from which, at first, both they and we must have shrunk back with horror. We cannot allege, that all the consequences, greatly as they are to be deplored, are not such as we might have anticipated with ease, or rather might have predicted with certainty, reasoning from the acknowledged principles both of speculation and experience. Could we not have foretold what would necessarily be the consequences of a system of slavery continued for centuries, where the Slaves, as in the West Indies, were to be of a peculiar race and colour, and under

under all the other circumstances of the African Negroes? We cannot, at least, plead a prejudice in favour of slavery, in consequence of having long been habituated to its evils. Surely if those who have lived all their lives in Great Britain, are tainted with such a prejudice, they are of all men inexcusable. I repeat it, therefore, we are more criminal than the West Indians, for having suffered such a system to gain an establishment, and to grow to its present size; and we shall be still a thousand times more criminal than they, if, with our eyes at length opened to its evils, we suffer it to continue unreformed.

But though from these considerations, as well as others which have been formerly mentioned, it has been with deep reluctance that I have dwelt on these invidious topics, would it be consistent not only with humanity and justice, but even with common fairness and truth, that transactions like those which have been here stated, when communicated from the highest authority; and, for the instruction and guidance of the British Legislature, laid before the House of Commons, should be suppressed, from any motives of personal delicacy; or if noticed, that just conclusions should not be drawn from them? I am almost fearful that I am wanting to the claims of duty, in not detailing the particulars of a
far

far more horrible narrative, which has also been laid before Parliament. For duties too serious, and even interests too high, for the admission of such an inferior principle as delicacy, are here in question. If such a system must still exist, surely it ought only to be with our fullest knowledge, the result of our most deliberate consideration; not because we are unacquainted with its horrors, from our having instinctively turned away our eyes from objects too painful to be beheld.

Consider if these enormities are too shocking to be seen and heard, what are they to be felt and suffered? When we are thoroughly acquainted with the abuses of the West Indian system, we may, perhaps, be able to mitigate, if we cannot cure them. If policy and interest are still to be admitted as a plea for injustice and cruelty, let us at least not take for granted, as if it were a self-evident truth, what I never can myself believe, that injustice and cruelty must forward the views of policy and interest. Let us scrutinize the evils point by point, and be sure of each individual particular of them which we leave in being, that on grounds of policy and interest it is indispensable. If we are to tolerate such enormous evils, let it be at least by weight and measure; let us deal them

them out, grain by grain, as absolute necessity shall require; and not in a wholesale way, give our sanction to such a mass of miseries, because the close inspection and scrupulous examination of them shock our delicacy, and wound our humanity. Let us remember what was beautifully said of this last virtue by one, than whom none possessed a larger share; " True humanity consists not in a squeamish " ear. It consists not in starting or shrinking " at such tales as these, but in a disposition " of heart to relieve misery. True humanity " appertains rather to the mind than to the " nerves, and prompts men to use real and " active endeavours to execute the actions " which it suggests."

To this long catalogue of the vices of the West Indian system, there remain yet to be added two others, which tend powerfully to aggravate almost all its various evils.

The first is, Absenteeship, particularly that of the more affluent Proprietor, who could afford to be liberal, whose presence among his Slaves would naturally produce a sort of parental feeling, and cause him habitually to interest himself in their comfort and improvement; and whose affluence might enable him to carry into effect the plans, whether

Absenteeship.

ther in the way of exemption or beneficence, which his liberality should devise.

I have not leisure to point out in detail the various bad consequences which follow from the Owner's absence; but they will naturally occur to any one who will consider the peculiar circumstances of the West Indian Slaves, in connection with this subject.

But let me point out one consequence which has been less attended to than it deserves to be, the unspeakable loss to the society, of that very class of men, not only in the legislature, but in private life also, who, from their rank and fortune, must in general be supposed to have received the best education, and to possess the most enlarged and liberal minds; who consequently would raise the general standard of morals and manners, whose presence, and the desire of being admitted into whose company, would be a check to dissoluteness; who would not only abound themselves in acts of kindness to the wretched Negroes, but who might make liberality popular, and render, more than it now is, the ill treatment of Negroes disreputable; for I trust it is already so in no small degree, where it is discovered. Many absentee Proprietors, of large property, even if they do, once or twice in
their

their lives, visit their estates; yet, while living in the West Indies, they consider themselves not at home, but only on a visit, and on a visit commonly which is not very agreeable to them, and which, therefore, especially when, as often is the case, constrained by œconomical motives, they mean to end, as soon as they have saved enough to enable them to live again in the mother country in ease and affluence. Hence they are too naturally persuaded to adopt the generally prevailing practice as to feeding and clothing, and other particulars; and, however desirous they may be of introducing a more liberal system, they are easily dissuaded from it, knowing that they shall not be able themselves to superintend the actual observance of their own regulations.

As for the far larger class of absentee Proprietors, who reside constantly in the mother country, though I give them all due credit for benevolent intentions, yet they are commonly precluded by their very ignorance of plantation affairs, from interfering with any confidence, or to any good purpose, in the detail of management. How little they are often acquainted with these particulars, I was not even myself aware till lately, when it appeared, that an old West Indian Proprietor, acknowledged

acknowledged by all who know him to be remarkable for the extent and accuracy of his information, and intimately conversant with all the detail of political and commercial œconomy, was wholly ignorant of its being the universal practice to work the Negroes in their field-work under the whip. This is the more remarkable, because the practice is not a partial or an occasional procedure, but the constant and universal mode; because for several years, men in general in this country, though personally unconnected with the West Indies, had been naturally led to turn their attention to the system of negro management.

I doubt not that the absentee Proprietor directs his manager to treat the Slaves with all due kindness and liberality; yet it must not be conceded with equal readiness, that the orders even of these benevolent Absentees will be faithfully executed. For in supposing this to be the case, we suppose a combination of incidents, and an assemblage of qualities, each of which, unconnected with the others, is sufficiently rare; how much more rare, then, must it be, to suppose them all concurring. We must suppose this benevolent Absentee to be affluent also, that he may be able to give effect to his benevolence. Benevolence, I trust and believe, will generally be found

found in the higher class of Proprietors; but I fear affluence, in proportion to their rank and way of living, is not so common. Again, we have also to suppose the more rare occurrence, not merely of equal but of far superior benevolence, in a man of inferior rank, fortune, connections, and manners, most probably of inferior education also. We must suppose this man of extraordinary benevolence to select for himself the situation of a manager in the West Indies, a somewhat unlikely choice; and that this benevolent owner, and this still more benevolent manager, happen to come together; I repeat it, still more benevolent, because this quality in the owner, though a generous, is a transient effusion, when the mind is in close contact with its object; or we may assign to it the higher character, of the habitual generosity of a just judgment, and a liberal heart. But such a judgment and such a feeling may often be found in a moment of serious reflection, in men, who from various infirmities, are not practically kind and beneficent in all the homely occurrences of daily life; especially under circumstances in which there are many little trials to be borne, and many vexatious obstacles to be surmounted.

But

But we are to suppose a manager whose benevolence is of this hardier and firmer kind. It must be a principle ever wakeful and observant; combined with judgment, and improved by experience; the very acquisition of which experience implies the having been long practically conversant with the system. We must suppose also, what is very extraordinary, that this long familiarity with prevailing abuses has not, in any degree, impaired the power to perceive, or the promptitude to redress them. In short, we are to suppose a principle so vigorous as to resist the strongest counteractions, and not only to maintain its existence, but to support a continued activity, under circumstances the most powerfully calculated to impair and destroy it.

But we have not yet done. Besides this extraordinary portion of benevolence, this rare manager must have some other qualities not less uncommon. He must not only have the firmness to dare to be singular, and to expose himself to the imputation of wishing to be thought to have more humanity than his neighbours, a sort of courage the most difficult of all to be found in our days; but, above all, he must resist the consciousness, that in return for all his humane exertions he may be misrepresented to his employer; that,
having

having acquired the character of a visionary schemer, who sends home comparatively small returns, and calls for great expences, he may, in consequence of such representations, be dismissed from his present office, and in vain solicit another. To find such a man, of so much benevolence, combined with so much resolute integrity, must be acknowledged to be no common occurrence. That such a man should be in the precise situation of overseer of a West Indian estate we should still less expect; and that this rare manager should meet with this more than commonly benevolent owner, is a still more curious coincidence. Yet all these expectations must be realized, for an Absentee's plantation to be regulated as it ought to be, under the present circumstances of the West Indies.

This subject is of such primary practical importance, that I must still be permitted to add one word more. Any man who will consider what his own feelings and temptations would be likely to be, were he the absentee Proprietor of a West Indian estate, will acknowledge the force of my reasoning; and they who may see no reason to suspect themselves, will be precisely those, concerning whom all other men would be apt to entertain the strongest suspicions. Were we ourselves

ourselves West Indian proprietors, we naturally should wish that the income of our estate might be as large, and the outgoings as small as might be; and though in a benevolent, or rather let me call it, a just mind, this wish would be qualified by the understood condition, that the Slaves should be sufficiently provided for; yet, ever allowing most honourable exceptions to the contrary, that which would in general constitute a manager's recommendation, which would obtain him a character, would be his increasing the clear profits of the estate. All this depends on principles of universal, infallible, and constant operation. It was the case in Mr. Long's time. He pointed out to the West Indian Proprietors, in the strongest terms, the mischief done by " overseers,* whose chief
" aim it was to raise to themselves a cha-
" racter as able planters, by increasing the
" produce of the respective estates; this is
" too frequently attempted, by forcing the
" Negroes to labour beyond their abilities;
" of course, they drop off, and if not re-
" cruited incessantly, the gentleman steals
" away, like a rat from a barn in flames, and
" carries the credit of great plantership, and
" vast crops in his hand, to obtain advanced

* Long's History of Jamaica, vol. ii. page 406.

" wages

" wages from some new employer in another district of the island. The Absentees are too often deceived, who measure the condition of their properties by the large remittances sent to them for one or two years, without adverting to the heavy losses sustained in the production of them."

Let me likewise again remind the benevolent absentee Proprietor to beware lest he is misled by the ambiguities of language. Let him bear in mind that when he receives from his manager in the West Indies, assurances that his Negroes have a *sufficient* supply of food, and clothing, and medical care; that their work is not *unduly* hard, nor their treatment *unduly* rigorous; that *sufficient* regard is paid to their comforts, and their feelings: Let me again remind him, that this *sufficiency* is not necessarily estimated by the measure of the claims and wants and feelings of a human being. Of course, I mean to speak only of managers in general. Individuals there are of that class, I doubt not, of a liberality and feeling, which would do honour to any rank. But it must be remembered, that it would be unreasonable to expect them to be exempt from prejudices and feelings, to which they are peculiarly exposed, and which have been so lately proved to prevail in the majority

rity of a body of men like the Assembly of Barbadoes, greatly superior to them in rank, connections, and fortune. If such a prejudice could shew itself also, and exert its influence in the sight of the world, and in the face of so many opposing considerations, how much more must it not be expected to operate, when there is no bystander to witness its acts, and when indolence, self-interest, habit, example, and various other motives, conspire to give effect to it?

Effect of the pressure of the times.

But if, in the way which has been lately stated, the Slaves suffered from absenteeship thirty or forty years ago, for it is so long since Mr. Long remarked the evil, how much must their sufferings have been aggravated in our days, when (this is the second circumstance to which I alluded some time ago) the increased extravagance of the age on the one hand, and the increased price of all articles of consumption on the other, furnish to every man, strong additional inducements for raising his estate to its utmost value? Above all, how powerfully must this principle operate in the case of those whose estates are considerably encumbered with debts? And this, remember, is actually the case of probably nine tenths of all West Indian Proprietors. Here in truth consists the grand obstacle in the way of all those regulations, in the present

sent system, which would call for any additional expenditure in the first instance. Proprietors, whose estates, after paying the interest of their mortgages, leave scarcely enough, in our times of pecuniary difficulty and pressure, for merely decent subsistence, much less sufficient to live upon in the way naturally acceptable to the West Indians, who are, in general, men of liberal and hospitable habits; such Proprietors, so circumstanced, must naturally be endeavouring in every instance to discover the minimum of charge, and the maximum of production. The manager of the estate will not be long in learning this, and his endeavours will be directed to the same objects. The effects of lessening the allowances of the Slaves may not be immediately visible, and he may really conceive that, without injury to them, somewhat may be saved for the master. But I will not pursue this invidious topic into its too obvious consequences. The professional Planter has just sketched a faint outline of some of the effects.*

Let

* The passage to which I allude, contains such important truths, and bears so strongly on the point now under discussion, that I shall take the liberty of inserting a large part of it. I should place it in the Appendix, but that, for various reasons, I wish not to introduce in the Appendix any article respecting the West Indian branch of the subject.

" To

Let me, however, remind all Proprietors who are thus circumstanced, that however inconvenient it may be to them, to increase,

for

"To superior morality I lay no claim; but I under-
"stood my interest, and happily, interest and morality
"were not in that case, as in many others, at variance.
"I lost very few Negroes in comparison with other gen-
"tlemen, even of such as were purchased out of Guinea
"yards, and surprisingly few of the infants born on the
"estate.

"It may be urged, as an objection to this system
"of management, that the expence attending it would
"be too great to be defrayed with such a portion of the
"produce of the estate as it is consistent with prudence
"to apply to that object alone. That the expences of
"estates will be considerably larger than at present I ad-
"mit, because it is proposed that the Negroes should be
"fed and clothed more liberally than they now are, and
"be more indulged during their indisposition; whence
"an excess of expence, and an apparent decrease of in-
"come: But let it be remembered at the same time,
"that an expenditure, when judiciously applied, is not
"a waste, but the investment of a capital with a view
"to productive return. It will be found so in this case;
"for, when Negroes are so treated, there will be fewer
"sick than in the common mode of management, and
"they will certainly be enabled to make much more
"vigorous efforts when engaged at their labour; for
"they will be more robust of body, more alert and con-
"tented in mind, so that, performing more work, the
"gross income of the estate, far from being reduced,
"will necessarily experience a considerable increase.
"But not only the gross income will be greater, but it
"may be presumed that fewer Negroes will die, and

"that

for a time, the outgoings, and subtract from the receipts of their estate, to go on as they are now doing, is sure and utter ruin. Will they say, that the course which I recommend, however politic ultimately, yet at the moment, and in their circumstances, deserves no better a name? I must reply, the professional Planter

" that more will be born, so as to afford a reasonable
" hope that your number may be kept entire without
" any foreign recruits; whence a saving in itself, proba-
" bly equivalent to the extraordinaries incurred by the
" proposed melioration of their treatment; and the ba-
" lance at the end of the year, so far from being against
" the planter, will probably be in his favour. Were it,
" however, otherwise, who would not submit to a small
" pecuniary loss, for the inappreciable advantage re-
" sulting from a mind contented with itself, and conscious
" of no neglect of duty? As to those who are unfortu-
" nately in such a situation, with respect to incumbrance
" and credit, as to be disabled from supplying their Ne-
" groes as they ought, it behoves them to consider whether
" by the utmost their undue savings can effect, they can
" possibly be retrieved from their embarrassments, and
" if they can, they ought seriously to ponder on the
" consequence by which their relief is to be obtained;
" that it must be by the blood of their own species—a
" horrid thought; and if they cannot, how much better
" would it be for them to surrender at once their pro-
" perty to their creditors, and to repose in the humble,
" though exquisite enjoyment of ease of mind, and a
" fair name, and to trust to recommendations for a
" future subsistence, which, in the West Indies, is never
" denied to the industrious, while it is frequently con-
" ferred on the undeserving."

Planter will tell them, that the opposite system of working down their gangs of Negroes, and making them good from the Slave-market, is murder added to ruin, murder too in its most painful and shocking, because a protracted form.

The topic on which I have just now touched, so lightly, considering its importance, reminds me of another circumstance, which, in various ways, has a most unfavourable tendency on the treatment and happiness of the Slaves; and which, though it has operated powerfully in the West Indies, has never, perhaps, produced such extensive effects as within the last twenty or thirty years. This is, the buying of West Indian property on speculation. Wherever this is the principle of purchase, it is for the most part connected with the formation of new settlements, and this is in various ways, some of which have been already specified, productive of unspeakable misery to the Negroes employed in forming them.

West Indian speculations injurious to the Slaves.

But besides this probable class of evils, where any one is engaged in planting speculations, there must naturally be a disposition to regard the undertaking as a mercantile transaction, in which the investiture of capital

tal is to be made as small, and the returns as large as possible; rather than as a landed property, or as (for that is the light in which a West Indian estate ought still more to be considered) as a little sovereignty of a feudal nature, the vassals of which have a claim to their lord's protection, with whom, therefore, he is instituting a connection of mutual duties, services, and attachments, which is to subsist on both sides through generations yet unborn.

I scarcely need state, that, most commonly, West Indian speculations fail; and in that failure, at whatever number of years it happens, is most probably involved the sale of such of the Slaves as survive, to a new owner. But I must forbear from enlarging on this important topic, and hurry you through what remains of our painful journey. It is a course furnishing, at every moment, numerous and interesting objects: But in the case of the greater part of them, I must be forced to content myself with doing little more than barely pointing them out for your own more deliberate consideration. Other duties now demand my time, and I should be strongly tempted to desist from my undertaking, from the consciousness that in such a brief and hasty progress, I cannot do justice to the great

interests

interests which are at stake, if I were not deeply impressed with a sense of the importance of stating at this time, though but imperfectly, the real views and principles of the Abolitionists.

To resume my subject. I have now stated the chief vices of the present West Indian system. But before I quit the discussion concerning West Indian abuses, I might appear wanting in justice to the cause, and even in deference towards many gentlemen of high respectability, if I were not to acknowledge, that the condition and treatment of the Negro Slaves were painted in colours which were almost a direct contrast to all which have been here used, by several West Indian Proprietors of great consideration and affluence; and still more by several persons of high rank, who resided for some time in the West Indies, either in a naval and military capacity, or, in some few instances, as governors of islands.

Admirals and other most respectable witnesses gave evidence of the good treatment of Slaves.

It is no disparagement to the characters of these justly respected men, to affirm, that this was not the stage which they trod to the most advantage. It is due to them however, to say, in general, that they came forward from the impulse of grateful and generous feelings.

While

While in the West Indies, they had been treated with that liberality and kindness which strangers never fail to experience in those hospitable islands. If they visited a country plantation, it was commonly on a scheme of pleasure; every countenance around them was lighted up with cheerfulness and gaiety; they themselves naturally partook of the same feelings, and looked on every object with a good-humoured eye.

But even when a longer residence afforded more ample means of acquiring information, they looked down from an elevation far too high to allow of their having a just perception of the state and circumstances of the poor depressed Negro Slaves. It will not, I trust, be deemed disrespectful treatment of men, towards whom, in common with their countrymen in general, I feel great respect and gratitude, to say, that they came forward under the influence of strong prejudices. And who needs be told of the wonder-working powers of prejudice, in colouring, adding to, or subtracting from the scene which it contemplates? What can render this more apparent, than that they had come to a conclusion, without touching on the premises on which it must depend. They expressed a decided opinion, that the abolition muft ruin the Colonies; an opinion which, it is obvious, muft necessarily depend on the practicability of keeping up, or increasing, the ftock of Slaves; and yet on the latter point they had formed no opinion. In others of their ftatements, the effects of prejudice were not less visible.

In truth, it scarcely needs be remarked, that these respectable visitors could know very little of the general treatment of the Negroes, of their allowance of food, and ordinary amount of labour, and ftill less of the temper and difposition of the manager, on which so much muft depend. If he were ever so severe, or even ever so cruel, the visit of an Admiral would not be his time for shewing these difpositions. In short, these gentlemen appeared almoft utterly unacquainted with those details, an accurate knowledge of which would alone warrant the opinions which they delivered. Such are the conclusions which we should naturally form, from a general knowledge of the circumftances of the case.

But, added to all these, we fortunately obtained access to one of the party, a Weft Indian gentleman, who resided many years in Jamaica; whose high respectability and ample fortune had not so eftranged him from the

the poor despised Negroes, as to prevent his seeing, and pitying their diftresses; and who, with a resolute benevolence and integrity, rarely found in these days, dared to come forward and deliver his evidence in behalf of that injured race.

He declared that he had often accompanied Governors and Admirals in their visits to the different plantations. That the eftates naturally being those of persons of diftinction, were such as muft be supposed to be under the beft management; and that all possible care would be taken to keep every disgufting object out of sight, that the feelings of those high personages might not be wounded.

There is also a remark which muft be made, concerning the evidence of several very respectable Weft Indian Proprietors, who appeared as witnesses. The Weft Indian body, it is obvious, would naturally look through the whole range of Proprietors, and call as witnesses those whom they knew to be moft affluent and humane. But nothing can possibly be so unreasonable as to suppose, that we are hereby furnished with any fair sample of the general treatment of the Negroes, which, as has been already ftated, muft necessarily vary according to the temper and

Opponents witnesses: Effects of Selection.

disposition

disposition of the owner) and also of their manager,) and still more than on his temper, on his being in affluent or distressed circumstances, on the nature of his views and undertakings. But from this selection of witnesses, which however was perfectly natural, the treatment and the allowances of some peculiarly liberal and affluent proprietors are taken as the treatment and allowances of all masters, in all their several varieties. Indeed, these witnesses themselves were disposed to take for granted, and thence to state, that their own was the general mode of proceeding, partly from the natural repugnance which is felt by men of liberal minds to say any thing which might have the appearance of boasting of their own peculiar liberality; partly, from the real ignorance of one man as to the conduct of another, in all matters of private management.

It would, however, be gross injustice to my cause, not to mention one instance, in which the effect of this mode of proceeding, in conveying, quite unintentionally I doubt not, a very exaggerated idea of the allowances and comforts of Slaves, was established by indisputable proof.* The Agent for the

* Vide Privy Council Report, Part III. Jamaica, A. N° 5.

Island

Island of Jamaica, a gentleman truly respectable and well-informed, with some other coadjutors of equal respectability, when questioned by the Privy Council as to the provisions allowed to the Slaves, stated; that the common allowance of herrings, which are used for the Slaves as a seasoning of their vegetable food, was from twenty to twenty-five barrels of herrings annually, to every one hundred Slaves. Now, taking an average of five years of peace immediately after a long war, from 1783 to 1787, the whole number of Slaves in the island being estimated at about 230,000, and the field Slaves, according to the usual calculation, as seven-eighths of the whole number, the barrels of herrings consumed ought to have been near 46,000 barrels. But the accounts of imports shew, that the average quantity of herrings, and all other cured fish, annually imported during the five years, not for the Negroes alone, but for all the inhabitants of the island, amounted to not half the quantity, to but 21,089 barrels. Surely this circumstance powerfully confirms the supposition, which, on our reasoning from what we know of the manner of selecting and bringing forward witnesses, would be suggested to our minds.

It is curious likewise to observe concerning both those moſt respectable witnesses who were formerly mentioned, and concerning several juſtly respected members of the Weſt Indian body who delivered their teſtimony, that their evidence covers a conſiderable extent both of time and space, and yet they make no diſtinction whatever as to periods and places. In every island, equally, during the whole period of their acquaintance with the Weſt Indies, the Slaves were treated as well as possible. Now the Weſt Indians themselves tell us, that the treatment of Negroes has been exceedingly improved within the laſt twenty or thirty years: if this be so, there were at leaſt defects in the syſtem formerly; yet in speaking of that former period, no such hint is given; but the treatment is ſtated to have been uniformly excellent. These declarations are manifeſtly incompatible.

The queſtion itself, whether the treatment has or has not improved of late years, is of great importance; but far too large and difficult to be here discussed. Still, as the assertion is often made, and as, in the opinion of some, it may be of great practical influence, a few words ought to be said on it. That there are fewer individual inſtances of cruelty now

now than formerly, I believe to be true. It is alleged, and I hope truly, that an improvement has taken place in the education and manners of the book-keepers, or overseers, who are in immediate and continual contact with the Slaves; and whose characters and tempers muſt therefore have a decisive effect one way or another on the treatment they receive. But the syſtem continues the same; and it is greatly to be feared that the increasing pressure of the times has tended in too many inſtances to abridge the ſtock, before but too contracted, of the Slave's comforts, and perhaps to increase his labours.

It is worthy also of remark, that the Weſt Indian colonies, and their inhabitants, are almoſt always mentioned, by the witnesses before mentioned, in general terms; and scarcely a hint is given us, that greater attention is paid to the comforts and feelings of the Slaves in one island, than in another. Now in the case of one island, and that next to Jamaica, by far the largeſt and moſt populous of them all, we have had such proof, I had almoſt used Shakespeare's expression, such damning proof, of the low estimate of Negroes, and of the treatment to which they are liable, as even our opponents themselves muſt own to be utterly inconsiſtent with the

accounts

accounts of those respectable witnesses of whom I have before spoken. And indeed in others of the islands we have the same facts established by individual testimony of the most respectable sort. Are we not, then, entitled to extend the application of the instances, and to consider them, such as indeed from their number also they must be regarded, as fair samples, by no means of the universal, but of the general condition and treatment of the negro Slaves?

Assertion, that Negro Slaves are happier than our Peasantry.

But another broad and general objection may be urged against the testimony of the same respectable class of witnesses, that it proves by far too much. For they tell us not only that the Slaves are in general treated with liberality and kindness; not only that they are protected by law equally with white men, in their lives and property; but that they are in a situation superior to that of the bulk of our English peasantry: and one most respectable and amiable man, of whose humanity no one thinks more highly than myself, declared, that they were so happy that he often wished himself one of them.

Such assertions as these might excite a smile, if the subject were less serious; but after the review we have taken of the degraded

graded state of this unfortunate class of our fellow creatures, in all it's humiliating particulars, we cannot but hear, with the greateſt pain, assertions, which, coming from characters so respectable, have but too manifeſt a tendency to prolong the duration of those enormous evils. The assertions can in themselves be only accounted for by the supposition, that they who made them were utterly ignorant of the particulars of the treatment and eſtimation of the Negro race. They may have seen, perhaps, the domeſtic Negroes collected at some season of feſtivity, and thence have too haſtily drawn an inference as to the general situation of the bulk of the Black population; of that far larger class, which daily works under the whip, and is subject to all the other particulars which have been mentioned, of degradation and suffering.

When from the Weſt Indies themselves I have heard the same assertion, that the negro Slaves are happier than our labouring poor, let me be forgiven for declaring, that such an opinion, formed not by transient visitors, but by those to whom a Negro sale, working under the whip, public and severe floggings of decent females, private punishments, and all the other sad particulars of negro humiliation

liation are thoroughly known, has, I own, created in my mind a reflection of a different character. I have by no means questioned the veracity of those from whom the remark has fallen, or imputed to them, I say it with sincerity, the smallest intention to deceive; but I have conceived myself to see in it an instance of that righteous ordination of the Almighty, by which it ever happens, that the system of slavery, and the same may be affirmed of every other gross infringement on the rights and happiness of our fellow creatures, is far from being so much clear gain, even to those for whose exclusive advantage it may appear to be instituted. It is not by the wretched Negro that the whole price is to be paid. Surely it is much, that the Master's understanding of the nature and amount of the value of liberty is so far impaired. Much also is paid in that effect which, ever since the world began, has ever been produced by slavery on both the morals and manners of the free art of the community in which it has prevailed.

It would be really an insult to the understandings and feelings of members of this free and happy country, to enter into any detailed comparison between the situation of a British peasant and a West Indian Slave.

It

It is almost in every particular a perfect contrast; and, for my own part, when, after asserting, with what correctness we will not just now question, that the Slaves are better fed, and clothed, and lodged, than our own peasantry; and when the conclusion has been so confidently drawn, that therefore they must be happier; the assertion has appeared to me to supply only another proof, in addition to the many already furnished, that our opponents in their judgments as well as in their feelings are apt to reason concerning the Negroes, as well as to act towards them, as if they were of an inferior species. Were we engaged in any inquiry concerning the brute creation, to ascertain these particulars might be to decide the question of their happiness or misery. But are feeding and clothing, and lodging, the only claims of a rational and immortal Being? Are the feelings of the heart nothing? Are the consciousness of independence, and the power of pursuing the occupation and habits of life which we prefer, nothing? Is the prospect of happier days, and of an improved situation for ourselves or our children, nothing? Where also are family endearments, and social intercourse, and willing services, and grateful returns? Where, above all, are moral improvement, and the light of religious truth, and the hope full of immortality?

It

It is indeed a merciful ordination of the Supreme Being, that men are often able to accommodate themselves in some degree to their situation, and to suffer less from it than we might suppose. We may therefore sometimes be apt to imagine our fellow creatures more miserable than they really are, because we should be extremely miserable in their situation; but this does not alter the essential nature of things, and annihilate the distinctions between happiness and misery.

But besides that in the negro Slave's condition there are but too many glaring unambiguous causes of positive suffering, many of those sources of enjoyment which are commonly open to the poor and the ignorant, are here excluded. It has juftly been observed, as an inftance of the goodness of the great Creator of all things, that though he has provided the world with but a scanty portion of those more curious substances, or more refined luxuries, which are never necessary to happiness, and which often serve only to gratify vanity; the articles which are really necessary for the comfort and well-being of man, are either supplied every where with inexhauftible profusion, or are at leaft of no difficult attainment. By a like gracious ordination, he has likewise rendered the enjoyments which are

moft

moſt ſubſtantially and permanently gratifying, universally accessible; the domeſtic affections, the social pleasures, the tender emotions, the sweets of hope, and recollection, religious hopes and consolations. All these are gratifications which virtuous poverty often enjoys in large measure, which wealth cannot purchase, nor greatness secure.

But in the Negro's cup few indeed of these cordial drops are to be found; while there are too many other ingredients which even to a negro palate must be unconquerably bitter. We are not, however, here left to infer their actual feelings, from considering what our own would be in their situation. We learn, from the professional Planter, how their spirits sink within them on their firſt acquaintance with the cart-whip system, and with what caution a provident manager will inure them to the discipline and treatment to which they are hereafter to be subjected. We have heard from others, of negro mothers lamenting the wretched prospect of their offspring.

But there is one decisive proof, that even custom does not render the Slaves insensible to the evils of their condition. It sometimes happens, rarely if ever I am assured to common field Slaves, but sometimes to domeſtics and

Decisive proof that Slaves are unhappy.

and artificers, that by the sale of the little productions and stock which they are allowed to raise, they may annually lay by a little peculium, which, it is due to the masters to declare, is never invaded. When the savings of many years have, at length, accumulated to a considerable amount, how do they dispose of it? With this sum, for which they have been struggling during the whole course of their lives, they go to their masters, and buy their freedom. By the sacrifice of their last shilling, they purchase their release from that situation which the West Indians would persuade us is a condition of superior comfort. Or, if they think that the little which is left of their own lives is not worth redeeming, they will purchase the freedom of a son, or a brother, or a sister; thus affording at once a proof of the value they set on freedom, and of their disinterestedness and social affection.

It ought likewise to be observed, that they who thus buy their freedom, are likely, from the habits of industry which the very circumstance of their acquiring so much property implies them to have had, to have smarted less than the general mass of Slaves under the whip of the driver. And what is it that they thus purchase at so high a rate?

a rate? Is it really freedom? the consideration, the security, equal rights, equal laws, and all the other blessings which the word liberty conveys to our minds? No: but degradation and insecurity; the admission into a class of beings whose inadequate protection, by the law and the public force of the community, is not in some measure compensated by the interest which their owner feels in the preservation of his property. They are still of the inferior cast, and must for ever continue of it—a set of beings, as Mr. Edwards himself informs us, " wretched in themselves
" and useless to the Public. These unhappy
" people, are a burthen and a reproach to so-
" ciety. It very frequently happens that the
" lowest white person, considering himself as
" greatly superior to the richest and best
" educated free man of colour, will disdain to
" associate with a person of the latter descrip-
" tion."* " No wonder that, as it is added,
" their spirits seem to sink under the conscious-
" ness of their condition. They are continu-
" ally liable to be injured and insulted with
" impunity, from the inadmissibility of their
" evidence; so that in this respect they seem
" to be placed on a worse footing than the
" enslaved Negroes, who have masters that
" are interested in their protection, and who,

* Edwards's History of the West Indies, vol. ii. p. 20.

" if

" if their Slaves are maltreated, have a right
" to recover damages by an action on the
" case."*

Yet this wretched and degraded state, the lowest, one would have conceived, and least desirable, of all human conditions, is eagerly coveted, is bought with the earnings of a whole life, by the Negro Slave. And shall we then be told that the situation of the latter is a situation of comfort, a situation superior to that of our British peasantry! Nor is it merely that the Slaves themselves desire their freedom, over-rating perhaps the evils of their actual state, and ignorant of what may be really conducive to their happiness. I would not so calumniate the West Indians, as to impute to them that they mock these poor people with a real evil, under the name of an imaginary good; yet we find masters remunerating long and faithful services by the gift of freedom, as their best reward; nay, more, we have seen the laws of the islands hold out the same boon as the most valuable recompence of the most distinguished public merits.

I cannot therefore but consider the earnestness of the Slaves to purchase, at so dear a rate, their admission into a class of beings,

* Edwards's History of the West Indies, vol. ii. p. 18.

which,

which, whether we judge from what we know of the circumftances of their situation, or from the accounts given of it by all intelligent writers (by none more than by Mr. Edwards himself), we should conceive the moft unprotected, ineligible and miserable condition of human exiftence in any civilized society, as a moft decisive proof of the wretchedness of the ftate of slavery. From the very nature of the case, it is probable, in some of the inftances, we know, that they who have thus purchased their freedom have been the Slaves of Mafters of affluence, under whom the treatment muft have been as mild and liberal, and the situation as comfortable, as the condition of a Weft Indian Slave is capable of being rendered. It therefore seems fairly to indicate that there are particulars in the situation and circumftances of a Weft Indian Slave in general, as such, which prove a source of great practical suffering; and perhaps it is a proof of the degree in which the Slaves are conscious of their own degradation. But it also well deserves to be noted, that we never find any, either of those Slaves who have bought their freedom, or of the free Negroes or coloured men, of whom there are above a thousand in many of the smaller islands, and in Jamaica several thousands, desiring to be again admitted into the condition of slavery.

P We

We know that in the middle ages it was not uncommon for poor men of free condition voluntarily to become vassals, that, in an age in which person and property were very imperfectly secure, they might obtain a master's protection; but the vassalage of the middle ages was not the slavery of the West Indies. In spite of all the evils therefore and degradation, incident to the state of Blacks who have no owner to protect them from injuries and insults, there never yet was, surely there never will be, an instance of an emancipated Negro returning to resume the yoke of slavery, notwithstanding all the security and all the comforts which we are assured this situation carries in it's train. May not also the state and circumstances of this class account for the numerous defects and vices which are laid to their charge? Their indolence is particularly noticed, and their never engaging in field-work is mentioned as discreditable to them: but can we wonder that none will subject themselves to the driver's lash, who are not absolutely forced to submit to such a degradation.*

On

* It is a mistake however to suppose, that, from any natural or moral infirmity, the Negroes are not as willing as the people of other countries to perform ordinary out-of-doors work for hire, as free labourers. This was decisively proved both in the Sierra Leone and Bulam Colonies.

On the whole, therefore, notwithstanding the favourable representation made of the condition and treatment of the negro Slaves by persons of high rank and acknowledged respectability; if you will seriously weigh the amount of the various vices of the West Indian system which have been here enumerated, you will be ready almost with certainty to conclude; that, under circumstances so extremely unfavourable to the multiplication of our species, the West Indian Slaves must annually and rapidly decrease in number. This, it will be remembered, was the first of the three propositions which I undertook to prove on the question concerning the keeping up of the Black population without importations from Africa.

<small>First Proposition proved.</small>

The second proposition was, that notwithstanding all the grievous abuses of the West Indian system, the decrease of the Slaves was on the whole very inconsiderable, if there were any decrease at all.

<small>Second Proposition.</small>

When

Colonies. Vide Sierra Leone Company's Reports, and Beaver's African Memoranda. This fact, through inadvertency, was not inserted in its proper place; but it ought not to be left unnoticed, because several authors have confidently stated the contrary as an undoubted fact. Their works were in general, I believe, written before the publication of the intelligence from Sierra Leone and Bulam.

P 2

When the Slave Trade became firft the subject of public discussion, His Majefty's minifters sent to the legislative and executive bodies of the different Weft Indian Islands, a number of queries, the answers to which contained a vaft body of information on the various particulars of the colonial syftem. A great addition was made to this ftock of information, by examining various persons of intelligence and experience in Weft Indian affairs. The whole was compiled into one bulky Report, and laid before both Houses of Parliament.

Jamaica Slaves Population. This Report contains the account of the population, both white and black, slave and free, of our several Weft Indian islands, as received from their respective governors. We are there furnished with the actually exifting number of the Slaves in Jamaica, which alone contained as many as all the other islands put together, at several different periods; the first, at the diftance of almoft a century; the laft, in the year 1787; together with the number of Slaves imported annually, during the whole period. In order to judge whether the Black population was in an improving or declining ftate, the whole term was divided into four periods:

The 1ft beginning with 1698 and ending with 1730.
The 2d - - - from 1730 to - - - - 1755.
The 3d - - - from 1755 to - - - - 1768.
The 4th - - - from 1768 to - - - - 1787.

And

And we had the satisfaction to find, from those unexceptionable documents, that,

In the first period, the excess of deaths above the births, of Slaves, or their annual decrease, was - - - - 3¼ p'cᵗ
In the 2d period, it was - - - 2¼
In the 3d period, it was lessened to - 1¾
And in the 4th, from 1768 to 1788, it was not more than - - - - 1·

Now, it is manifest, that if the ratio of decrease had been continually lessening, as appears on the very face of the account, and if, during the whole of the last period of twenty years, the annual loss had been but 1 per cent., having been 1¾ per cent. during the former immediately preceding period of thirteen years, that loss would be somewhat more than 1 per cent. at the beginning of the last period, and somewhat less than 1 per cent. towards the end of it. But even this loss of 1 per cent. was itself accounted for, by an extraordinary series of hurricanes and consequent famines, from which it was stated that fifteen thousand Slaves lost their lives; and still more, the 1 per cent. included the loss on all the Africans who were imported during that period. This, which is termed the loss in the seasoning, has been estimated, by high West Indian authorities, to be, including the

loss

loss in the harbour, between 1-4th and 1-3d of the whole number imported; by some it has been rated ftill higher. This mortality was supposed to be in a considerable degree occasioned by the Slaves having been commonly landed in a highly diseased ftate, owing in a great measure, as was supposed, to crowding, and other evils on shipboard: And the Assembly and Council of Jamaica eftimated that 1¼ per cent. of all the Africans imported died in the short period, probably not above a fortnight, between the ship's entrance into port and the day of sale. Adding together the whole loss fairly to be ascribed to these various causes of mortality, of which all depending on the voyage would obviously cease with the importations, they would more than account for the whole 1 per cent. loft during the laft period; and we should be warranted in concluding, that the whole number of Slaves in Jamaica were at length actually on the increase.

It will add to your confidence in the conclusion which so clearly results from the above calculations, to know that they were carefully drawn by that great and able minifter before referred to, among whose extraordinary powers, peculiar clearness and accuracy in calculation was universally acknowledged to possess

sess an eminent place. Indeed this result ought not to surprize us, for we were assured by Mr. Long, many years before, " that upon moſt of " the old settled eſtates in the island of Jamaica, " the number of births and deaths every year " is pretty equal, except any malignant dis- " order happens."

Calculating on the same principles, and from Weſt Indian accounts, it appeared that in Barbadoes also, the annual loss of Slaves has been of late under 1 per cent. Indeed if the loss had been so small in Jamaica, it probably was not greater in moſt of the other islands, into which, in general, the importations had been less considerable, and in which, from their several circumſtances, the population was likely to be, to say the leaſt, full as well kept up as in Jamaica itself. Thus the second proposition was eſtablished, that, notwithſtanding the general prevalence of so many and great abuses, the annual decrease was very inconsiderable.   *Second Proposition proved.*

The third proposition, that therefore an increase might in future be expected, muſt doubtless rest on the basis of probable inference; but in a case like this, in which an appeal is made to a principle of sure and unerring operation, as eſtabliſhed by universal experience, we may hold our conclusion   *Third Proposition.*

almoſt

almoſt with the certainty of absolute demonſtration. If the many exiſting abuses would account for a great annual decrease, yet there had been no decrease at all, or a very ſmall one; it clearly follows, that if the prevailing abuses could be done away, or even conſiderably mitigated, we might anticipate in future a great and rapid annual increase.

<small>Opponents moſt powerful objections.</small>   Our chief opponents of abolition in Parliament objected neither to the premiſes on which our reaſonings concerning the Weſt Indian population were grounded, nor to the concluſions which we drew from them. They acknowledged, as has been already ſtated, to the utmoſt extent, the guilt and cruelty of the Slave Trade. But they urged, that it would be fair to give the Weſt Indians time for the completing of their gangs of Slaves, and for the ſubſiding of their prejudices; and as they warmed in argument, advancing in their poſitions, they contended, that from the facilities afforded by the local circumſtances of the iſlands for ſmuggling, it would be found impracticable to aboliſh the Slave Trade without the aid of ſuch regulations as could only be enacted by the Weſt Indian Legiſlatures themſelves. They truſted, however, the time would ere long arrive, when, by the general conſent of all parties, this hateful traffic might be abandoned.

abandoned. A respite till the remainder of the century was alone asked, a period of eight years, and on the 1st of January 1801, the reign of juſtice and humanity was to commence, and a new and happier day was to begin to dawn on the wretched Negroes. Meanwhile, no new settlements were to be formed, a limited number of Slaves only was to be annually imported; and other regulations and measures were to be adopted, with a view to the general abolition of the Trade in human beings.

Time would fail me, were I to attempt to lay before you in detail the various discussions which subsequently took place. It may be enough to ſtate, that the Abolitioniſts apprehended, that if Parliament, acknowledging the foul injuſtice and cruelty of the African Slave Trade, should suffer it to continue for several years on any such weak and vague grounds as those of not shocking the prejudices, and acting contrary to the wishes of the Weſt Indian proprietors, and on such other pleas as were urged by our opponents, when it had been diſtinctly proved by the greateſt political authorities, who, differing on moſt other subjects, entirely concurred on this, that the measure so far from being ultimately injurious to the Weſt Indians, would subſtantially and permanently

nently promote their interests, it would be in vain that we should flatter ourselves that any determination to abolish the Slave Trade at the end of eight years would ever be adhered to.

If obligations so powerful, if duties so clear and urgent, could be now so easily evaded, surely at the end of eight years some new pleas would be set up for the continuance of the trade, and the Abolitionists themselves would then be told, that, having formerly recognised the right of sacrificing the dictates of justice and humanity to considerations of expediency, they ought in common consistency to grant a new respite on the same or better grounds. Thus, period after period would be claimed from us, so long as ever the planters should choose to purchase, or as Africa should have victims to supply.

What has since passed shews that there was but too much reason for these apprehensions; for, notwithstanding that a period was fixed by a majority of the House of Commons; though a period, far longer than the longest which was then asked, has since elapsed; though it was distinctly stated that importations ought henceforth to be allowed only for keeping up the cultivation at its actual state; though

219

though numbers, prodigiously greater than any which were then stated as necessary for filling up gangs, and preparing the islands to meet abolition, have been since imported; yet the same difficulties have still been experienced, the same objections have still been urged. The wickedness and cruelty of the Slave Trade have been frankly confessed, while all our endeavours to put an end to it have been opposed with undiminished earnestness.

As to the objection, grounded on the impossibility of preventing Slaves from being smuggled into the islands, it was argued with undeniable force, that the power of this country to prevent the smuggling of Slaves to any considerable extent, had been proved by abundant and undoubted experience. Some trifling supply might be thus introduced, but in cases wherein it was far more difficult to prevent a contraband trade, regulations had been enforced somewhat strictly, which were opposite to the known and avowed interests and feelings of all the inhabitants of the West Indian islands. *Objection concerning Smuggling, answered.*

But the consideration which appeared to weigh most powerfully against an immediate abolition, was the expediency, if not the absolute necessary: *Grand objection: Co-operation of Colonial Legislatures necessary:*

lute necessity, of the co-operation of the West Indian Legislatures. They, it was hoped, would enact such internal regulations as would rectify any abuses which might prevail in the system of negro management. Several of the Colonial Legislatures, it was said, had lately passed, or were now passing Acts for improving the condition and treatment of the Slaves. Similar laws might be anticipated in others of the islands; and these reforms having taken place, the domestic stock of Slaves would gradually increase; the importation would diminish, and the Slave Trade would ere long die of itself.

Considered. It must be to suppose the Abolitionists absolutely void of all common sense, to imagine that they were not well aware how greatly the introduction and establishment of the necessary reforms in the negro system would be facilitated by the planters being willing to adopt them. But, from the very first, there was but too much reason to fear that no hearty co-operation would be afforded on their part.

In the first place it should be remembered, that they appeared to be impressed with a persuasion, that though the profit was theirs, the guilt and shame were exclusively our own;

own; and it was not probable that they would voluntarily consent to dissolve a contract so much to their advantage. Soon after the abolition was first proposed, this sentiment was stated in the most explicit terms by the Assembly of Jamaica. "The African trade (they say) " is purely a British trade, carried on by British " subjects, residing in Great Britain, on capitals " of their own. The connection and intercourse " between the planters of this island and the " merchants of Great Britain trading to Africa, " extend no further than the mere purchase of " what British Acts of Parliament have de-" clared to be legal objects of purchase." But independently on all other considerations, the spirit of party had gone forth, and the operation of that powerful cause would alone prevent the West Indians from forwarding the views of those whom they regarded as their determined opponents; especially since their concurrence might be supposed to imply a recognition of the various abuses and evils of the West Indian system. The Abolitionists therefore found themselves very early compelled to abandon all hopes of obtaining the abolition of the Slave Trade, through the enforcement of regulations to be prescribed by the colonial legislatures. It was not going too far to argue, that the colonial assemblies neither

ther were able, nor, if able, would they be willing to produce the desired effect.

<small>Colonial Legislatures neither able nor willing to effect the abolition, by regulations as to the detail of management of Slaves.</small> It must be manifest to any one at all acquainted with the principles of human nature, and still more clear to any one who knows the peculiar circumstances of our West Indian settlements, that any laws which might be passed by the legislatures of the islands, would not of themselves be adequate to the end in view. Granting that the legislatures might fix the quantity of food and clothing which all masters were to allow their Slaves, that they might also prescribe the degree of labour to be exacted, the punishments to be inflicted, the instruction to be given, and other regulations with a view to moral reform: How could they see to the execution of their own laws? Put the case of a similar law, applicable to servants in this country; how impossible would it be found to enter into the interior of every family, and with more than inquisitorial power to ascertain the observance or the breach of the rules which should have been laid down for our domestic economy. How much more difficult in the West Indies, where the testimony of Negroes not being admissible, there would be no means of bringing proof of any violations of the rules prescribed. But supposing the means of enforcing

ing the regulations to be found, how odious, how utterly intolerable would such a system be found in it's execution! Would it be borne even in this country?

But let it be remembered, that this kind of inquisition would be still less endured in the West Indies than it would be here. For, it has been often observed, and it is undeniably true, "that wherever slavery is established, " they who are free are peculiarly proud and " jealous of their freedom." Mr. Edwards has more than once declared this to be true with respect to the inhabitants of our West Indian Colonies, and this principle would assuredly cause them to regard with jealousy, and resent with indignation, any interference of the officers of government in the management of their private concerns and family affairs, among which their treatment of their own Slaves must fairly be included.

But in truth all such general regulations of the kind here supposed, entering into all the detail of domestic economy, and prescribing the precise quantum of food, clothing, labour, punishment, and medical care, must be, in their own nature, inherently defective. The quantity of food which they should direct, might in some cases be greater, in others

others less, than would be necessary; accordingly as the land which the Negroes had for growing their own provisions was more or less in quantity, more or less productive. Again, the medical care, the labour, the instruction, the discipline, the correction which might be called for on some estates, would not be required on others. And then all these provisions, so vexatious and invidious in their nature, were to be observed, not merely gratuitously, but it was to be expected that people would submit to them, would lend themselves to the enforcing of them, for the purpose of accelerating the period of abolition; an event which they had frankly declared they conceived would be in the highest degree injurious to their interests. Surely no credulity could be sufficient to make any one believe that laws of such a kind, and for such a purpose, and with such a premium on obeying them, could ever be carried into execution.

Proofs subsequently furnished, that no hope from Colonial Legislatures. But if these and other arguments rendered it abundantly clear, when the question was first discussed, that the colonial legislatures neither could nor would apply any adequate reform to the existing abuses, so as effectually to cooperate in measures for the abolition of the Slave Trade, there is now at least no ground

ground for doubt on that head. The queftion has been since brought to the teft of experiment. For, an endeavour to obtain the concurrence of the colonial legiflatures has since been made under the moft favourable circumftances of which the nature of the cafe could possibly admit; and yet it is not saying too much to declare, that the endeavour has utterly failed.

On this as on other occasions, different motives would operate on different men, in prompting them to concur in the measure. For my own part, I sincerely declare, that to the respectable gentlemen who took the lead on that occasion, I give the fulleft and moft unreserved credit for having been actuated by an earneft desire of reforming the Weft Indian syftem. But it muft be acknowledged that the transaction in some of its parts, especially since we have had new light reflected back on it from recent Weft Indian communications, exhibits an appearance of having been befriended by some of its promoters with a view rather to defeat, than to promote, the abolition of the Slave Trade. Be this however as it may, in the year 1796 a Committee, consifting of the moft respectable Weft Indian proprietors, having been appointed to take into consideration what fteps should

should be taken respecting the Slave Trade, resolved among other things, "That, for the "joint purposes of opposing the plan of Mr. "Wilberforce, and establishing the character "of the West Indian Planters, it is essential "that they should manifest their willingness "to promote actively the cause of the Ne- "groes, by such steps as shall be consistent "with safety to the property of individuals, "and the general interest of the colonies;" and they requested a most justly respected member of the House of Commons to move in Parliament, "That an address be presented "to His Majesty, requesting him to recom- "mend to the colonies the adoption of "such measures, as may promote the in- "crease, of the Negroes, gradually diminish "the necessity of the Slave Trade, and ulti- "mately lead to its complete termination; "and also as may conduce to their moral and "religious improvement, and secure to them "the certain, immediate, and active protec- "tion of the law." This address was moved and carried with the warm support of all the West Indian party in Parliament; and was transmitted to the Governors of all the islands by the Duke of Portland, accompa- nied by letters urging the colonial legislatures to second the wishes of the House of Com- mons; private and confidential letters being written

Applications to the Colonies.

written to explain to the Councils in the different islands, the amicable purpose with which this otherwise perhaps questionable measure had been proposed, and assuring them, " that the adoption of some legislative " provisions relative to the Negroes was in- " dispensably necessary, not only to stop for " the present, but gradually to supersede the " very pretensions at a future period, to a " measure of direct abolition of the Slave " Trade by the mother country."

Thus the concurrence of the West Indian legislatures was requested by their own tried friends and counsellors, on that most acceptable and pleasing ground, of superseding the abolition of the Slave Trade. It might have been conceived, that, by the administration of such a powerful opiate, the *esprit de corps* of the islands would be lulled asleep; and, though it might even be from motives less pure than those of their friends at home, that they would at least adopt the line of conduct which had been recommended.

But how different has been the issue! You are already apprized of the conduct of the island of Barbadoes, to which Lord Seaforth, most honourably glad to avail himself of an opportunity of introducing the mea-

Colonial answers.

sure

sure under such favourable auspices, recommended the rendering a capital crime, the wilful murder of a Negro, which is now punishable only by a fine of about £. 11. 10 *s.* sterling.

The Assembly of Jamaica assert, " that " the right of obtaining labourers from Africa " is secured to them on the moſt solemn en- " gagements; and that they never can give up, " or do any act that may render doubtful, this " essential right." The General Council and General Assembly of all the Leeward islands ſtate, " that the right of procuring labourers " from Africa, has been secured to us by re- " peated Acts of Parliament, &c. We, there- " fore, never can abandon it, or do any thing " that may render doubtful this essential " right." The language of these answers is but too intelligible. But some communications lately made to Parliament, render it if possible ſtill more clear than it before was to all considerate and impartial men, that it is in vain to expect much effect from the regulations which any colonial acts may prescribe.

It may here perhaps be proper to ſtate, that since the abolition of the Slave Trade came into queſtion, acts have been passed for securing better treatment to the Slaves. It is no more however than juſtice to the Island of of Jamaica, to take this opportunity of declaring, that the Legislature of that island had passed a law rendering the murder of a Slave a capital crime, and containing various other salutary regulations, before the motion for abolishing the Slave Trade had been brought forward; though at the same time a fact then became public, which affords a curious proof how little the treatment of Slaves is really affected, one way or another, by public laws. For it appeared from the Assembly's own communication, that, for three years immediately preceding this laft reformation, an interval happening to take place between the repealing of a former consolidated Slave law for the protection and security of the Slaves, * and the passing of a new one, there were for three years together no laws whatever in being for the protection and security of the Slaves; and yet it was not found that the smalleft difference in the treatment of the Slaves had been occasioned. They were juft as well secured without laws as with them. In truth, as was before ftated, the real protection of a Slave muft lie in his mafter's disposition to protect him.—But to resume the discussion.

* Vide Privy Council Report, Nov. 12th 1788; 2d Report of the House of Assembly of Jamaica,

What has been already urged may perhaps appear sufficient to prove, that all the colonial laws for reforming the vices of the West Indian syftem, muft be practically inefficient. Nor can any farther argument be necessary, in order to enforce a conclusion so manifeftly resulting from the circumftances of the case. To some persons however it may render the point ftill more clear, to know, that the inefficacy, to say no worse, of the late Colonial Slave Acts, is decisively eftablished even on Weft Indian authority itself.

For, about two years ago, on the application of His Majefty's Secretary of State to the Governors of the Weft Indian Islands, for information as to the manner in which the late Acts for the better protection of Slaves had been executed, it clearly appeared, that though those laws had been paſſed so few years before with so much pomp and circumstance, yet that their provisions had never been carried into effect. This applies not merely to the impossible regulations, so to term them, prescribing the precise quantity of the food and clothing, and labour and punishment of the Slaves, but to all those regulations which really were of perfectly easy execution. There had been the same entire neglect of the religious and moral regulations, in which the Owner's

Owner's duty was clear and easy, even granting that his success might be difficult and doubtful.

This utter neglect of the Slave laws might alone have tended to give effectual confirmation to the suspicion, that the laws had been intended for the protection of the Slave Trade, rather than of the Slaves. This indeed was plainly stated by a British Officer, who was resident in one of the islands in 1788, when one of the earliest and best of these boasted laws was enacted. It was the general language of the Colonists at the time, that it's only real operation would be, to supersede any similar measures which might otherwise be adopted by the British Parliament. But much to the honour of the Governor of the only island from which any satisfactory information has been returned, he has distinctly stated,—" The Act of the Legislature, " entitled, " An Act for the Encouragement, " Protection, and better Government of " Slaves," appears to have been considered, " from the day it was passed, until this hour, " as a political measure to avert the inter- " ference of the mother country in the ma- " nagement of Slaves. Having said this, " your Lordship will not be surprised to learn, " that

" that the 7th clause of that Bill has been
" wholly neglected."

It may be proper to mention, that the clause which has been thus wholly neglected, was enacted for the express purpose of securing, as far as possible, the good treatment of the Slaves, and ascertaining the causes of their decrease. Some farther information, much to the same effect, was contained in a letter to the Secretary of State, from another correspondent, concerning the encouragement which the law had required to be given to Slaves to marry.

After this, can any reasonable expectations be entertained, that the Colonial Legislatures will cordially concur in any measures for the abolition of the Slave Trade? Can the Abolitionists be deemed uncandid, for not greatly confiding in any statutes which those assemblies may enact, in co-operation with the British Parliament, for the abolition of the Slave Trade?

<small>Laws for the protection of Slaves ineffectual in the old French, Spanish, and Portuguese settlements.</small> It ought earlier to have been stated, as an additional proof of the inefficacy of all legal regulations for the government and protection of Slaves, that they have fallen into practical disuse even in countries in which the masters do not themselves enjoy that political freedom
with

with which all such regulations are peculiarly at variance; and where, it might have been preconceived, a government perfectly despotic possessed abundant means of giving effect to its own regulations.

The better treatment of the Slaves in the Spanish and Portuguese Settlements, is much more to be ascribed to the influence of their religious zeal, and it's happy consequences, than to the institution of a Protector among the one, or to the provisions of the Directorio on the other.

Again, under the more despotic system of government which was established in the French islands before the revolution, the Code Noir, and various other edicts, which from time to time had been issued, concerning the treatment of Slaves, were become a mere dead letter. It is a curious proof, how much the practice and the opinions and feelings produced by it may differ from the law, that the free coloured people had for an entire century been legally entitled to that equality of rights and privileges with the whites, the granting of which, by the national assembly of the mother country, produced so violent a ferment among the white inhabitants of St. Domingo; and the retractation of which, after its having
been

been granted, followed by fresh grants and fresh retractations, produced the confusion which terminated in the loss of that flourishing colony.

Legal protection of Slaves in an abject state of slavery either impracticable or unsafe.

But besides that fundamental objection to statutes, for regulating the treatment of Slaves, and securing for them, to use the words of the colonists themselves, the *certain, immediate, and active protection of the law,* that they must prove utterly inefficient; I must frankly acknowledge my opinion, that all those legal regulations which, in the various particulars of treatment, interfere between the Master and Slave; which interpose between them some external authority to which the Slave, when ill used, is to have a right to apply for protection and redress; unless, as I before observed, they are not executed, must prove in practice unspeakably dangerous. This is true at least where Slaves are in a state of such abject slavery as that which has so long prevailed in our West Indian islands, and where the Slaves so greatly outnumber the free men, and the difference between Slave and Freeman, is marked and palpable. In extreme cases of ill treatment, or rather in cases of enormous cruelty, it might be practicable to apply some remedy, by the means of that regulation which was established in Athens, and

and which, with additions moſt grateful to a humane mind, prevails, we are assured, in the Spanish islands, of allowing the Slave when extremely ill treated, to be transferred to another owner. But this regulation is not applicable to those particulars of treatment, which are conſtant and syſtematic, such as underfeeding, overworking, and other general vices of management, whether arising out of degradation, absenteeship, speculation, the pressure of the times, or any other of the causes which have been above specified. And it is these syſtematic vices which conſtitute the real evils in the condition of the bulk of our Slaves.

In these cases of syſtematic management, of daily and almoſt hourly recurrence, the interposition of a new tribunal of appeal for checking the maſter's authority, and compelling him, by the dread of penalties, to be more liberal in his allowances of food and reſt, and more abſtemious as to labour and punishment; in short, to force him to amend the Slave's treatment in future in all the undefinable particulars into which it ramifies, or even to compensate to the Slave his paſt ill usage, would in practice be soon found productive, not only of extreme discontent, insubordination, and commotions on private properties, but of the moſt

fatal

fatal consequences to the safety of the whole colony. Sunk as the Slaves at present are, we are assured they do not feel into what a depth they have been depressed. We are told that they are not shocked, as we are for them, by the circumſtances of a Negro sale, or by the other degrading particulars of their treatment; the spirit of the man is extinct, or rather dormant within them. But remember, the firſt return of life after a swoon is commonly a convulsion, dangerous at once to the party himself, and to all around him. Impart to the Slaves the consciousness of personal rights, and the means of asserting them; give the Slaves a power of appealing to the laws; and you awaken in them a sense of the dignity of their nature, you call into life a new set of moſt dangerous emotions; of emotions, let me repeat it, beyond measure dangerous, while you continue the humiliating and ignominious diſtinctions to which they now unconsciously submit. When you encourage your Slave to take account of his rights, and measure them with his enjoyments: when you thus teach him to reflect on the treatment he is receiving; to compare his own condition with that of Slaves under other maſters; to deliberate about obtaining redress; and, at laſt, to resolve to seek it: when you thus accuſtom

cuftom him to think, and feel, and decide, and
act; to be conscious of a wrong; to resent an
injury; to go and relate the ftory of his ill-
usage, thus daring to harbour the idea of
bringing his mafter to punishment and shame:
when you even enable him to achieve this
victory; Do you think that he will long endure the wrongs he now tolerates? It is a
remark, if I miftake not, of an ancient hifto-
rian, who had the power above all others of
placing before his reader the scene he represents, that in that celebrated inftance in which
a whole army, being hemmed in on all sides by
the enemy, was compelled, according to the
barbarous practice of ancient warfare, to submit to the shameful condition of going under
a sort of gallows, that each man was rendered
most sensible of his own dishonour, by seeing
the shameful appearance of his comrades in
that disgraceful exhibition. And can you
think that, when affection combines with
indignation, a Negro will bear to see the
wife of his bosom, or a mother the children
of her rearing, driven through their daily
work like the vileft of the brute creation;
and that too when each man can consult with
his fellow, when all they see around them
almoft are blacks? Above all, but here I anticipate——when St. Domingo, and the lessons
which it inculcates, occur to the mind.

Surely

Surely enough has been said to shew, that there is no alternative, no practical medium, between keeping the Slaves sunk in their present state of extreme degradation, an idea for which no one, I trust, will be found hardy enough to contend, and introducing the milder system of what may not improperly be termed Patriarchal vassalage (to which the abolition is an indispensable preliminary) as the state of training and discipline for a condition in which they may be safely admitted to a still more advanced enjoyment of personal and civil rights.

<small>Mr. Burke's plan respecting the SlaveTrade.</small> And in this place, where we are considering the different modes which have been proposed for effecting the abolition of the Slave Trade, it may be proper to notice another plan of gradual abolition, which has been often mentioned, though it has never been yet produced. No one can doubt that attention is justly due to it, when they are told that it claims the late Mr. Burke as it's author. In duty to that great man himself, as well as to the cause which I am defending, this matter should be explained. Some years before the abolition of the Slave Trade had been named in Parliament, Mr. Burke's attention had been drawn to that object. His stores of knowledge were so astonishingly ample and various, that it is

difficult

difficult to suppose any subject on which his great mind was not abundantly furnished. But certainly very little was known, even by men in general well informed, concerning the nature and effects of the Slave Trade on the coaſt, but much more in the interior of Africa. Nor had we then obtained any of that great mass of information concerning the Weſt Indian syſtem of management, which was procured through the authority and influence of Government, and which could no otherwise have been obtained. Mr. Burke, however, drew up the heads of a plan for regulating the mode of carrying on the Slave Trade in Africa, and a syſtem for securing the better treatment of the Slaves in the Weſt Indies.

When, after the whole subject had been thoroughly investigated, a motion for the immediate abolition of the Slave Trade was made in the House of Commons; Mr. Burke honoured it with his support. He indeed ſtated, that he himself had formerly taken up ideas somewhat different, with a view towards the same end; but he added, expressing himself in that strong and figurative ſtyle which muſt, methinks, have fixed the matter of his speech firmly in the memory of all who heard him, that he at once consigned them,

them to the flames, and willingly adopted our mode of abolition. I can with truth declare, that in private conversation, he afterwards expressed to me his concurrence in our plan. It is a little hard, therefore, that the authority of that great man should now be pleaded againſt us. Still harder, that this should be the only use made of it, that, inſtead of any attempt to give effect to his intentions, his plan of abolishing the Slave Trade should be rendered practically subservient to the continuation of that traffic. In short, that his name should be used in complete opposition to his example. As to the nature and effect of his proposed plan, I had the opportunity of perusing it only haſtily, and I have endeavoured, hitherto in vain, once more to procure a sight of it. It is ſtill however I believe in being, and will I truſt appear in some authentic form.

The plan itself was probably no more than a rough draught, or rather his firſt thoughts on a subject, for forming a right judgment on which, a full and exact knowledge of facts muſt be particularly necessary. That on any subject, even the first thoughts of so great a man claim the higheſt deference, I willingly allow. But may I not be permitted to indulge a persuasion, that, from farther information than it
was

was possible for any man then to possess, concerning the nature and effects of the Slave Trade in the interior of Africa, into which no traveller of credit had then penetrated for some centuries, Mr. Burke would have been convinced of the inefficacy of the regulations he proposed to establish for the coast. Of his West Indian regulations, I will only say, that while, unless completely neglected in practice, they would probably have excited an opposition even more efficient than abolition itself; while they would have been open from beginning to end to all objections, grounded on interference with the internal legislation of the colonies; they would, more than any other plan ever heard of, have been liable to the objections which I have lately urged against imparting personal rights and the privilege of complaining to a legal protector, so long as the Slaves remain in their present condition of extreme degradation.

With this plan for abolishing, as by a strange perversion of terms it is styled, instead of confirming and perhaps perpetuating, the Slave Trade, by the gradual operation of colonial statutes, a plan which, though tried under the most favourable of all circumstances, has absolutely failed; which has been declared even by West Indian authority itself

Greater efficacy of abolition.

to

to have been proposed for the sake merely of getting rid of the interference of the British Parliament; which has been clearly proved to be utterly inefficient as to practical execution, and which, if it could be executed, would immediately become inconceivably dangerous—With this measure, founded on principles essentially and unalterably incompatible, either utterly inefficient or mischievously active, compare the effects of the measure which we propose, the abolition of the Slave Trade.

The bad effects of the continual introduction of African Slaves are so manifest as scarcely to need suggesting. The annual infusion into the West Indian Colonies of a great number of human beings, from a thousand different parts of the continent, with all their varieties of languages, and manners, and customs, many of them resenting their wrongs, and burning with revenge; others deeply feeling their loss of country and freedom, and the new hardships of their altered state; must have a natural tendency to keep the whole mass into which they are brought, in a state of ferment; to prevent the Slaves in general from emerging out of their state of degradation; and to obstruct, both in them and in those who are set over them, the growth of those domestic feelings and habits, and the introduction

troduction of those more liberal modes of treatment, which might otherwise be deemed both safe, and suitable in the case of Slaves whose characters were known and who were become habituated to their situation. But the grand evil arising from the continuance of importations from Africa, is, that till they are discontinued, men will never apply their minds in earnest to effect the establishment of the breeding system.

But all farther importations being at length stopped, the Slave market now no longer holding forth any resource, the necessity for keeping up the stock would at once become palpable and urgent. All ideas of supply from without, being utterly cut off, it would immediately become the grand, constant, and incessant concern of every prudent man, both proprietor and manager, to attend, in the first instance, to the preservation and increase of his Negroes. Whatever may have been the case in the instance of men at once both liberal and opulent, the mass of owners have, practically at least, gone upon the system of working out their Slaves in a few years, and recruiting their gangs with imported Africans. The abolition would give the death-blow to this system. The opposite system, with all its charities,

R 2   would

would force itself on the dulleſt intellects, on the moſt contracted or unfeeling heart. Ruin would ſtare a man in the face, if he did not conform to it. The sense of intereſt so much talked of, would not as heretofore, be a remote, feeble, or even a dubious impulse; but a call so pressing, loud, and clear, that its voice would be irresiſtible.

But the grand excellence of the operating principle of this reform is, that it will ſtand between the absentee maſter and his Slaves; and while it will promote the intereſt of the former, it will secure for the latter the actual enjoyment of the effects of his benevolent intentions. Managers would henceforth be forced to make breeding the prime object of their attention. And every non-resident owner would express himself in terms of an experienced Barbadian proprietor of superior rank and fortune; " That he should consider " it as the fault of the manager, if he did " not keep up the numbers of his Slaves." The absent owner would have the beſt security of which the nature of the case admits for his Slaves being treated with liberality and kindness. The operative principle thus supplied would exactly answer the desired purpose. It would adapt itself to every variety of situation and circumſtances. It would
penetrate

penetrate into the interior of every plantation; it would ensure a due quantity of food; it would provide againſt too rigorous an exaction of labour, and enforce the adoption of those reforms which should be found requiſite for increasing the population. Many of the improvements which muſt at once be introduced are perfectly manifeſt. But, ingenuity once set at work in this direction, a thousand discoveries will be made, a thousand reforms adopted, and, a manager's credit and character now depending on the increase of the Negroes, not as hitherto on that of the immediate and clear returns from the eſtate, the former would henceforth become the great object of his ſtudy in the closet, and of his conduct in life and action.

The professional Planter's work shews the improvements which may be suggeſted by a ſingle individual of intelligence and experience, living on the spot, and superintending the whole ſyſtem with an observant eye. What, then, may be expected when the ingenuity and attention of a whole community are set at work in the same direction; to effect the introduction of moral reforms, the settlement of families, the discouragement of adultery; the countenancing, by example as well as precept, among book-keepers or overseers, of morality

rality and decency, the neglect of which, by persons of that class, has been hitherto productive of many injurious consequences.

Let us hear therefore no more of the Slaves invincible habits of profligacy and sensuality, of their not being susceptible of the reftraints, obligations, duties, and comforts of the marriage ftate.

Wonder not that they are now sunk into habits of gross debauchery. Not man alone, but beings in general, throughout the whole range of animated nature, inftinctively seek the indulgencies and enjoyments suited to their condition and capacities. Depressed therefore nearly to a level with the brute creation, the negro Slaves inftinctively adapt themselves to their level, and are immersed in merely animal pursuits. Hence it is, that those very Negroes, who in Africa are represented as so eminent for truth, so disinterefted in kindness, so faithful in the conjugal and domeftic relations, so hospitable, so fond of their children, of their parents, of their country, gradually lose all these amiable dispositions with the enjoyments which naturally arise out of them, and become depraved and debased by all that is selfish and mercenary, and deceitful, timid and indolent, and tyrannical.

tyrannical. Would you raise them from this depressed condition, remember the disease is of a moral nature. It admits therefore only of a moral cure. Take away those particulars which degrade and vilify, and thus expel from the syftem those circumftances which depress the Slaves below the level of domeftic life.* Endeavour in such ways, and by such inftruments, as by experience are found beft fitted for the purpose, to impart to them the ineftimable blessings of religious inftruction and moral improvement and reform, many of them would soon shew the happy effect of these inftructions, by a conduct and demeanour manifeftly the result of higher principles; for I muft once more raise my voice againft that gross misconception of the character of the Negroes (an impeachment of the wisdom and goodness of their Creator no less than of our own), which represents them as a race of such natural baseness and brutality as to be incapable of religious impressions and improvements. Encourage marriage and the rearing of children in the only proper way; by settling the Slaves in family life, with their cottage and gardens, and with such other immunities and comforts and diftinctions as will make them be respected by others and teach them to respect themselves.

Syftem of management, how to be reformed.

---

* Inftitute schools for their children.

I am

I am aware that it has been by no means uncommon for such masters as have made the domestic increase their object, to give rewards to mothers for rearing their children. Surely they have forgot, that Nature, I had almost said instinct, would take care of this for them, if they would but pursue the previous course she so manifestly dictates. It is not by a reward to be given at the end of a year or two, that continual attention can be purchased, with all the ten thousand cares and assiduities and kindnesses which both by day and by night the weakness of infancy requires; they are to be bought by a different price; they are to be prompted and repaid by maternal tenderness, by domestic sympathy, and parental interest. Give but to the Slaves a home; let the children be safely born, with a tolerable prospect of happiness; and let the mothers be allowed immunities and indulgencies, especially a little time from field work, morning and evening, to attend to their infants; bring them thus acquainted with conjugal duties and conjugal feelings, with the comforts and emotions of family life, awaken in them the dormant sympathies of domestic affection, and they will soon become creatures of a higher order, for it is in the soil of domestic life that all the charities of our nature spring up and flourish. A new set of feelings will begin to unfold themselves,

themselves. The Slaves in general will learn to feel the value of a good character, to covet the acquisition and strive for the maintenance of it. They will make it their study to gain a master's good opinion and confidence. With hope to animate, and gratitude to warm, how soon should we witness willing industry and hearty services. To these would justly be added, for in this imperfect state the addition will doubtless be required, the fear of a master's displeasure, and the wholesome restraint of punishment for the indolent, and refractory, and vicious. The harshness of their present bondage being transformed into the mildness of patriarchal servitude, they will become capable of still greater blessings, and more ennobling privileges. The Slaves being now admitted to be not incapable of moral obligations, they will surely be acknowledged to be fit for the lower civil functions; and, above all, there will be no pretence for maintaining that grand disqualification, which alone is sufficient to taint their whole condition with the bitterness of degradation and suffering, the utter inadmissibility of their evidence.*

Thus

---

* Why should not a right of giving evidence, with perhaps some other civil distinctions, be granted to any Slaves who have lived creditably in the marriage state, for three or five years. They might think little of
these

Thus they would gradually and insensibly be transformed into a native peasantry.

Is it possible to contemplate the change which has been here slightly traced, without emotions of the moſt lively delight? I will not now indulge myself in the pleasing task of detailing the several ſteps of this gratifying process; but I muſt ſtate, that in many of the islands, probably in them all, the quantity of food muſt be increased; in the articles of clothing, lodging, and medical care, improvements muſt be adopted; especially the hours of working muſt be lessened, and wherever it is possible, task-work muſt be introduced; above all, that degrading practice of working the Slaves under the whip muſt be abandoned. Think not that it will be enough that females, when clearly pregnant, shall be spared the more laborious duties of field work. No; nor even that all the young women, without exception, shall be no longer worked under the driver's lash; from which, in the judgment of a moſt respectable and intelligent planter, innumerable miscarriages happen in the earlier periods of pregnancy.

these distinctions at first; but accompany them with some outward mark, and they will produce their effect. No distinctions are more impressive, than those which are arbitrary, and the essential nature of which is little understood.

pregnancy. The syftem of whip-working itself muft be entirely exploded, and in it's place muft be subftituted the operation of those principles which are elsewhere found universally sufficient for their object, the hope of reward, and the fear of punishment.

In all these particulars I am but recommending the several reforms enforced with so much more authority by the professional Planter, to whom I have so often referred. All these are preliminary reforms, which must precede, or rather accompany that moft efficient and beneficial of all improvements, the combined effect of religious and moral cultivation, with the comforts of being settled in families, and the obligations and duties of conjugal and domestic life. That it may require reflection, attention, and discretion to introduce this happy change, I mean not to deny; it will require also, that a proprietor should make up his mind to some present diminution of income, for the sake of larger ultimate returns. Possibly even some arrangements of law may here become expedient; nor will I even affirm, that in one or two particular islands there may not be inftances (though it is with reluctance that one would acknowledge such a case) in which proprietors may have found it their intereft hitherto to

work

work down their gangs, and supply vacancies from the Slave market, to whom therefore the new syſtem may be injurious, the rather, because it would of course find their Slaves nearly ground down by the want of necessaries and the excess of labour.

But with such moderate exceptions as must necessarily be anticipated in any change so great, it may be truly affirmed, to be the excellence and glory of the measure we propose, that it is likely almoſt from the very firſt to dispense blessings to every individual connected with it, in every ſtep, from the firſt to the laſt, throughout the whole of it's progress.

Often it happens in human affairs, that ends the moſt beneficial muſt be obtained by painful and diſtressing means. Inveterate diseases can rarely be cured without disguſting or painful remedies. But how gratifying is the consideration, that in the present instance, not only is our ultimate point the seat of security and happiness, but the way by which we travel to it is a way of pleasantness and peace. It's effects cannot be produced at once, but we are all the while tending to their complete enjoyment, with an uniform and uninterrupted course. The Slaves will daily

grow

grow happier, the planters richer. The whole will be like the progress of vegetation; the effects are not at firſt perceptible, but the great principle, operating in ten thousand inſtances, will gradually change the whole face of things, and subſtitute fertility and beauty in the place of barrenness and desolation.

And all this happy transformation we anticipate, not from carrying into execution the speculations of the moſt intelligent and able men, but by quitting the ways of injuſtice and cruelty, and by entering on those happier paths, which, by the gracious ordination of Heaven, are, on the long run, ever found to lead to safety, prosperity, and happiness. It may be right to ſtate one consideration, which may suggeſt the probability, that even from the firſt the island ſtock of Slaves may not be found inadequate to the increasing demands to be made on it.

It is proved by indisputable reasoning, as well as by uniform experience, that where slavery exiſts, there is always an immense waſte of labour; there is a tendency to accomplish, by mere force, all which is elsewhere effected by machinery. How far this has been the case in the Weſt Indies, is pointed out by various authors, and particularly with great ability,

Waſte of labour wherever slavery prevails.

lity, and perfect knowledge of the subject, by a late writer.*

In order, therefore, to form a just estimate of the means of cultivating the West Indies, after the abolition shall have taken place, we must superadd, to a population gradually increasing, and advancing so much the more rapidly from the removal of the obstacles to breeding, and the positive causes of increase which have been already stated, that great and incalculable increase in the efficiency of the force actually employed, which will be effected by its becoming the immediate and pressing interest of the proprietors to economise in the labour of their Slaves, and to avail themselves of all the means by which labour may be abridged, and the same produce may be raised by fewer hands.

Immediate abolition preferable to gradual, both in the West Indies and in Africa.

Allow me also to remark that, now especially, when the planters have had so much time, since the first proposal of abolition, for filling up their gangs, the change is likely to operate more favourably on both sides of the Atlantic, in consequence of it's being immediate and complete, not gradual in it's opera-

* See the publication of Mr. Canes, a most experienced and benevolent West Indian proprietor.

tion.

tion. In the West Indies, where there is to be a great change of practical views and objects, a change too which will be very unwillingly adopted, men are far more likely to make up their minds to the new system, and to set about acting upon it with vigour, if it be clearly and decisively necessary, than if there be still some supply, though in a diminished proportion, to be obtained from the Slave market. Supposing them in the first year to fail in their endeavours to obtain a share of the Slaves allowed to be imported, they may hope to be more fortunate in the second. Meanwhile the hope of a resource in the Slave market will prevent their exerting themselves in earnest in establishing the system by which they might secure an internal increase; and thus they might be drawn on from year to year to their own ruin, to the public injury, and to the misery of their unhappy Negroes.

Again, in Africa, were we at once to give up the Slave Trade, the native chiefs and factors, who have hitherto entirely depended on it for their supply of spirits, fire-arms, ammunition, and other European articles, having no resource in their old occupation, would set themselves in earnest to some other mode of employing their domestic Slaves, in
order

order thereby to procure the desired stock of European articles. But were the trade to be abolished by degrees, they, as in the former case, would hope to obtain a share, though it should be a smaller share; and this expectation would be sufficient to prevent their engaging spiritedly in any undertaking of agriculture or commerce.

It may seem to be anticipating an argument which ought to receive a separate consideration; but let me also remark, that our retiring gradually from the trade, would greatly favour the entrance of other nations into the poſt we had before occupied. It would be utterly impossible for them to find capital or other means sufficient for undertaking the whole of so extensive a commerce; but were we to give it up by degrees, they might possibly be able, by great efforts, to obtain the means of carrying on, part after part, what we should have abandoned.

Abolitioniſts falsely deemed inconſiſtent for not emancipating the Weſt Indian Slaves.
And here, perhaps, it may be right to answer a ſtrange objection, which our opponents, at a loss, surely, for sound arguments, have urged againſt us. I may be able also at once to vindicate the Abolitioniſts from two opposite charges, which have been brought againſt them. One class of their opponents,
in

in spite of repeated and moſt positive assurances to the contrary, have imputed to them the deſign of immediately emancipating the Slaves. Can it be neceſſary to declare, that the Abolitioniſts are full as much as any other men convinced, that insanity alone could dictate such a project. On the other hand, by another class of opponents, they have been charged with being unfaithful to their own principles, in not immediately emancipating the Slaves already in the islands, as well as immediately putting a ſtop to our ravages in Africa. Sometimes it has been argued, that we ourselves prove by our conduct in this inſtance, that the laws of juſtice muſt occasionally concede somewhat to considerations of expediency. That therefore they do but extend a little further than we, the limits of that concession, when they propose that the Slave Trade itself, with all its horrors, should be suffered to continue.

It scarcely would be requisite to expose the sophiſtry of this argument, if it had not sometimes proceeded from men of underſtanding, whose use of it however can only be accounted for by the supposition, that they are utterly unacquainted with the circumſtances of the case.

Supposing

Supposing they were themselves to discover an unfortunate human being, who, by long imprisonment and severe treatment, had been driven into a state of utter madness; would either juftice or humanity prompt them to grant at once to this unfortunate man the unconftrained enjoyment of his natural liberty? On the contrary, would not these principles rather inculcate the duty of endeavouring by proper medical regimen, by falutary reftraint, and if necessary even by the harsher expedient of wholesome discipline, to reftore him to his senses, and qualify him for that freedom which he might afterwards enjoy?

The Weft Indian Slaves are in a ftate which calls for a course of treatment founded on similar principles. It would be the grossest violation and the mereft mockery of juftice and humanity, to emancipate them at once, in their present unhappy condition. God forbid (with moft serious reverence I use the expression) that we should not desire to impart to the Negro Slaves the blessings of freedom. No man, I believe, eftimates liberty more highly, or loves it better, than myself. True liberty, of course, I mean, the child of reason and law, the parent of order and happiness; such liberty, as that, of which they must

must be dull indeed who do not understand the nature and feel the value, who have lived in the enjoyment of the blessings which it dispenses under the form of a British Constitution; while they have beheld also its perfect contrast, both in nature and effects, in the wild licentiousness of a neighbouring kingdom.

It is indeed a " plant of celestial growth," but the soil and climate must be prepared for its reception, or it will not bring forth its proper fruits. These are fruits, alas! which our poor degraded Negro Slaves are as yet incapable of enjoying. To grant it to them immediately, would be to insure not only their masters ruin, but their own. A certain previous course of discipline is necessary. They must be trained and educated for this most perfect state of manly maturity; and, by a singular felicity of coincidence, the stoppage of all further importations from Africa, with all the consequences which it introduces in it's train, is the very shortest and safest path by which the Slaves can travel to the enjoyment of true liberty.

Besides the great argument urged by the opponents of the abolition, that of not being able to maintain their stock of Slaves at its present

Other objections to Abolition.

present number and force, without importation from Africa, a position which, I truſt, has been now moſt satisfactorily refuted by decisive appeals both to speculation and experience; other allegations also were made concerning the injurious consequences of the abolition, and of these it may now be proper to take a brief review.

It should however be borne in mind, that they all depend on the determination of the great queſtion concerning the keeping up of the population, except so far only as the African Slave Trade is in queſtion; and, with the exception before made, of persons connected with places whence this bloody traffic is carried on (now, to the honour of the kingdom, but two, London and Liverpool), none have been found such ſteady advocates for the Slave Trade, as to contend for its continuance merely for it's own sake.

The opponents of abolition, and especially some of our great colonial antagoniſts, have confidently ſtated, that our measure would effect the speedy deſtruction of our Weſt Indian colonies; and that in consequence of the loss of national capital which we should ſuſtain, and from our no longer importing the productions of our Weſtern colonies, the abolition

tion would bring down utter ruin on the commercial, manufacturing, maritime, and financial interests of the empire.

I am far from denying the political, commercial, and financial advantages we have derived from the West Indies, or the benefit resulting to us, as a maritime nation, from the distant situation of those possessions. Still it is impossible to admit the principles of calculation, any more than the reasoning, of our opponents, when they state the whole loss which the public will sustain by the abolition of the Slave Trade. *Abolition injurious to our Commerce, Manufactures, &c. &c.*

They commonly begin by putting down as loss, very nearly the whole value of our exports to Africa, together with that of all the ships and sailors employed in that branch of commerce. They enlarge much also on the evils resulting from the suddenness of the shock, by so large a share of the national capital, as well as of our ships and seamen, being all at once thrown out of employment; they then pass over to the West Indies, and sum up the value of the West Indian estates of all kinds belonging to British subjects, with their buildings, Negroes, and other stock. To these they add the value of all the exports and imports, to and from the West Indies; with all the revenue derived from them, and the shipping and sailors which they employ; and then they tell us, that, adding the value of all these various articles together, we shall find the amount of our loss.

With respect to the African branch of the foregoing statement, all who believe with me, that the Africans are not incapable of civilization, and that when the fatal barrier shall be broken down, which along the whole western frontier has shut out all the improvements to be derived from a bloodless intercourse with more polished nations, they may gradually advance to a state of social order, comfort, and abundance; all who entertain hopes like these, will anticipate the immense amount of the commercial transactions which Britons in future times may carry on with that vast continent; and surely our descendants will, at the same time, wonder that their forefathers, on principles even of mere commercial gain, could be blind to the advantages to be derived from diffusing our manufactures through a region which constitutes almost a third part of the habitable globe.

Even our opponents themselves will acknowledge, that the suddenness of the shock is alone to be regarded. The objection on this

this ground was quite satisfactorily, though briefly refuted, in the concise statement formerly referred to. It appears, that, even before the abolition of that large part of the Slave Trade which consisted in supplying foreigners, and the French and Dutch conquered settlements with Slaves; the capital employed in the Slave Trade was but about one thirty-fifth part of the whole of our capital employed in foreign trade; and it was very truly affirmed, that " very few
" changes ever take place in the political
" arrangements of the state, or in it's mea-
" sures of commercial œconomy, which are
" not attended with a much greater shifting
" of capital, than the abolition of the Slave
" Trade, however sudden, could have effected
" in the periods of it's greatest prosperity."

The assertion, that we should be injured by suddenly throwing out of occupation the ships and seamen employed in the African Trade, was shewn to stand on still weaker grounds. When at it's very highest amount, an amount far higher than it will ever again reach, unless we even replace the branches which we have actually lopped off, it employed not one-sixtieth part of our whole tonnage; not one twenty-third part of our seamen. But so far as our seamen are in consideration,

consideration, it will scarcely be disputed by any Naval Officer, that we should gain by the extinction of the Slave Trade.

With respect to the West Indian part of the price, as calculated by our opponents, which Great Britain must pay for obeying the dictates of justice and humanity, by abolishing the Slave Trade; we must remark, that they forget that the revenue at least, derived from the taxes raised on West Indian productions, is paid by the subjects of this country. Other objections of detail might be made to their calculations. But, passing by these, let me observe, that, above all, they utterly forget, that in this reasoning they take for granted the whole question in dispute; for the Abolitionists maintain, that, while the abolition would produce a gradual increase of our exports to the West Indies, from the improving condition of the bulk of their population; our revenue, our imports, and our marine, dependent on them, would be fixed on a basis far more safe and durable than that on which they now rest. But in considering the question on the grounds of policy, it is ever to be kept in mind, that the alternative is not, whether or not we shall take a step which is affirmed, on one side, to be big with mischief, while the opponents only maintain, on the other, that it will about an equal proportion; but as some derive great gains, others are proportionably losers. In some few of the smaller islands, the profit on the capital was ſtated to be somewhat, but only a little more.

The facility of purchasing labourers afforded by the Slave Trade has tempted multitudes to their ruin. Sometimes a great number of Slaves, for which no adequate preparations were made, have been put to the moſt unhealthy and laborious of all employments, the clearing of new land, and forming of new settlements. Accordingly, it has followed for the moſt part but too naturally, that the Slaves have perished, and the eſtate has been either thrown up, or sold for the benefit of the creditors.

These are no new speculations. Mr. Long, above thirty years ago, dilated on the evils of this syſtem in the ſtrongeſt terms. He even went so far as to recommend, with a view to the prevention of them, a temporary ſtoppage of the importation of Slaves from Africa; and he confirmed his reasoning by appealing to the experience of one of our North American colonies, which, when involved in the deepeſt diſtress by the operation of similar circumſtances, had been retrieved from a ſtate of almoſt

almost utter ruin by the adoption of a similar expedient.

We have had an opportunity of receiving but too decisive a proof of the bad effects of suffering the opposite system to go on without restraint. Even twenty-six years ago they had exhibited a display of ruin, which was scarcely equalled by the effects of any regular and permanent cause of evil, in any other age or country. It would scarcely have appeared credible, if it were not established by the records of a public court, that in twenty years, from 1760 to 1780, the executions on estates in the Sheriff's court amounted in number to above 80,000, and were to the amount in value of £. 32,500,000 currency, or about £. 22,500,000 sterling. Again; of all the sugar estates in the island at the beginning of the same period of twenty years, nearly one half were, at the end of it, either thrown up as not worth cultivating, or were in the hands of creditors, or mortgagees, or had been sold for their benefit. *

This was many years before the abolition of the Slave Trade had ever been proposed;

* Vide Report of the Committee of the House of Assembly of Jamaica, in the Papers presented to the House of Commons.

and

and one would have conceived, that the consequences of the syftem which had been so long pursued, might alone have produced a disrelish for it, and have predisposed the Colonifts to adopt another which was recommended by the higheft authorities. Prejudice, however, and party spirit, were too powerful for reason and sound policy, as well as for humanity and juftice. And what has been the result ? The affairs of the colonies have gone on from bad to worse, until the diftress being extremely aggravated by another cause, to be presently noticed, the great island of Jamaica is represented, by its own legislature, in a ftate, to use the compendious terms of a very able and experienced Weft Indian proprietor, of general diftress and foreclosure of property.

During all this time a debt to the mother country, before prodigious, has been gradually accumulating; or rather, perhaps, to say the truth, the merchants of London have for the moft part become the real proprietors of colonial eftates; while the resident, and even sometimes the absentee planters, have been little more in reality than their ftewards and agents.

You will naturally be aftonished at the facts which have been here ftated; you will naturally ask, what temptations can have
been

been sufficiently strong to prompt men to go on in such a continued course, with speculations which have proved in the main so unprofitable? It is really difficult to account satisfactorily for the phœnomenon. Much is certainly to be ascribed to the operation of that principle in our nature, the gambling principle as it may be termed, the existence and effects of which have been so well explained by Dr. Adam Smith; the disposition to overrate our probable success, and to assign too little weight to contingencies which may disappoint our expectations. However, in the present instance, besides this general cause, we may discover several specific causes of sure and highly powerful operation.

The West Indies are a very wide field, and some few instances of great and rapid success attract more notice than the far more numerous cases which terminate in ruin. The British merchant's profit from consignments ensures a somewhat ready disposition to assist adventurers in planting. When also, as often happens, there is a glut of Slaves in the West Indian market, as they are an expensive article while they remain unsold, the planter can buy them on a proportionably longer credit. Two and even three years are not seldom allowed; the Planter therefore is tempted

tempted to purchase Slaves even if he does not greatly want them, in the hope, that before the time of payment arrives, they will have more than worked out their coft, by the sugars which their labour will have brought to market. In like manner the British merchant trufts, that before the bills drawn on him shall become due, the sugars in his hands will meet them. Thus encouraged, the planter buys. Meanwhile the Slaves muft be set to work; and the inadequate funds of their mafter, the same cause which curtails their food and abridges their other comforts, causes them to be worked the harder. They sicken and drop off, and perish in what is called the *seasoning*, a mode of death sufficiently important and notorious to have obtained this epithet; a somewhat singular one, considering that the climate of the Weft Indies and Africa are so much the same. Yet this is a syftem, which, ruinous as it is, has a natural tendency to increase; which may grow even to an indefinite extent. The evils of it, however, though too long unacknowledged, are now at leaft felt by all who are not blinded by intereft or passion. An immense mass of the national capital has thus been invefted, I had almoft said has been sunk, in our Trans-Atlantic Empire. In one respect it may be said, that, in accordance with the principles so clearly

developed

developed by the great political Economist who has been already named, our commercial accumulations have found their way to the land, and have become an agricultural capital. But it is to land many thousand miles removed from the mother country.

Excessive accumulation of capital in the West Indies.

I admit all the advantages, to their utmost extent, which we derive, considered as a maritime nation, from these distant possessions. But there are peculiar circumstances in their situation, which must make every considerate politician acknowledge how much more it would have been for the benefit of this country if a part of that capital had been employed at home. What is expended in the improvement of our own soil is so much permanently added to the wealth, resources, and population of Great Britain. It is well digested, and well assimilated nutriment; and it adds proportionably to our muscular strength. It is inseparably a part of ourselves; it must share our fortunes; and in all times and circumstances contribute to our benefit. Even the wealth which is acquired by British subjects in the East Indies is brought home to be spent in our own country. It improves our land, or it increases the funds to be employed in commercial or manufacturing enterprizes.

How

How differently circumstanced is that part of our national capital, which is invested in the West Indies. It is in a situation where it is peculiarly open to seizure; and where, in consequence, it often invites the attack of an enemy, while at the same time it is defended at an immense expence of the lives of our fellow subjects. From a fatal principle of internal weakness, it may at once be dissipated by the explosion of an insurrection, or it may be separated from us by other events which no one can call impossible. Not only would our gain, from a large part at least of this capital, have been greater in amount, if it had been invested within our own island; but still more, the gain, whatever it might have been, would have been held by a less precarious tenure. Of West Indian, even more truly than of any other riches, it may be affirmed, that they are apt to make themselves wings and fly away.

But notwithstanding the decisive proofs which have been adduced, of the ruinous consequences of the existing system; notwithstanding the tried efficiency, and salutary operation, of those great principles, to which, in the event of the abolition, we look for the advancing safety, happiness, and greatness of our Western Colonies; notwithstanding,

still

still more, the acknowledged authority of that great man, whose opinion of the tendency of the abolition to promote the solid and permanent prosperity, as well as security, of the West Indies, was so repeatedly declared—I am yet aware that the statement of the contrary opinion by the Colonists themselves, and by their agents and correspondents in this country, greatly biasses the judgment of many considerate and respectable men.

<small>Probable causes of the opposition to abolition.</small> Allow me therefore to make a few observations on this head, and to consider a little whether there may not be other causes besides reason and argument, from which the continued opposition of what is termed the West Indian body may probably be owing in no inconsiderable degree.

It is not surprizing that a great effect has been produced by the declaration of so numerous and respectable a class of the community as that of the West Indian body, that the abolition would be ruinous to their interests; especially, considering that there has been full scope for the operation of party spirit, we should not be surprized to find this opinion held somewhat strongly and generally by the colonial world, and their numerous connections. Yet surely we have been too much

much accustomed to hear men predicting the moſt fatal consequences from incidents and measures, which have been depending, when the event has afterwards proved that their fears, if not utterly groundless, have been at leaſt excessively magnified; to conclude that the mere circumſtance of such apprehensions being entertained, is a sufficient proof of their having a sound foundation. We have already ſtated a ſtriking inſtance of this kind, in the progress of this very conteſt—that of the violent opposition which was made by all the parties concerned, to the passing of the Slave-carrying Bill; a meaſure which a very few years after was acknowledged, as it is still universally confessed, to have been beneficial to them all. One of the moſt efficient of the opponents of abolition, in 1792, frankly acknowledged this common deluſion; and even declared, that he anticipated the period when the queſtion of abolition itſelf would afford another inſtance of it's having occurred. He ſtated a particular fact in confirmation of his opinion; which, as the ſtory is not long, it may be worth while to relate.

" There was a species of slavery prevailing
" only a few years ago in some boroughs in
" Scotland. Every child that carried a coal
" from

" from the pit, was the bound slave of that
" borough. Their emancipation was thought
" by Parliament to be material; and was
" very much agitated in the House. It was
" urged by those who opposed the emanci-
" pation, that, let every man's genius be what
" it might, yet that those pits in which the
" work, from it's nature, was carried on
" under ground, were quite an excepted case;
" and that without the admission of slavery in
" this particular inftance, the collieries could
" not be worked; that the price of coals
" would be raised to a moft immoderate
" height; and all the neighbouring manufac-
" tories, which depended on them, would
" essentially suffer in their interefts. After
" several years ftruggle, the Bill, however,
" was carried through both houses of Parlia-
" ment. Within a year after, the whole idea
" of the collieries being in the leaft hurt
" by the abolition of this sort of slavery,
" vanished into smoke, and there was an end
" of the business."

I hope therefore, that, notwithftanding the declared sense of the bulk of the Weft Indian body, I may, without being thought presump-tuous, ftill declare, that renewed consideration has only confirmed my judgment, that the abolition of the Slave Trade would be ultimately

mately and permanently beneficial to the West Indians themselves.

It is not lightly that I have taken up the persuasion, which has been intimated more than once, that the determined hostility with which the abolition of the Slave Trade has been opposed by the bulk of the West Indian body, is, in a multitude of instances, the effect of party spirit rather than of rational conviction after full and fair investigation. It is in the case of the West Indian party as in that of parties in general, a few men of superior zeal and activity give the tone to the rest. The residents in the islands, the greater part of whom are either engaged in planting speculations, or are looking forward to such speculations, are the real instigators of the opposition. The West Indian merchants lend them their zealous and powerful aid; and the proprietors in this country head the party, partly from an implicit confidence in the judgment of others, partly from a liberal feeling, which renders them unwilling to desert the cause of their fellow planters abroad; and if they take any share at all in the contest, their rank and fortune render it natural for them to take the lead.

By far the greater part however a   actual

actuated merely by deference for the opinion of others; and by that *esprit de corps* which first renders men unwilling to differ from their friends, and which, by degrees, produces warmth, and at length vehemence, by mutual intercourse, sympathy, and collision.

In truth, what force of mind does it not require in a considerate man of any feeling, aware of all the low surmises, the invidious comments, the unkind constructions, the altered countenances, not to speak of the real loss of influence and connections to which he may expose himself, to resolve, on refusing to join the general party, and to adhere to his resolution; in such circumstances as those of the West Indian body; or, even still more, to quit the party he has joined, when a sense of duty commands the sacrifice. It is indeed but too true, that almost in any instance, and never perhaps in any more than in that of the West Indian connection, to break through the trammels of our party, demands the most strenuous, and, judging from experience, we should say, one of the most difficult of all efforts.

For men to emancipate themselves from this bondage, it requires not so much an uncommon degree of judgment and foresight, not even so much of impartiality and candour,

dour, as it calls for such a share of firmness and independence of mind as rarely indeed falls to the lot of men in any times, and less than almost in any other, in our own, in which fashion and party rule with such a rigorous despotism, as if it were to revenge on us our not submitting to any other yoke. Yet are there not a few West Indian Proprietors, both in and out of Parliament, who, though owners of large colonial possessions, have refused to join the West Indian body; who are exempt from West Indian prejudices, and who, to their honour, are resolved that the source from which their annual income is derived, shall not be polluted by injustice and cruelty.

There are also various individuals connected with the colonies, whose complete personal acquaintance with the whole system of West Indian management has given them an opportunity of discovering it's vices, and has prevented their becoming the dupes of party violence or sophistry. And though, in quitting a formed party when we have once joined it, we obviously have greater difficulties to encounter, and obstacles to overcome, than even in originally refusing to combine with our brethren in constituting it, yet one splendid conquest of this kind has been made well it deserves

deserves such an epithet, for he, who knows any thing of human nature, knows full well, that these are the most difficult of all masteries.

Yet this difficult conquest has been achieved by one of those gentlemen who originally took the lead, in committing to the colonial legislatures the service of superseding the necessity of abolishing the Slave Trade by internal regulations. He has since abundantly proved that he did not support the measure, in order merely to defeat the efforts of the Abolitionists, and with a real view of prolonging the continuance of the Slave Trade; but that he conceived, that the question then at issue was, whether that traffic should be abolished by the Colonial Assemblies or the British Legislature: and now, that the former have refused to accept the commission which the House of Commons offered to intrust to them, he has embraced the other part of the alternative, and cordially co-operated in the attempt to abolish by the Imperial Parliament. Instances of such conduct as this are rare; for being rare, they are the more honourable. The mind loves to dwell on them. Perhaps, from never having been a party man myself I may feel their excellencies with peculiar force.

I might

I might offend the delicacy of this gentleman, by mentioning his name; but surely without his leave I may venture to describe him. I fear there are but two or three others with whom, in all the following particulars, he can be well confounded. I may ſtate him, then, to be the Jamaica Proprietor, in whom I believe humanity and kindness to his Slaves are hereditary virtues; and who, having more waſte but cultivable land, than almoſt any other Jamaica landholder, had more to gain by the continuance of the Slave Trade, while he has been among the firſt to abandon, or rather to aboliſh it; who has ever had his eyes more open than moſt other proprietors to the abuses of the Weſt Indian syſtem, and his endeavours more warmly and actively exerted to correct them; being more exempt than moſt others of his brethren from Weſt Indian prejudices, but often, I fear, counteracted by the prejudices of others; who has been desirous especially of promoting those moral reforms which would above all other improvements tend to the comfort of the Slaves, and the security and prosperity of the islands.

This is not general and indiscriminate praise; each commendation has it's object. May he go forward in the path on which he has so honourably entered, and may he be followed
by

by descendants, inheriting his principles as well as his property, who may perfect the work which he has commenced.

<small>Power of party spirit in the West Indians.</small> That the principle of party spirit is adequate to the production of moſt powerful effects; that it may be even sufficient to prompt men to act in manifeſt opposition to a clear, direct and valuable intereſt, has been decisively eſtabliſhed in the case of our Weſt Indian Proprietors themselves in a very recent inſtance. For, what but this party spirit could cause them to support the continuance of that branch of the Slave Trade which consiſted in supplying foreigners with Slaves, and ſtill more, which could prevent their even ſtrenuously and eagerly anticipating the efforts of the Abolitioniſts for ſtopping the supply for the cultivation of the immeasurable expanse of the South American continent. In the colonies which we there conquered, near twenty millions of the capital of this country were actually inveſted during the short period after their conqueſt, for which we remained in possession of them during the laſt war; and, on their being reſtored by the peace, all this vaſt sum contributed to the improving and enriching of the colonies of a power which unhappily even then could be considered only as the vassal of our already too powerful rival.

rival. The proprietor in our old islands will not deny that those continental settlements not only have injured him by greatly increasing the quantity of colonial produce in the market, but that, enjoying very decided advantages over our older islands, from a more fertile soil, from being exempted from hurricanes, from the opportunity of feeding the Slaves more plentifully, and at a cheaper rate, they have been to him the cause of very great loss and embarrassment. Had this evil been suffered to advance, the ruin which muſt have followed from it, though gradual, would have been sure and complete. From that misfortune the Abolitioniſts have relieved him, by obtaining the Order of Council, since confirmed and sanctioned by an Act of Parliament, for ſtopping the importation of Slaves, not only into foreign colonies, but even into those possessions, chiefly in Guiana, which in the present war have been again conquered from the enemy. And surely we may assume to ourselves some credit for having willingly rendered to them, our opponents, the greateſt benefit which they could receive. But while we are engaged on this topic, let me call on the Weſt Indians in our own ancient possessions, for whom again I muſt declare I feel moſt good will, as those

who

who have long been our fellow subjects, in company with whom we have weathered many a storm and rejoiced after many a victory; let me call on them to bear in mind a very probable source of extreme injury to their particular interests, which will be opened on the restoration of peace, if the Slave Trade be not abolished.

Supposing us to retain the conquered settlements, the importation of Slaves cannot be withheld from the proprietors in those colonies, while we allow it to their fellow subjects; yet, if granted to the former, by far the larger part of our whole export from Africa will be allotted to their use. Their settlements will be every year increasing; new cargoes of colonial produce will be poured by them into the market, and the planters in our old islands, for whom and for whose interests we ought to feel most concern, will be plunged deeper and deeper into a gulf, in which, by their own confession, they have already sunk almost irretrievably. But supposing us even to give up the conquered West Indian settlements on the restoration of peace, still Trinidad will remain to us; and that large and fertile island would of itself be sufficient to furnish such an immense quantity of fresh colonial

colonial produce as almost to consummate the ruin at least of our more ancient and less fertile colonies.

To resume the discussion in which I was lately engaged. Let me again declare, that so much do I ascribe to the effects of that party-spirit of which I have treated so largely, that I am convinced, if the colonial proprietors were not warped by prejudice, and heated by *esprit de corps*, such of them as are really well acquainted with the subject in it's various parts and bearings, would be in favour of abolition; they would agree with me, that, excepting only some particular interests, the present West Indian system, and, above all, the Slave Trade, as it's basis and ground-work, are contrary to sound policy, no less than to justice and humanity. In truth, this question has been already decided; for, we have been assured by the same respectable gentleman who was before alluded to, that, above thirty years ago, the following question was discussed in Kingston, the capital of Jamaica, in a society formed of the first characters of the place, " Whether the Trade " to Africa for Slaves was consistent with " sound policy, the laws of nature and mo-" rality."—The discussion occupied several meetings, and at last it was determined, by a

majority,

majority, that the Trade to Africa for Slaves was neither consistent with sound policy, the laws of nature, or morality *.

"The chief ground on which the advocates for the Slave Trade rested their opinion (he thinks) was, that God had formed some of the human race inferior to others in intellect, and that Negroes appeared to have been intended for Slaves; or to that purpose."

Let this incident, and the conclusions which it suggests, be well considered. It deserves to have the more weight, on account both of the understanding and character of the individual who gave the account of it; for, no man living was ever less likely to confound any hasty expressions of men of warm and feeling minds, or of men of speculation or ingenuity, who might like to defend a paradox, with the real deliberate judgment of men of reflection, practical knowledge, and personal experience. Observe, the only ground on which the Slave Trade was defended, even in Jamaica, was that of the Negroes being an inferior species. This opinion, as I formerly remarked, was the original foundation of the Slave Trade, and it is the only ground on which it can be rested with the smallest

* See evidence taken before the House of Commons.

pretence

pretence to reason, justice, or humanity. Happily, the friends of these wretched beings have, at length, obtained the recognition of their human nature; but as yet it is a barren and unprofitable right, if, while we grant them to be men, we treat them as if we still deemed them of an inferior species. But still more this incident shews, that they, who, from their local circumstances and pursuits were most conversant with this great subject in all it's parts, had adopted, above thirty years ago, the position which Mr. Pitt asserted so confidently, and proved so unanswerably, that the Slave Trade was contrary not to justice and humanity only, but to sound policy also; and if even so long ago they entertained this opinion; what, if relieved from the blinding effects of prejudice and party, would be their judgment now, when all the facts and principles, on which the Slave Trade system must have been proved impolitic, have received an almost unspeakable accession of force, and when the arguments, by which it's policy could alone be contended for, have since been almost entirely done away? I regret that I have not time for enlarging on this topic. But any man who has obtained any insight into this question will readily discern the several considerations to which I allude.

But

<small>No hope of West Indian body's opposition ceasing.</small>

But notwithstanding I ascribe so much of the opposition which has been made to us, to the operation of party spirit, yet I dare not hope that the flame is likely to become weaker, or at length to die away. On the contrary, there is a store of aliment fully sufficient to maintain it in continual and even interminable vigour. For after all that I have stated, of it's being rather the spirit of party, or at the utmost a mistaken apprehension of loss, than a just sense of interest, which animates the efforts of the great mass of West Indian Proprietors, yet there are many who, it cannot be denied, are prompted by a true persuasion that the abolition of the Slave Trade will materially lessen their gains. Of this number is that great, respectable, affluent, and, as we have fatally experienced, most powerful body, the West Indian Merchants. I cannot deny that many, perhaps almost all of this class, may have a direct interest in the extension of West Indian cultivation. Though planting speculations may not answer to the immediate undertakers, they may answer to the merchant in this country; and he might gain by the cultivation being pushed to an extent which would utterly ruin the planters. He pays himself in the first instance both for the articles furnished for the supply of the estate, and for his profits on the importations from

from abroad; and if he have prudence sufficient, which however is seldom the case, to prevent his advancing too much on any one estate, so as to compel him to become the proprietor of it, he is certainly engaged in an advantageous branch of business. Hence he is always the foremost to petition against the abolition.

Together with the merchants, I must except also that considerable body, often of respectable men, who have gone over to the West Indian islands in inferior capacities, and who mean to engage in planting undertakings. The stoppage of the importations from Africa would retard, at least, if not destroy these speculations. This is a class of men, in whose interests I confess I take a lively interest; but not an interest sufficient to induce me to sanction the destruction of thousands of my fellow creatures annually, for the sake of allowing them more convenient opportunities of rising in life. I confess their interest is a matter of much more concern to me than those of the greater and more adventurous speculators. I ought, perhaps, also to except the last-mentioned class of persons. Though, in common, to afford them the opportunity of engaging in these West Indian speculations, be only to afford them

them an occasion of accomplishing their own ruin; yet they conceive they have an interest in the continuance of the Slave Trade, and therefore they are not actuated only by party spirit. This class is likely to increase. The few great prizes in the West Indian lottery will tempt adventurers to engage in it; and it is in vain to hope that the colonists will ever concur in the abolition of the Slave Trade, so long as there is room left for new speculations; that is, so long as there remains, in the Western hemisphere, any unsettled land capable of cultivation, and as any Negroes can be brought from Africa to work it. So long as there is any scope left for new speculations, so long there will be a set of new speculators residing in the islands, who will form the real instigators of the opposition to the proposal for abolishing the Slave Trade; and these, joined by the great mercantile body at home, will carry along with them the bulk of their brethren, the colonial proprietors resident in this country.

It is for the benefit of these classes, not for that of our old colonial proprietors, that the Slave Trade is in reality carried on. For it is undeniably true, nor will it, I presume, be contested, that by far the larger proportion of all the Slaves we import, have always been and

and will ever be deftined to the formation of new settlements, not in maintaining and keeping up eftates which had been already completed.

But surely the queftion has ere now occurred to you, When or where is this syftem to terminate? Is it to go on till our colonial settlements are brought into a ftate of complete cultivation? It may be worth while to spend a few moments in examining the consequences of such an admission; they were traced out by a high authority, who ftated, that, even of the great island of Jamaica itself, the quantity of uncultivated land was two-thirds more than that already in cultivation.*
To suffice for the cultivation of the other parts, the complete number of 600,000 more Negroes, living at the same time, would be necessary, in addition to 256,000 now there. The calculation went on to consider the numbers which muft be imported, and the length of time which, under all the wafte of human life which attends the present deftructive syftem, muft elapse, in bringing the Island of Jamaica into complete cultivation by Slaves. It was found that, supposing the rate at which the cultivation and population would increase in

* This is fully confirmed by the Assembly of Jamaica. See Privy Council Report.

future, to be the same as that at which they had increased hitherto, that it would not be accomplished in less than two hundred and twenty years, and it would require the exportation from Africa of greatly more than a million of our fellow creatures. For reasons which could be stated, the period here mentioned is much too short. But besides the Island of Jamaica, there are St. Vincents, Grenada, Dominica, above all, Trinidad, and the unknown extent of our future continental acquisitions, which would claim juſt the same right to have their cultivation completed.

Such muſt be admitted to be the fair consequences of prosecuting the Slave Trade, for the purpose, plainly enough avowed by the coloniſts in Jamaica, of bringing into cultivation the whole of the land which is ſtill uncultivated. Would even the moſt determined friends of the Weſt Indians on this side of the water go this length? I speak not of thoſe, if any such there be, who love the Slave Trade on account of its own inherent excellencies; nor of the Weſt Indian merchants, nor yet of the African trader. But would the less devoted friends of the Slave Trade go the length of admitting this principle? I truſt they would not. Muſt they not then concede, that the only principle on which

which they can act consistently, must be that of carrying on the importation of Slaves for the sole purpose of keeping up, not of extending the cultivation. Indeed, when this great cause was argued in the House of Commons in 1792, all, I believe, of our opponents, excepting only those who were personally connected with the Slave Trade, admitted fully and frankly the principle of not opening new lands. They objected not to the ground which was taken by that great man to whom I have already so often alluded. Would the most attached friend, he asked, of the Slave Trade, think of founding a new colony, or of setting up a new Slave Trade? And it was justly and undeniably argued, nor was the position contested, that the formation of new settlements in our old islands was just as much the planting of a new colony, as if the same settlements were made in any newly discovered country. There was no difference in principle between the two cases. It was a new and voluntary establishment, made with our eyes open to all the guilt which the enterprise would involve, and all the horrors of which we professed to be sensible. The force of these arguments, when used in 1792, was granted to be irresistible; but, as if it were in absolute contempt of them, and of the practical conclusions to which they lead, we are plainly warned

warned by the colonists, against supposing that they will ever consent to stop the importations from Africa, so long as any vacant and cultivable land remains on which to plant them. These facts, with the aweful considerations which result from them, let me most seriously urge on the conscientious deliberations of those who, contrary alas! to the expectation indulged by that great man whom I have before so often mentioned; by their fatal proposal of gradual, instead of immediate abolition, dashed the cup of happiness from the lips of the wretched African, at the very moment when at last he appeared likely to taste it, and who thus proved in fact the most efficient supporters of the Slave Trade. A vast majority in Parliament were then so much alive to the principles of justice and humanity, that all direct opposition would have been utterly ineffectual. But this kind of half measure, however unintentionally, exactly answered the purpose of our enemies, by giving time for the zeal of men to cool, and providing an expedient by which, aided by a little of that self deception which we are all apt to practice on ourselves on suitable occasions, they might feel the complacencies arising from an act of justice and humanity, without paying the price or making the sacrifice which those principles required.

The gradual abolitionists especially bound to consider these facts.

Let

Let me be forgiven if I speak ſtrongly, where I feel so very deeply. It is not only because the gradual Abolitioniſts have been, in fact, the only real ſtay of that ſyſtem of wickedness and cruelty which we wish to abolish; though that assertion is unqueſtionably true; but it is trying beyond expression that they should be the real maintainers of the Slave Trade, who reprobate it in terms of deteſtation as ſtrong as any which we ourselves can utter. Nor do I mean (the declaration is made with solemnity and truth) that these expressions are not sincere. If they were not proved to be so by the general character of those who use them, my personal knowledge of some of them, and the eſteem and regard I entertain for them, excludes the contrary supposition. Yet I cannot but believe, that, could they have clearly foreseen what would be the practical effect of their opposition, it would not have been continued for an hour.

Let them now, however, remember the grounds and principles on which they resiſted our measure; that they themselves ſtated the queſtion to be only between two different modes of abolishing the Slave Trade. They alleged, indeed, with others, the difficulty of preventing Slaves being illicitly imported into the

the colonies; but this was obviously an evil which never could prevail to any great extent, nor did they lay any considerable stress on it. Abjuring the most remote idea of contending for the interminable continuance of the Slave Trade, the utmost they asked was, that a short respite should be granted. The year 1800 was afterwards specifically named; the West Indians would be able, in the interval, to fill up their vacancies, to complete their gangs; in short, to improve their population, so as to be prepared to meet the new order of things.

But the gradual Abolitionists chiefly urged, that we were too hasty and violent, and that by our precipitancy we should defeat our own purpose. For, without the concurrence of the colonial legislatures, it was alleged, we could not carry our measure into effect; they advised that time, therefore, should be allowed for softening the prejudices and cooling the warmth of the colonists.

What has followed since that period? The Slave Trade, instead of eight, has now lasted fourteen years. Far more time, therefore, has been allowed the Planters for completing their gangs, than was originally proposed by any one who did not avow himself a friend to to the perpetuity of the Slave Trade. A far greater number of Slaves, also, than was then in any one's contemplation, has since been imported. So far, therefore, the Islands are better prepared for the measure.

But above all, it is now clear that we muſt abandon all hopes of bringing the colonial legislatures to consent cheerfully to the termination of the Slave Trade. Was it possible for the proposition to come before them, not only in a more acceptable form, but with a more gradual approach; and, if I may so say, at the end of a longer viſto, than when it was presented to their notice by some of the most respectable of their own body, by men who had uniformly opposed the abolition in the British Parliament, and when they had, therefore, every reason to believe that the importation of Slaves would never be actually ſtopped until the measures, which were to make that importation no longer necessary, should have had, according to their own report, an effect so complete and satisfactory as to render the abolition no longer in the leaſt objectionable; yet so ſtrong are the prejudices of the coloniſts, that, even in answer to this communication, they frankly declared againſt abolition at any time and in any form. They intimate plainly that they look forward
to

to the complete settlement of all the cultivable but now waste land throughout the whole of our West Indian islands.

Supposing, therefore, that the gradual Abolitionists even still retain their original opinion, that the concurrence of the Colonists is necessary to our complete success, yet considering the immense magnitude, as acknowledged by themselves, of the evil which all this time has been going on with even increased ravages; would it not be fair that they should now, at least, consent to try the effect of our less satisfactory measure? Would not this be the mode of conduct pursued by men in all the common affairs of life, when really interested for the accomplishment of any object? Supposing them to labour under some painful or dangerous disease, which was making havoc of their constitution, and wearing them down with excruciating torture, and that a particular plan of treatment should be proposed to them; supposing that, (though the plan should be recommended by various medical men of the most acknowledged superiority of skill, who, though often differing, entirely agreed in this particular, and prescribed with the most sanguine confidence,) they should yet fear the plan would not answer, perhaps that it was in some

way

way or other impracticable; supposing them also to prefer a second plan, recommended by some other practitioner; yet if there appeared to be in the way of the adoption of this second plan some practical obstacle which they could not remove, Would they suffer the disease to go on with it's ravages, rather than adopt the first plan, from which they might not themselves expect much benefit, but which might yet be preferable to doing nothing at all?

But supposing, to make the case more nearly parallel, that the disease was to have continued for many years; that the proposers of the first plan had declared from the very first, that the second plan could not be carried into execution; that time and other circumstances had proved the truth of their prediction as to the past, and that, to say the least, the prospect was not brighter for the future; would not a man thus circumstanced be disposed at least to suspend his opposition, and, if he could not give the plan, which he still feared would be ineffectual, his active support, yet would he not at least cease to obstruct the trial of it, when at the utmost he could only object, that he feared that the impracticability would be found to attach to the first plan, which had been

proved

proved by experience to belong to the second?

Are we not in public life continually compelled to act on the principle of embracing the measure which we do not, in itself, judge to be near so eligible as another, which, from it's not appearing to others in the same light as to us, is practically unattainable? And was there ever an instance, if such an one can possibly exist, in which this mode of proceeding was so imperiously enforced on us as in the present, when we consider to what an extent the work of death is every year going on in Africa: for here it may be truly said, *Deliberat Roma, perit Saguntum.*

Were I not convinced that the objection against which I have been here contending was urged by men of fair and honourable minds, I should not have entered so largely into this discussion. But with that persuasion, I cannot but indulge the hope, that even though their original objection may appear to them to retain all it's force, they will at least not obstruct the trial of a measure which pleads the authority of such respectable names, and which affords the only practical hope, though they may think it but a faint hope, of putting an end to a system which every year that

that it lasts is producing, as they affirm not less than we do, an almost incalculable amount of misery.

Let me also remind these gentlemen, that if we immediate Abolitionists conceive them, the gradual Abolitionists, to be, though unintentionally, the real practical friends and supporters of the Slave Trade, we at least are not the only persons who hold that opinion. The West Indians, who frankly declare they never can consent to the abolition, nay even the Slave Traders themselves, evidently shew that they conceive these gradual Abolitionists to be their real adherents. Against them ought to have been directed the serious opposition of our African and West Indian opponents, while we were mere objects of derision and contempt. We were a set of well-meaning visionaries, who were proposing what, even if carried into effect, would be found utterly impracticable. Whereas they were men of sound practical understanding, who had wisdom to devise effectual measures for executing all which their virtue might suggest. This is not urged with levity, it is seriously and earnestly pressed. Nor is it a statement without instruction. It has often been justly urged, that we may collect much as to the character of any man, or the tendency

dency of any measure, by observing them not only in themselves, but, when that investigation is difficult and doubtful, by observing who are their enemies and who are their friends. Tried by this principle at leaft, we know what judgment would be passed on the gradual Abolitionifts.

<small>Slave Trade injurious to our Marine.</small> Another argument which, especially in the outset of the discussion, was strongly, and with great confidence, urged against us by our opponents, was, that the African Trade is a nursery for seamen; and that its abolition would therefore be highly injurious to our naval strength. This part of the subject was very early taken up by Mr. Clarkson, a gentleman whose services, throughout the whole conduct of this great cause, deserve the higheft commendation. He asserted, as the result of a long and laborious inquiry, that of the sailors employed in the African Trade, between a fifth and a sixth actually died; and that the African ships seldom brought home more than half of their original crews. Nothing was more vehemently repelled, or more obftinately denied, than these positions, till, at length, having long borne with these clamorous contradictions, the mufter-rolls of the African ships were moved for and laid before Parliament; documents which had

been

been kept in the possession of our opponents, and which cannot therefore be supposed to have been fabricated or coloured to serve our purpose.

From these papers Mr. Clarkson's calculations were fully juftified. It appeared, that of 12,263 persons, the number of the original crews, there had died 2,643, the average length of their voyages being twelve months; whilft, on the contrary, in the Weft Indian trade, in which the length of the voyage was seven months, of 7,640, the number of the original crews, there had died only 118. But the loss by deaths was not the whole loss to the country; for, besides the broken constitutions of the survivors, which rendered many of them, for the reft of their lives, incapable of the duties of their profession, so many left their ships in consequence of ill usage, that they seldom brought home more than half the persons they had taken out. This laft circumftance was attempted to be accounted for, from the natural capriciousness of sailors; and it was said, that they ran away in as great number from the Weft India as from the Guinea ships. The direct contrary appeared from the mufter rolls, and this too, though, from the different ways of paying them in the two trades, their forfeiting little

or

or nothing by quitting the West Indiamen, but much by quitting the Guineamen, the reverse might have been naturally expected. Much more might be said on this subject. Especially, such scenes of cruelty towards those unhappy men might be opened to your view, as would excite at once the concern and indignation of every man, who feels for that class of his fellow citizens to which this nation owes so much both of her security, her affluence, and her glory.

The evidence taken before the House of Commons contains but too many humiliating instances of this kind; and in consequence we find the most respectable naval commanders acknowledging that the Slave Trade is no nursery of seamen. This truth was even frankly confessed by a Noble Admiral on whose general testimony our opponents set the highest value. But I will quit the present topic, only remarking, that as at the outset of the discussion none of our assertions was more strongly controverted than that concerning the loss of seamen, which can now be no longer denied, we may hence claim some credit on those points which are still in dispute. The incident shews at least that it is not necessary that our opponents should be correct in order to be positive.

Again,

Again, great stress was laid on the consideration, that were Great Britain to desist from the Slave Trade, other nations would still continue it, and that the trade would not therefore cease to exist. The only difference would be, that the trade which formerly we had ourselves carried on, would henceforth be carried on by others; and how would Africa, how would the cause of humanity, be hereby a gainer? To this argument, many answers were returned. But before I proceed to state them, can I forbear remarking, that there would have been no place for such an argument as this, but for that fashionable though pernicious doctrine of the present day, that we are to regulate our practice by considerations of expediency, that vague, fluctuating, and often vicious instructress, instead of the sound, plain, and immutable dictates of justice. It is self-evident, that by stopping the importation into our own colonies, we destroy a large proportion at least of the evil.

Another objection to abolition:—if we should abolish, foreign nations would still carry on the trade.

During the continuance of the war, all the Dutch, and some of the French colonies, being in our hands, the supply to such of the French as are still unconquered being stopped, that of the Spanish being much interrupted, and the Portuguese settlements also deriving their supply from the more southern part of the

the Slave coaft, the whole of that vaft region which conftitutes what may be called the solid subftance of the African continent, would be almoft entirely exempt from the ravages of the Slave Trade. Nor is this temporary abolition desirable, merely in the view of its affording to that wretched country a short breathing time from her miseries. If the war should be of any duration, we may hope, that the Africans may form ne whabits, and, having adopted less guilty expedients for obtaining the commodities with which they are supplied by the Europeans, may, in some parts at leaft of the coaft, not resume the traffic in human beings, when the war shall be at an end.

All that could be said concerning the future conduct in this relation, of France, Spain, and Portugal, muft be mere speculation. But, let us ask, in regard to those several nations, Where is the capital to be found? Surely whatever might have been alleged formerly concerning the possibility of British capital being transported into foreign countries for this use, it will scarcely now be urged; it will surely at leaft not be credited, that in the present ftate of the continent, any British subjects will be mad enough, let their ftrange and unnatural craving after this trade in flesh and

and blood be ever so importunate, to truſt their capital in the way which this argument supposes, out of the only country in which either person or property can now be deemed secure.

We ought also to observe, that in both the Spanish and Portuguese colonies, the Slaves are far better treated, and the breeding ſyſtem much more encouraged, than in those of the other European nations. There is in them also far less of the spirit of commercial speculation and enterprize than in our own. Denmark has long since shewn her willingness to abandon the Slave Trade, and private information confirms the supposition which the circumstances of the case suggeſt, that her not having yet carried into full effect her declared resolution, that the human traffic should cease with the year 1800, may fairly be ascribed to our conduct and example.

The United States of America were absolutely precluded, by a fundamental article of the confederation, from abolishing the Slave Trade before 1808, by any general law operating over the whole of the union. But it was one of the firſt acts of all, except I believe one, of the individual ſtates of which the union consiſts, to abolish this traffic; and when a

x 2 law

law was lately passed in South Carolina, allowing the importation of Slaves, Congress shewed its sense of the transaction by imposing on the importation of Slaves into South Carolina itself, the higheſt duty which the conſtitution permits. The importation of Slaves also into Louisiana was entirely prohibited. All these are ſtrong indications of a disposition in the Government of the United States to abolish the Slave Trade; and they confirm the assurance which has been received from the beſt informed gentlemen of that country, that in 1808, when Congress will have a clear right to put an end to that traffic, it will not be allowed the respite of an hour.*

So far for the Slaves which are exported weſtward from the coaſt of Africa. As to the supply which is sent to the countries eaſt of Africa, it has long been comparatively trifling in amount; and by far the larger part of those immense regions which furnish the European exports, are too diſtant to allow of

* These expectations have been juſt now confirmed by the welcome tidings, that, on the recommendation of the President of the United States, Congress are passing an act for abolishing the Slave Trade on January 1ſt 1808.

Slaves

Slaves being carried out of them eaſtward to a profit.

But may we not be allowed to assume a higher tone, and to ask, if this practice, though by a ſtrange perversion of words it is called the Slave Trade, ought indisputably to be considered as a moſt enormous crime, rather than a commerce, Is it not clearly our own duty to abſtain from it, and to prohibit and to punish the perpetration of it by our own subjects, however it may ſtill prevail in other countries?

It might serve to discover the monſtrous tendencies of this argument, to those whose moral principle is so dull and dark as not inſtinctively to reject it, to consider to what lengths it might fairly carry them: for why might it not equally be alleged as a sufficient plea for performing every other act of profitable wickedness, which we might conceive, though perhaps unjuſtly, would be performed by others if not by ourselves. Let any one consider what would be the consequences of admitting such a principle into the intercourse of nations.

Is this, then, a principle to which we will give our solemn sanction, unless we mean

x 3   fairly

fairly to avow that we have one set of religious and moral principles for Africa, and another for the rest of the world?

Apply the principle to private life, and consider what would be it's consequences. But there happily the law of the land would soon interfere to check it's application. And here, indeed, from first to last, is our misfortune in this whole business of the Slave Trade; that the practices, for the abolition of which we are contending, are such, as by the laws of every civilized community are punishable with death; but, unhappily, there is no tribunal (no earthly tribunal) to which the criminals are amenable. And is this a time above all others, and are the present circumstances of nations precisely those in which such a principle of conduct becomes the Imperial Parliament of Great Britain? Or, if the reproach which has been cast against us be really true, and we are only to be moved by an appeal to our self-interest, is this a time when it is politic or even safe to avow such a principle, and to inculcate such a lesson?

But how, it was indignantly asked, could this enormous evil be ever eradicated, if every nation were thus prudentially to wait
till

till the concurrence of all other nations should be obtained? Let it also be remembered that, on the one hand, no nation has plunged so deeply into this guilt as Great Britain; on the other, that none could be so likely to be looked up to as an example, if she should be the firſt decidedly to renounce it.

But does not this very argument, grounded on the probable conduct of other nations, apply a thousand times more ſtrongly in a contrary direction? How much more reasonably might other nations point to us, and say, Why should we abolish the Slave Trade, when Great Britain has not abolished? Great Britain, free, juſt, and honourable as she is, deeply also involved as she is in this commerce above all other nations, not only has not abolished, but has refused to abolish! (This was the language of a great man, many years ago). Alas! it may now be added, and after even at length resolving to abolish, has receded from her resolution!

A long and scrutinizing inquiry has taken place, the subject has been thoroughly canvassed. Her Senate has deliberated again and again; and what is the result? She has gravely and solemnly determined to sanction the Slave Trade. Her Legislature therefore is is doubtless convinced that it has been falsely charged with injuftice, cruelty, and impolicy. What need then have we to look any further? Why should we examine or deliberate? What more satisfactory proofs could our own inveftigation bring forth, of the juftice and policy of the Slave Trade?

Thus, then, it would appear, on a more impartial view, that, inftead of being juftified in our continuing to prosecute the Slave Trade, by the probability that other nations would ftill carry it on, we with but too much colour of reason may be charged with being, if not the authors, yet at leaft the confirmers of their disposition to persevere in it; and to our account may at laft appear to be in a great measure imputable the entire mass of the guilt of this enormous wickedness. We cannot, it is to be feared, now undo all the evil which our misconduct has occasioned; but, as we have long been foremoft in the crime, let us, however tardily, endeavour to be at length exemplary in our repentance.

Slave Trade supported on grounds of justice. Of all the sources whence arguments could be drawn in support of the Slave Trade, that of juftice would perhaps leaft have been anticipated by those who have seen how from firft to laft it sets at nought the

the rights and happiness of our fellow creatures. The argument was put, however, with some plausibility, so as on a very superficial view to appear to have a faint colour of equity. It was argued, that we had encouraged the West Indians to engage in colonial speculations; that these speculations could not be carried on without supplies from time to time of African labourers; that therefore, to prohibit the importation of Negroes, was to ensure the failure of those very speculations into which we had encouraged the West Indians to embark.

It was a sufficient reply, that if the West Indians would but reform the glaring abuses of their system of management, abuses to which not only every humane but every just mind must be anxious to put an end; importations of Slaves from Africa would be rendered perfectly unnecessary, by the natural increase of their domestic stock; while from the stopping of these importations, various and highly important advantages would follow, to the West Indians themselves as well as to the empire at large. But supposing the case to have been otherwise, and that the West Indians might be likely to suffer in their property from our abolition of the Slave Trade; the inference suggested by justice,

tice, I say not by self-interest, but by justice, would be, that the West Indians should be compensated out of the treasury of the mother country, or rather, that the loss should fall in equal shares on all the several parties. But for justice to be supposed to inculcate, that because (from our being ignorant, it is to be hoped, of the real nature and effects of the Slave Trade) we had been accustomed to ravage the unprotected shores of Africa, and bring away by force a number of innocent men, women, and children, to carry them in the hold of a Slave ship in fetters, across the Atlantic, and consign the survivors and their descendants for ever to a state of hopeless and most degraded bondage;—to argue, that, because for two centuries we had pursued this course of wickedness and cruelty, or because, which is not fact, we had even engaged to continue it—that we are bound by the obligation of duty to admit the equity of such a prescription, or to fulfil such an engagement, is certainly a most extraordinary lesson for justice to be supposed to inculcate.

Supposing us to be the debtors of the West Indians, what right have we, as was so well urged by my excellent friend, Mr. Gisborne, to pay British debts with the flesh and

and blood of Africans? The absurdity of this argument, not to mention it's profane usurpation of the sacred name of juftice, is too manifeft to require any further comment.

But it may be proper in this place to say a few words concerning compensation. It was ftated by the great minifter to whom I have so often had occasion to allude, than whom no one was more intimately conversant with the commercial syftem of this country, that it had been our general practice to make from time to time such regulations in the different branches of our commerce, as considerations of policy or finance might require; and excepting cases in which the circumftances had been peculiar, it had not been usual to grant compensation to those who might suffer from the change. The abolition of the Slave Trade ought therefore to be regarded as one of the contingencies which are foreseen and underftood in general, though not in the particular form and inftance in which they may happen; one of those accidents to which persons who engage in commercial or any other speculations render themselves liable, relying only on the wisdom and juftice of the legislature, that, in administering it's important truft of watching over the general welfare of the community, it will, as

far

far as possible, consult also the advantage of every particular class, and not lightly sacrifice any individual interests.

The truth of this doctrine was completely established by the great man above referred to, who contended, founding his arguments on general reasoning, and confirming them by a reference to particular statutes, that Parliament had at no time given any pledge that the Slave Trade should be continued, or that the losses incurred in consequence of it's suppression, had any losses been likely to take place, should be made good by the public.

Still as it might seem hard, if not absolutely unjust, that one set of men should be the sufferers, when the crime, though committed chiefly for their benefit, was one in which others had participated with them, it was declared by the chancellor of the exchequer, that one class of persons, those alone who might otherwise with reason complain of hard measure, if not of unjust treatment, should receive compensation on any fair case of injury being made out to the satisfaction of impartial commissioners. This was the class of persons who had bought lots of uncultivated land of Government, in the ceded or any other islands. It might be presumed, that they had engaged
in

in the speculation, with expectations of being able to bring them into cultivation by imported Africans; and therefore if they had performed their share of the conditions of the purchase, they were entitled to require the state to perform it's share also, or to pay them an equivalent.

But when the colonial syftem, as now adminiftered, except perhaps in some particular cases, has not only been injurious to the Slaves, but on the long run to the mafter also; when it is at length declared by a very intelligent Weft Indian, that the colonifts, by adopting those reforms for which juftice and humanity should alone furnish sufficient motives, will ultimately derive the moft subftantial benefits, though possibly they may suffer some temporary inconveniency; when, at the same time, the prejudices againft these reforms are so powerful, that a direct, palpable, and valuable intereft alone, will probably be adequate to overcome their effect; in such circumftances as these, it is undeniably obvious, that to hold forth an offer of compensation to all, who, after the abolition, should allege that they had suffered from that measure, or who should even furnish plausible proof that it had been injurious to their interefts, would not only be to subject ourselves to immeasurable

measurable and moft inequitable claims, but would be to interpose an insurmountable obstacle in the way of all reforms of the Weft Indian fyftem, or, to speak more correctly, it would be to give a premium on the continuance and even extension of the old abuses. It is, however, moft of all aftonishing, that our opponents attempt to vindicate the Slave Trade on grounds of religion also. The only argument which they urge with the slighteft colour of reason is, that slavery was allowed under the Jewish dispensation. The Jews were exalted by the express designation of heaven to a ftate of eminence above the ftrangers who sojourned among them, and the heathen who dwelt around them, from either of whom, as a mark of their own dominion, God, who has a right to assign to all his creatures their several places in the scale of being, allowed them to take bondmen and bondwomen, treating them, however, with kindness, remembering their own feelings when they were slaves in Egypt, and admitting them to the chief national privileges, to the circumcision, to the passover, and other solemn feafts, and thus inftructing them in the true religion. Besides this, the slaves were to be set free at the year of Jubilee, or every fiftieth year, a command which was alone fufficient to prevent their accumulating in any great number.

and on grounds of religion.

But

But they who thus urge on us the Divine toleration of slavery under the Jewish Theocracy, should remember that the Jews themselves were expressly commanded not to retain any of *their own nation*, any of their *brethren* in slavery, except as a punishment, or by their own consent; and even these were to be set free on the return of the sabbatical, or the seventh year. Inasmuch therefore, as we are repeatedly and expressly told that Chrift has done away all distinctions of nations, and made all mankind one great family, all our fellow creatures are now our brethren; and therefore the very principles and spirit of the Jewish law itself would forbid our keeping the Africans, any more than our own fellow subjects, in a ftate of slavery. But even supposing, contrary to the fact, that our opponents had succeeded in proving that the Slave Trade was not contrary to the Jewish law, this would only prove that they would be entitled to carry it on if they were Jews, and could, like the Jews, produce satisfactory proof that they were the chosen people of God. But really it would be consuming your time to no purpose, to enter into a formal proof, that fraud, rapine, and cruelty, a contrary to that religion, which commands us to love our neighbour as ourselves, and to do to others as we would have them

them do to us. I cannot persuade myself that our opponents are serious in using this argument, and therefore I will proceed no farther with this discussion. Besides, even granting that it were possible for any of them to be seriously convinced that Christianity does not prohibit the Slave Trade, I should still have no great encouragement to proceed, for,—it may be prejudice, but I cannot persuade myself that they are so much under the practical influence of religion, that if we should convince their underſtandings, we should alter their conduct. After having thus ſtated the various grounds on which our opponents argued againſt the abolition of the Slave Trade, it ſtill however remains for me to mention two or three additional considerations. For want of time I shall not dwell long on them. But let me recommend them to your most serious reflection, for they are of unspeakable importance. It is not using too ſtrong language to affirm, that if all the arguments which have been hitherto adduced in support of the abolition of the Slave Trade, were weak and unsatisfactory, the measure is urged on us by these considerations alone, with such commanding force, that it would deserve the name of infatuation not to agree to it, and that on grounds not merely of abſtract right and

Other Conſiderations which enforce the neceſſity of abolition.

and duty, but of regard for the well being of our West Indian Colonies themselves, and for the prosperity of the British Empire.

The first consideration which I shall mention is that of a danger of unspeakable amount, to which at length, though surely somewhat too late, even those who have been most blinded by prejudice begin to open their eyes. It seems at last to be discovered, that Negroes are men; that as men, they are subject to human passions; that they can feel when they are injured; that they can conceive, and meditate, and mature; can combine and concert, and at length proceed to execute with vigour what they have planned with policy. Such being the lesson which the Island of St. Domingo has taught to those most unwilling to receive it; the immense disproportion between the Blacks and Whites in our islands, perhaps ten or even fifteen to one, is a subject of most just and serious dread, and the danger is extremely aggravated, by the difference between the two descriptions being so plain and palpable, that the more numerous body is continually reminded of its own force. What but insanity would go on every year augmenting a disproportion already so great!

Insurrections:— danger of.

But

But it is highly important also to consider, that the continuance of the Slave Trade not only aggravates the danger of the West Indian settlements, by increasing the disproportion between Blacks and Whites, but still more by introducing that very description of persons which has been acknowledged by the most approved West Indian writers to be most prone to insurrections. Here let us refer again to the historian of Jamaica. "The "truth is," says he, "that ever since the "introduction of Africans into the West "Indies, insurrections have occurred in every "one of the colonies, British as well as fo- "reign, at times."* Again, "The vulgar "opinion in England confounds all the Blacks "in one class, and supposes them equally "prompt for rebellion; an opinion that is "grossly erroneous. The Negroes who have "been chief actors in the seditions and mu- "tinies which at different times have broken "out here, were the imported Africans."† Again; "If insurrections should happen "oftener in Jamaica than in the smaller "islands, it would not be at all surprising; "since it has generally contained more Ne- "groes than all the windward British islands

* Vol. ii. p. 442—3.   † Ibid. p. 444.

"taken

" taken together : it's importations in some
" years have been very great:

"In 1764 imported, - - - - 10,223
"And from January 1765 to July 1766, a year and a half, - - - } 16,760

" So large a multitude as 27,000 introduced in
" the space of two years and a half, furnishes
" a very sufficient reason, if there was no
" other, to account for plots and mutinies."*
Let it be remembered, that since Mr. Long's
book was published, in 1774, there have been
retained probably above 200,000 Negroes;
and add to these the importations which have
subsequently taken place in our other islands,
and remember, that, as even Negroes can confederate, and the Slaves in the several islands
might mutually assist each other, all the
islands are interested; that fresh accessions of
Negroes should not be permitted in any one:
then estimate if you can the sum of the danger
which has been too long suffered to accumulate without restraint, and which is every
year still increasing.

Even at the very moment in which I am
writing, I hear rumours of an insurrection in
one of our smaller colonies, Grenada; and
though I cannot trace the report to any authentic source, yet it is impossible to deny

* Vol. ii. p. 442.

that it is highly probable. The importations into this island have been of late years larger, considering it's size, than into moſt of our other islands; thence the report derives additional probability. But to all the foregoing considerations, add that new aggravation of the dangers of our Weſt Indian colonies, that, almoſt within the visible horizon of our largeſt island, the Negroes have been taught but too intelligibly the fatal secret of their own strength. Here also the Planters may learn, were it not before abundantly clear, how ardent is the Negroes' love of liberty, and what a price they are willing to pay for it. The season is critical—not a moment is to be loſt. The British Legislature should consider the present as a happy interval, in which, perhaps, an opportunity is yet providentially afforded them, of averting the gathering storm. If they pause, it will be too late.

Let it not be said, that the Weſt Indians themselves can beſt judge of the reality of the danger, and that they do not greatly regard it. It might, indeed, have been expected, that the necessity of compulsion would here be superseded by every man's concern for his own interest and safety. But that takes place in this case, which often happens where

danger

danger is apprehended to the whole community, from practices in which men engage for their own individual advantage. Each particular inftance of this practice seems to add but little to the amount of the general danger, or but little in proportion to the advantage which the individual expects to derive from it. The danger besides is uncertain, however probable; and he shares it in common with the whole community. The benefit he conceives certain, and the gain is all his own. Is not this then precisely the ftate of circumftances in which the legislature should interfere as the general guardian of the whole community, and prevent the intereft and happiness of all from being endangered by individual avarice, obftinacy, or foolhardiness. But it would not be wonderful if the resident Weft Indians themselves were not conscious on what hollow ground they ftand. It is nothing new that they who are moft exposed to a great danger are the leaft aware of it; that, like the short-sighted inhabitants of Puzzoli, or Terra del Gréco, they alone are insensible to the approaching lava which is about to desolate their dwellings. It happens in this, as in other inftances, familiarity with the danger naturally generates insensibility to it, and the very persons who are moft exposed to its evils, are most blind to its reality and magnitude. But the legislature, as a provident guardian of the whole community, should exercise its watchful superintendance, and take that step which is the natural preliminary to all radical reform, and to all effectual measures for the future safety of the islands. But, to state the truth, it is not merely by familiarity with the great danger which we have been describing, that the resident colonists are rendered insensible to it. This insensibility results in no small degree from the extreme degradation of the Negro race. The resident White is so accustomed to regard them as of an inferior species, that he is no more apprehensive lest they should learn the fatal secret of their own strength, and combine for their own deliverance, than lest such a combination should take place among the horses or cattle, or any other inferior animals, which may therefore, without danger, be suffered to increase their numbers to any amount.* Is it possible to see

* Nothing can shew more clearly the degree of this security, than that the Jamaica newspapers have been allowed to print, not only the detailed account of all our parliamentary debates about the abolition of the Slave Trade, but even the particulars of the St. Domingo transactions.—Surely the West Indian Petitioners to the House of Lords were ignorant of these facts, or rather perhaps they thought the Abolitionists were ignorant of them, when the mere discussion of the question here was stated to be so alarming.

men thus lulled into a fatal insensibility to such a great and obvious danger, without recognizing once more that righteous ordination of the Almighty, by which, when human laws are inactive, he provides natural punishment of our infringement on the rights and happiness of our fellow creatures.

But the dangers to our great island of Jamaica, arising out of its proximity to St. Domingo, are not yet exhausted. Contemplate the state of St. Domingo. See how it is placed; almost in contact with Jamaica. Consider its size, and its vast Black population. And since recent events have so clearly proved that Negroes can reason, and feel and act like ourselves; we may form no unjust judgment of the probable sentiments and emotions of these free Negroes, by imagining what in similar circumstances would be our own.

Take then the Negroes of St. Domingo, justly jealous of the Europeans, and resolved carefully to watch over and defend those newly-acquired liberties which they have so dearly purchased. They hear of cargoes of their wretched countrymen continually torn from their native land, and doomed for life to a state of vassalage. They see that, all

around

around them, their African countrymen are still detained in that same state of bitter bondage from which they have themselves so lately emerged. They know that the Colonists in all the islands regard them with mixed emotions of hatred and fear, and would rejoice in being able again to rivet on their chains. Do they not see, in the present degraded state of their brethren, and remember in their own, that there is a grand fundamental ground of distinction between Blacks and Whites, a radical separation and even opposition of interests; a real, enduring principle of hostility?

May they not reasonably be supposed to think that they owe it alike to their honour and their security to vindicate the rights of their sable countrymen? May they not apprehend, that if they do not, while they can, assist their brethren in the neighbouring colonies to assert their freedom, and drive out their taskmasters, the white inhabitants of the other islands will not only preserve their empire over the Blacks already subject to them, but be continually plotting for the destruction of freedom in St. Domingo? May they not justly fear lest the European Powers, when their present differences shall be made up, should hereafter combine their efforts to restore,

restore, even in St. Domingo itself, the yoke of slavery?

Such, it is not unnatural to suppose, will be the reasonings and sensations of the St. Domingo Negroes. But experience has in vain afforded us proofs of the watchfulness, address, and versatility of our indefatigable enemy, if we do not suppose it possible that Bonaparte, by his agents, will reinforce those natural surmises; that by suggesting, through his emissaries, to the Negroes of St. Domingo, the dangers to which they are exposed, and the means of averting them, he will endeavour to stimulate them to invade Jamaica, and to stir up in all our islands insurrection and revolt. Those whom he has in vain attempted to make the victims of his rapacity, he will thus render the instruments of his revenge.

Let any one read the "Crisis of our Sugar Colonies" with seriousness, and he will acknowledge the amount, the variety, the probability, of the dangers to which our West Indian settlements are exposed. Their reality as well as their magnitude must equally be confessed by every man whose judgment is not totally obscured by interest, or whose discernment

cernment is not altogether blinded by familiarity with the objects which he views.

Our population drained.

The next of the important topics to which I lately alluded is one on which, from prudential motives, I will press lightly; but which I muſt commend to the moſt serious attention of my readers, not merely from considerations of humanity, but even of self-intereſt. The Weſt Indies have long been regarded as the grave of our soldiers and seamen, but never surely with so much reason as of late years. For a new disease has broken out, so terribly waſteful in it's effects, and so little subject hitherto to the controul of medicine, as to furnish too juſt cause for fearing leſt there should be such a constant drain of the population of the mother country, as from the numbers consumed on the one hand, perhaps even ſtill more on the other, from the dangerous effects on our naval and military service (I truſt I shall be underſtood, though, from motives of caution, I rather hint than express my meaning) to render the protection of our transatlantic colonies incompatible with our internal security. This is a topic on which I will not press; but in proportion as I abſtain from the alarming discussion, leſt I should in any degree aggravate one of the evils which I apprehend, let it be deeply and seriously

seriously weighed by every considerate mind. Even independently of intereſt, shall not the voice of humanity be heard? Is it nothing to send the brave defenders of our country, and the flower of our youth, to a peſtilential climate, where they fall not in the field of battle, not contending with the enemies of their country, but where they perish unknown, and therefore ingloriously, often even falling the victims of their own fears, from beholding such multitudes around them continually swept away.*

But that which I must press upon you is, that all these sufferers, or at leaſt an immense majority of them, are the victims of the Slave Trade. For it is this pernicious traffic, which by the double operation of continually increasing the disproportion between the Blacks and Whites on the one hand, and of obſtructing on the other those salutary reforms which would change by degrees this depraved, degraded mass into a happy peasantry; makes you shrink back with terror from defending the islands by their own internal resources, though we cannot but acknowledge that they would hereby be rendered utterly invincible by any European

* See Dr. Pinckard's late work; Notes on the Weſt Indies.

force which the great nation, or any others of our enemies, might bring against them.* And here a fresh prospect of misery opens to our view: here come in a new set of sufferers from the Slave Trade, not the less to be attended to, because, as yet at least, they do not themselves trace the bitter stream from which their cup is filled, to its original source; the numerous train of widows and orphans and relatives, whose nearest connections have fallen the victims of the diseases of the western world. I am persuaded, that if the full effect of the Slave Trade in this relation were generally known, the general feelings of the nation, more powerfully, alas! excited for our own subjects than for the unhappy Africans, would have produced throughout the British Isles one universal cry of indignation against this arch enemy of the happiness of mankind. Here is another of those instances, several of which in the course of this investigation we have had occasion to remark, wherein, through the righteous retribution of Heaven, wickedness and

---

* The petition of the Assembly of Jamaica, in 1775, plainly recognizes the source of danger here alluded to. "Weak and feeble (says the Assembly) as this colony "is, from its very small number of white inhabitants, "and its peculiar situation, from the incumbrance of "more than 200,000 Slaves," &c. &c.

cruelty

cruelty are not allowed, even in this world, to go unpunished; by which the irreligious and unfeeling are taught to respect the happiness of others, if from no higher motive, yet from regard to the preservation of their own.

And now surely you must be prepared to admit without hesitation, and in its full extent, the declaration made by Mr. Pitt in the House of Commons, that the Slave Trade was the greatest practical evil that ever had afflicted the human race. Such indeed it would be found, had we but leisure to take the real weight of all the various evils which it includes; and surely it might well become us to enter into this examination. But it would almost exceed the powers of calculation, after having traced the Slave Trade into all its various forms of suffering, to estimate the amount of them all.

Summary view of the miseries produced by the Slave Trade.

Let us, however, spend a few moments in adding up the great totals of which it consists, that we may be the less likely to deceive ourselves, as in such cases men are apt to do, by underrating the evils of which we are the cause, and consequently the amount of guilt with which we are chargeable.

To begin with Africa. If we would form
a fair

a fair calculation of the aggregate sum of misery caused by the Slave Trade, we muſt remember that it is by no means to be eſtimated by the numbers which we actually carry away into slavery: Nor yet by adding to them all the wretched relatives, families, and connections who are left behind: Nor yet by superadding the devastation and misery which, to those who may not actually be caught and carried off, may arise from all the several predatory expeditions occasioned by the Slave Trade, either directly or in retaliation of former aggressions originating from the same cause: Nor ſtill by adding the deſtruction and desolation produced by national wars (for of these the Slave Trade is often the origin), with peſtilence and famine, and all the various forms of misery which follow war in its train: Nor even yet by subjoining the wretchedness of those, with all their families and friends, who are the victims of injuſtice and treachery, masking themselves under the forms of law, or availing themselves of the native superstitions.

But let us endeavour to make the case our own, and to consider what it would be to live in a country subject to such continual depredations by night, and such treachery by day. These evils affect the whole condition

of

of society; they poison the happiness of every family, nay, it may almoft be said of every individual in the community. All the nameless but sweet enjoyments comprised within the idea of home, to all of which security is necessary, are at once destroyed; and Parke assures us that no people taste these pleasures with a higher relish than the Negroes.

Consider the intensity of the sufferings which the Slave Trade occasions in Africa, and the number of the sufferers; remember throughout what an immense extent these evils prevail, and the time they have continued.

To this vast mass of African misery, add up all the various evils of the middle passage. See there the husband and father, wife and mother, who have been torn from the deareft objects of their affections, and are now carried away, they know not whither, in their floating prison. Take in, their never having been before at sea, their confinement, their posture, with all the other diftressing particulars of their situation; is not too much to say that you see them enduring exquisite bodily suffering. But, much more, consider the sorrows of the mind; see them dying of a broken heart, from the loss of their friends
and

and country, from their remembrance of the past, and their prospect for the future. In this state forced to bear the coarse brutality of the sailors, and urged by stripes, with a stomach loathing food, to eat; and with limbs galled with fetters, to dance; while their hearts are wrung with agony. Consider then that in every individual Slave ship there are most likely multitudes of these wretched beings; many of them men, as Mr. Parke tells us, of some education; some of them men of considerable rank in their own country: but the whole cargo, as it is hatefully termed, consists of husbands and wives, of parents and children—all had a home—all had relatives.

But to the sufferings of the wretched Slaves themselves, we must add those of the sailors also, who are too often treated with extreme barbarity. Of the latter, there are not a few who, though their lives are spared, lose their health, their sight, or the use of their limbs, not merely from the unwholesome nature of the climate of Africa, but from various peculiarities attendant on the Slave Trade.

Nor ought we to omit the moral injury which our country sustains from the number of persons who are rendered ferocious and unfeeling

unfeeling by the hardening nature of their conſtant occupation.

It would be difficult to add up the different items, much less to discover the precise sum of the misery which may fairly be placed to the account of the Slave Trade in the Weſt Indies. Here, however, let me firſt remark, and it ought to have been observed in the case of Africa likewise, the Slave Trade is juſtly chargeable with the prevention of all that do- domeſtic happiness and social comfort and prosperity which would follow from the introduction of the domeſtic system which it naturally supersedes. But when we proceed to the positive articles of this account; when we endeavour to sum up the total of the immense number of individual sufferers: Again, when to these we add the sufferings and the waſte of our brave defenders, by sea and land, with the sorrows of their surviving relatives; and when we consider the unknown amount of evil, which, from the effect on the minds of our soldiers and sailors, may at some time or other result from this class of ravages, evil possibly commensurate with the ruin of our country: When we remember that it is the Slave Trade which prolongs the internal weakness of our Weſt Indian colonies, that it is this weakness
which

which invites attack, and thence creates the necessity of defence at such a profuse expenditure of the lives of our countrymen; and that the facility of conquering these possessions operates powerfully as a temptation to our enemies to commence war, with all its unknown miseries and dangers: By what new denomination shall we in any degree fairly express the real sum of these several items?

There is still, however, another class of evils on which I have occasionally touched, which will appear of the highest amount to all considerate men, to whom the best interests of their country are dear, and who have been accuftomed to trace the operation of those causes which have led to the decline and fall of nations.* These are the moral evils both of the Slave Trade, and even, ftill more, because of greater extent, of the system of Weft Indian slavery. It is the fashion of the present day to pay little attention to evils

* For the illuftration of this part of the subject, and of many other topics which I have slightly touched, I muft refer my readers to Mr. Brougham's Colonial Policy; a work from some parts of which I muft express my decided dissent, but which contains a moft valuable fund of commercial and financial, political and moral facts, and suggeftions on all the various subjects connected with colonial interefts and affairs.

of

of this class; but they are not on this account less real or less efficient. Their nature and force have been acknowledged by all writers of eminence, whether ancient or modern, who have treated either of the prosperity or decay of the great nations of antiquity.

The system of slavery, especially of slavery in it's more hateful forms, never did nor ever will prevail long in any country, without producing a moft pernicious effect, both on it's morals, habits, and manners. This is an invidious topic, on which I will not enlarge; but let it's amount be duly eftimated by all who are interefted for the independence, the prosperity, or the happiness of their country. When all these various masses of misery are piled up into one, who shall attempt to take the dimensions of it's enormous bulk. Yet we muft acknowledge, that from it's very size it produces less impression on mankind in general. This principle may be termed a law of our nature, and we suffer from the effect of it in every part of our great cause. I firmly believe that it is here the Slave Trade has found it's chief security. Had it not been for the operation of this cause, both Houses of Parliament, I had almoft said the whole nation, would have risen with one indignant effort, and have forced the Slave

Traders

Traders to desift from their cruel occupation. Could we but place even the people of Liverpool themselves, where they could see with their own eyes the progress, from first to last, of this series of crimes and cruelties; could we but confine their attention so that they might have but one object before them at once, and might view it in all it's parts distinctly, with all it's circumftances and relations, I firmly believe they would themselves abjure that inhuman traffic for which they are now so ignominiously preeminent.

But the enormous dimensions of this mass of misery are such, that our organs are not fitted for the contemplation of it; our affections are not suited to deal with it; we are loft in the immensity of the prospect; we are diftracted by it's variety. We may see highly probable reasons why our allwise Creator has so conftituted us, that we are more deeply affected by one single tale of misery, with all the details of which we are acquainted, than by the greateft accumulation of sufferings of which the particulars have not fallen under our notice. Could I but separate this immense aggregate into all its component parts, and present them one by one to your view, in all their particularity of wretchedness, you would then have a more juft impression of the immensity

mensity of the misery which we wish to terminate. This cannot now be done; but let us, in concluding our melancholy course, employ a few moments in taking some family, or some individual Negro, and following him through all his successive stages of suffering, from his firſt becoming the victim of some nightly attack on his dwelling, or from his being sentenced to slavery for the benefit of those who condemned him, to the final close of his wretched life. I will not attempt to describe his sufferings; eſtimate from your own feelings what muſt be his, in all the various situations through which he passes.

Conceive, if you can, the agony with which, as he is hurried away by his unfeeling captors, he looks back upon the native village which contains his wife and children who are left behind; or, supposing them to have been carried off also, with which he sees their sufferings, and looks forward to the dreadful future; while his own anguish is augmented by witnessing theirs. Accompany him through his long and painful march to the coaſt; behold him, when the powers of nature are almoſt exhauſted by fatigue and affliction, urged forward like a brute by the lash, or, with ſtill more bitterness of suffering, seeing the fainting powers of his wretched

wife

wife or daughter roused into fresh exertions by the same savage discipline. * Behold him next brought on shipboard and delivered over to men, whose colour, appearance, language, are all ſtrange to him, while every object around muſt excite terror. If his wretched family have not been brought away with him, he is tormented by the consciousness that they are left deſtitute and unprotected, and that his eyes will see them no more. If his wife and daughter have been carried off with him, he sees them dragged away to another part of the ship, while he is debarred from their society, and often even from the sight of them; what muſt be his anguish, from being conscious not only that they are suffering many of the same evils as himself, but ſtill more, from knowing that they are exposed to all those brutalities, the idea of which muſt be moſt cutting to a husband or a father; while his misery becomes more intense, from the consciousness that they are close to him, though he cannot alleviate their misery, or protect their weakness.

See our wretched family or individual arriving at the deſtined port, and then call to mind the abominations of the sale of a

* See Mr. Parke's account of his journey to the coaſt from the interior.

negro

negro cargo. See the wretched individual or family exposed naked like brutes, and the same methods taken as with their fellow brutes, to ascertain whether or not their limbs and members are perfect. See them forced to jump or dance, to prove their agility; or, still more affecting, see them afraid, each lest the other only should be bought by some particular purchaser, and therefore displaying their agility, while their hearts are wrung with anguish, in order to induce the buyer to take them both. Perhaps the different branches of the family may be bought by different owners; they may probably be taken to different islands, and the poor hope of wearing away together the wretched remainder of their lives is disappointed; or, if they are purchased together, see them taken home to the estate, and entering upon their course of laborious and bitter degradation; while, looking forward to the future, not a single ray of hope breaks in to cheer the prospect, no hope of any alleviation of drudgery or degradation for them or for their children, for ever! Suppose our wretched Slave at length reduced to the level of his condition, and, either with his own family or with a new one, suppose him to have his hard lot in some little measure mitigated by a very slight taste of domestic and social comforts. It might well be thought, that, except eept for the hardships and sufferings inseparable from such a state of slavery, where even the necessaries of life muft depend on an owner's affluence, in a country where we know that an immense majority are extremely embarrassed in their affairs—the bitterness of death would be now past; but a negro Slave does not die so easily; again probably, possibly again and again, he is to be subjected to the brutalities of a sale, and to the pains of separation from all that are moft dear to him.* He is taken perhaps to form a new settlement, and forced to the severe labour of clearing land, in a peftilential soil and climate, without any of those little accommodations which ingenious and induftrious poverty might in a course of years have collected around him, in his old habitation. This, however, if a severe is ftill a short suffering, from which death soon releases him, and is far preferable to the sad fate of those, who linger out the tedious remainder of life, separated from all who have known them in their better days, and without any of those kindly props to lean upon, which the merciful ordainer of all things has provided, for sustaining the weakness, and mitigating the sorrows of age,

* Let it be considered what immense numbers of Negroes have of late years been removed from our older islands to Trinidad, or to Guiana.

To

To look around, and to see not a single face of friendship or relationship, no eye to cheer, no staff to lean upon; surely the comfortless close of such a Negro's comfortless life, though not of equal intensity of suffering with many of the evils of the former scenes through which he has passed, is yet, from the deep tinge and uniform melancholy of its colouring, as affecting a state, to the humane mind, as any whatever in a life abounding in all the varieties of human wretchedness.

Such from first to last is the condition of human existence, to which that abhorred traffic the Slave Trade annually consigns many thousands of our unoffending fellow creatures. This is a most astonishing phenomenon, when we consider the general character of the people of this country; when we call to mind the unparalleled benevolence and liberality which are found among us; when we take into account, that not a new species of distress can be pointed out, but that almost immediately some meeting takes place, some society is formed, for preventing it. Is it not utterly astonishing, that Great Britain should have been the prime agents in carrying on this trade of blood? Posterity will scarcely believe it. We, the happiest, render the Africans the most miserable of mankind!

Conclusion.

It is a humiliating and an aweful, but, I fear, it is an undoubted truth; that it is in part, at least, because we ourselves overflow with comforts, that we are so indifferent to the happiness of this vaſt portion of our fellow creatures. It is, in our corrupted nature, too naturally the effect of prosperity to harden the heart. Yet I firmly believe, that could many of our opponents see with their own eyes but a slight sample of the miseries the Slave Trade occasions, they would themselves be eager for its termination. But, alas, Africa and its miseries are out of sight. Business, pleasure, engagements, the intereſts and feelings of the hour, leave little time for reflection, and therefore little access to the feelings. Sympathy here likewise operates againſt us. For we are readily led to sympathize with a great Weſt India Proprietor; but not with a miserable negro Slave. Yet, let me ask (in this happy country the case cannot really happen), what should we think of any man, who, for some even considerable and clear, much more for any dubious intereſt, was to make a single family as miserable as the Slave Trade renders thousands of families every year? If he were to keep them month after month and year after year in continual alarm, from the apprehension of some nightly attack; if at length the apprehension

apprehension were to be realized, the attack to be made, and the wretched beings, flying from the flames, were to be seized and carried off into slavery; if he were thus to tear a father or mother from their children, or to seize unawares and hurry away some helpless children from their parents ; What would be his remorse, if he had even innocently been the occasion of rendering a before happy family the scene of lafting sorrow and misery? What should we think of any man, who would not be forward to dry the tears of such a family, and restore them, if possible, to comfort, or who would not willingly expose himself to danger, in order to prevent their suffering such a miserable fate. Let every one then remember, that, by giving his vote for the abolition of the Slave Trade, he will prevent the perpetration of innumerable crimes, like the worft of those here mentioned, and the suffering of the bittereft of these miseries. How few, if one single man could be found, who would support the Slave Trade, were it but possible to bring before each individual, of the whole number of those who may vote for it's continuance, his own specific share of the whole mass of crimes and miseries. The exact amount, either way, will one day be known!

Forgive

Forgive me if I seem still to linger; if I appear unwilling to conclude. When I call to mind the number and the magnitude of the interests which are at stake, I know not how to desist, while any fresh argument remains to be used, while any consideration not as yet suggested occurs to me, by which I may enforce my intercession in behalf of the most injured of the human race. But though the mind be naturally led to the Africans, as the greatest sufferers, yet, unless the Scripture be a forgery, it is not their cause only that I am pleading, but the cause of my Country. Yet let me not here be misconceived. It is not that I expect any visible and supernatural effects of the Divine vengeance; though, not to listen with seriousness to the accounts which have been brought us of late years from the western hemisphere, as to a probable intimation of the Divine displeasure, would be to resolve to shut our ears against the warning voice of Providence. To mention no other particulars, a disease new in it's kind, and almost without example destructive in its ravages, has been for some time raging in those very colonies which are the chief supporters of the traffic in human beings; a disease concerning which we scarcely know any thing, but that it does not affect the Negro race, and that we first heard of it after the horrors

rors of the Slave Trade had been completely developed in the House of Commons, but developed in vain.

But it is often rather in the way of a gradual decline, than of violent and sudden shocks, that national crimes are punished. I muſt frankly therefore confess to you, that in the case of my Country's prosperity or decline, my hopes and fears are not the sport of every passing rumour; nor do they rise or fall materially, according to the successive reports we may receive of the defeats or victories of Bonaparte. This consideration opens the view into a wide field, and I muſt abſtain from so much as setting my foot on it. I will only remark, that a country circumſtanced in all respects like this, under an auspicious Providence, and using our various resources with energy and wisdom, has no cause whatever for despondency. But he who has looked with any care into the page of history, will acknowledge, that when nations are prepared for their fall, human inſtruments will not be wanting to effect it; and, left man, vain man, so apt to overrate the powers and achievements of human agents, should ascribe the subjugation of the Romans to the consummate policy and powers of a Julius Cæsar, their slavery shall
be

be completed by the unwarlike Auguſtus, and shall remain entire under the hateful tyranny of Tiberius, and throughout all the varieties of their successive maſters. Thus it is, that, moſt commonly by the operation of natural causes, and in the way of natural consequences, Providence governs the world. But if we are not blind to the course of human events, as well as utterly deaf to the plain instructions of Revelation, we muſt believe that a continued course of wickedness, oppression, and cruelty, obſtinately maintained in spite of the fulleſt knowledge and the loudeſt warnings, muſt infallibly bring down upon us the heavieſt judgments of the Almighty. We may ascribe our fall to weak councils, or unskilful generals; to a factious and overburthened people; to storms which waste our fleets, to diseases which thin our armies; to mutiny among our soldiers and sailors, which may even turn againſt us our own force; to the diminution of our revenues and the excessive increase of our debt: men may complain on one side of a venal miniſtry, on the other of a factious oppostition; while amid mutual recriminations, the nation is gradually verging to it's fate. Providence will easily provide means for the accomplishment of it's own purposes. It cannot be denied, that there are circumſtances in the situation of this

Country,

Country, which, reasoning from experience, we muſt call marks of a declining empire; but we have, as I firmly believe, the means within ourselves of arreſting the progress of this decline. We have been eminently blessed; we have been long spared; Let us not presume too far on the forbearance of the Almighty.

Broomfield,
Jan. 28th, 1807.

Printed by Luke Hansard & Sons,
near Lincoln's-Inn Fields.

APPENDIX.

APPENDIX.

AFRICA.

EXTRACTS FROM THE OLDER AUTHORS.

From Travels of the Sieur d' Elbée, sent by the French W. I. Company to Ardrah, in 1670.—Astley's Voyages, vol. iii.

THOUGH the king has a great number of wives, yet but one has the title of queen; who is she that bears him the first son. Her authority over the rest, whom she treats rather as her servants, than as her companions, is so great, that she sometimes sells them for slaves, without consulting the king, who is forced to wink at the matter. An affair of this kind happened while the Sieur d'Elbée traded here. The queen, having been refused by the king some goods or jewels she had an inclination for, ordered them up privately, and in exchange sent eight of his wives to the factory, who were immediately stamped with the Company's mark, and sent on board.

These poor princesses had sunk under so severe a stroke, if the Sieur d'Elbée had not shewn them some distinction, by treating them in a kind manner; so he carried them in good health to Martinico.— (p. 72.)

Depredatory Acts occasioned by the Slave Trade.

Extract from a Voyage to Congo, and other countries, in 1682, from Astley's Voyages, vol. iii. by Jerom Merolla, &c.

Depredatory Acts occasioned by the Slave Trade. He, said he, was sure it was not the intention of the duke (the Duke of York) that christians should be bought and sold as slaves; nor that such as he (meaning the captain) should be allowed not only to trade, but to rob and infest the shores wherever they came, in the same manner as another English captain had done there the year before; who, as soon as he had taken in all his lading, fell to wasting the country, and forced away many of the natives into slavery, and killed many others whom he could not get away. —(p. 174.)

Bosman's description of Guinea, about 1690 to 1700, in Astley's voyages, vol. iii.

Coto Coast.—Their trade is that of slaves, of which they are able sometimes to deliver a good number, but never enough to load a ship. These they chiefly steal from the inland country. But this commerce is uncertain; in some years there are no slaves to be had, the Europeans having no settlement here. (p. 2.)—Their most profitable trade is stealing men inland, whom they sell to the Europeans.—(p. 3.)

The same author says, that the people of little Popo depend chiefly on plunder, and the slave-trade, in both which they exceed those of Coto; for, being endowed with a much larger share of courage, they rob more successfully; although to freight a ship with slaves, requires some months attendance. In 1697, the author could get only three slaves here in three days time, but they promised him two hundred in three days more; which not caring to trust to he sailed to Whidah. There he learnt that they had succeeded so well in their incursions, as to bring down

down above two hundred; which, for want of other ships, they were obliged to sell to the Portuguese.—(p. 4.) *Depredatory Acts occasioned by the Slave Trade.*

Philips informs us that the Whidah blacks are constantly at war with the Ardrah and Allampo men, the Quamboors and Achims. All the plunder is men and women, to sell for slaves.—(p. 53.)

Sieur Brüe's (many years Director General of the French Senegal Company, and who resided in Africa eleven years) Voyage to the Isles of Bissas and Bissagos, on the Western Coast of Africa, in 1701; —*from Astley's Voyages, Vol. ii.*

The Sieur Brüe having received an assortment of goods by a fleet from France, sent notice to the Damel, or king of Kayor, between the rivers Senegal and Gambia, as he had promised, and wrote him word, that if he had a sufficient number of slaves, he was ready to trade with him.—This prince, as well as the other negro monarchs, have always a sure way of supplying this deficiency, by selling their own subjects; for which they seldom want pretensions, of some kind or other, to juſtify their rapine. The Damel had recourse to this method: knowing the Sieur Brüe would give him no credit, as he was already in the Company's debt, he seized three hundred of his own people, and sent word to the Sieur Brüe, that he had slaves to deliver for his goods, if he would come to Rufisco, where he waited to receive him.—(p. 29, 30.).

The Damel wishing for more goods than his slaves would purchase, the Sieur Brüe proposed having a licence to take so many of his people; he refused to consent, saying, it might occasion a disturbance amongst his subjects; and so he was forced to want the goods he desired for that time.

Depredatory Acts occasioned by the Slave Trade.
The chief sometimes penetrated far into the country, always returning well loaded with slaves and spoil.—(42.).

This is the negro manner of making war—it is a great chance if they come to a pitched battle. Their campaigns are usually mutual incursions, to plunder and carry off slaves, which they sell to the traders on the coast.—(p. 42.)

The isle of Bassao is very populous, and would be much morre so, if it were not for the frequent incursions made by the Biafaras, Balantes, and Bissagos negroes, who often infest the coasts.

The Europeans are far from desiring to act as peace-makers among them, which would be contrary to their interest; since the greater the wars are, the more slaves. These wars of theirs are never long; generally speaking, they are incursions, or expeditions, of five or six days.—(p. 98.)

He then describes the mode of their warfare: When the emperor of Bassao judges proper to invade his enemies, he sounds his bonbalon, and immediately the officers of his troops repair with their soldiers, armed, to the place directed; there they find the king's canoes of war, of which he has a fleet of twenty-nine or thirty. They put twenty men in each canoe :—they embark them, full of hope, and order matters so as to reach the enemy's country by night. They land without noise; and if they find any lone cottage without defence, they surround it; and after forcing it, carry off all the inhabitants and effects to their boats, and immediately reimbark.

If the villages be strong, they are not fond of attacking them, but rather plant themselves in ambuscade on the ways to some river or spring, and endeavour to surprise and carry off the natives.

On

On the leaft advantages of this kind gained, they return in as great a triumph as if they had obtained a complete victory. The king has, for his duties and the use of his fleet, the half of the booty. The rest is divided among the captors. All these slaves in general are sold to the Europeans, unless they be persons of some rank, whose friends can redeem them, paying two slaves, or, five or six oxen.— (p. 98).

Depredatory Acts occasioned by the Slave Trade.

Of the Bissagoes he says: They are passionate lovers of brandy. Whenever a ship brings any, they strive who shall be the first, and stick at nothing to get it. The weaker becomes a prey to the stronger. They forget the laws of nature; the father sells his children; and, if they can seize their parents, they serve them in the same manner. Every thing goes for brandy."—(p. 104.)

Barbot's Travels, about 1700.—Astley, vol. ii.

Barbot, speaking of the blacks, says, rather than work they will rob and murder on the highway, or carry off those of a neighbouring village, and sell them for slaves.—(p. 255.)

They go farther yet; for some sell their own children, kindred, or neighbours. This, Barbot tells us, has often happened. To compass it, they desire the person they intend to sell, to help them in carrying something to the factory, by the way of trade; and when there the person so deluded, not understanding the language, is sold and delivered up as a slave, notwithstanding all his resistance and exclaiming against the treachery.

Le Maire tells an odd story on this occasion, which Barbot says he heard in Africa. A man, it seems, had formed a design of selling his son, who, suspecting his intention, when they came to the factory, went aside to the storehouse and sold his father.

Depredatory Acts occasioned by the Slave Trade. father. When the old man saw them about to fetter him, he cried out, he was his father; but the son denying it, the bargain held good. The son met his desert, for, returning with his merchandize, he met a negro chief, who stripped him of his ill-gotten wealth, and sold him at the same market.

Abundance of little blacks, of both sexes, are also stolen away by their neighbours, when found abroad on the roads, or in the woods, or else in the lugaus, or corn-fields, where they are kept all day, to scare the small birds that come in swarms to feed on the millet.—(p. 256.)

Labat.—Astley's Voyages, vol. ii. p. 259.

The French have been forced sometimes to make use of violent means, when they cannot get the princes to discharge these forced loans, by pillaging some village, and making slaves of the inhabitants; after which they have balanced accounts with his majesty, and paid for as many as they had taken above their due. But these measures, says the author, don't always succeed; and even though one was sure of getting paid this way, yet that it would be better not to make a practice of it, for fear of drawing the resentment of the country upon a man, which, sooner or later, he would feel to his cost.—(p. 258.)

Le Maire's Travels, about 1690.—Astley's Voyages, vol. ii.

Sometimes the king of Senegal makes incursions on the weakest of his neighbours, driving off their cattle, or making slaves of them, which he sells for brandy. When his stock of this grows low, he locks it up in a small chest, giving the key to one of his favorites, whom he dispatches, perhaps thirty leagues off,

off, and thus saves his liquor by putting it out of his power to get at it. If he has no opportunity of exercising his tyranny on his neighbours, he makes no scruple of living on his own subjects, staying with his court, which consists of two hundred of those who have learnt all the worst qualities of the whites, till he has eat up the inhabitants; and, if they presume to complain, selling them for slaves. —(p. 260.)

<small>Depredatory Acts occasioned by the Slave Trade.</small>

As long as the brandy bottle lasts the prince is drunk: no answer is to be expected till all the liquor is out. When he grows sober, he gives his audience of *congée*, presenting the factor with two or three slaves, which he sends to have taken up in the nearest villages. Unhappy are they who at that time fall into the hands of his guards, for they stay to make no choice.—(p. 260, 261.)

Travels (about 1730), of Francis Moore, Factor several years to the Royal African Company of England.

The king of Barsalle, so soon as he has wasted what he has gotten, either by taking an enemy's town, *or one of his own*, he must look out for some new prize to give it to his men.—Astley, ii. 261.

Rohone, where the king of Barsali commonly resides, stands near the sea, about one hundred miles from Joar, which lies in the same kingdom. When he wants goods or brandy, he sends a messenger to the governor of James Fort, to desire he would send up a sloop with a cargo, which the governor never fails to do. Against the time the vessel is arrived, the king plunders some of his enemy's towns, selling the people for such goods as he wants, which commonly is brandy or rum, gunpowder, ball, fire-arms, pistols, and cutlasses for his soldiers, and coral and silver for his wives and mistresses. If he is at war with

Depredatory Acts occasioned by the Slave Trade.

with no neighbouring king, he falls upon one of his own towns, and makes bold to sell his own miserable subjects.

His usual way of living is, to sleep all day till sunset, at which time he gets up to drink, and goes to sleep again till midnight, when he rises and eats; and if he has any strong liquors, will sit and drink till day-light, and then eat and go to sleep again. When he is well stocked with liquor, he will sit and drink for five or six days together, and not eat one morsel of any thing in all that time. It is to this insatiable thirst after brandy, that his subjects freedoms and families are in so precarious a situation*; for he often goes with some of his troops, by a town in the daytime, and returns in the night, and sets fire to three parts of it, placing guards at the fourth, to seize the people as they run out from the fire: he ties their arms behind them, and marches them either to Joar or Rohone, where he sells them.—(p. 261, 262.). The king furnishes the Europeans with slaves very easily: he sends a troop of guards to some village, which they surround; then seizing as many as they have orders for, they bind them up and send them away to the ships, where, the ship mark being put upon them, they are heard of no more.

They usually carry the infants in sacks, and gag the men and women, for fear they should alarm the villages through which they are carried; for these actions are never committed in the villages near the factories, which it is the king's interest not to ruin, but in those up the country. It often happens, that some escape, and alarm the country, which, taking arms, join the persons injured, and pursue the

---

* Compare this with Captain Hill's and Wilson's, and especially with Mr. Wadstrom's evidence.

robbers.

robbers. If they catch them, they carry them be- *Depreda-*
fore the king, who then denies his commission, and *tory Acts*
sells them on the spot for slaves. What is further *by the Slave*
remarkable, if any of the injured people appear as *Trade.*
evidence still in bonds before the king, they are also
adjudged to be slaves, and sold as such.*—(p. 268.).

Voyage of Atkins to Guinea, about 1720.
Astley, vol. ii.

Panyarring is a term for manstealing, along the whole coast.—(p. 320.)

Voyage of Smith, about 1727—*employed under the African Company.*

December 18, they sailed from Sierra Leona, and on the 25th anchored at Gallinas; here lay the Queen Elizabeth, Captain Creighton, before mentioned, who invited Capt. Livingstone to take a Christmas dinner with him, and shewed him a letter from one Benjamin Cross (third mate of the Expedition, Capt. Mettisse) who had been *panyarred* by the natives of Cape Monte, three months before, and detained there by way of reprisal for some of their men carried off by an English trader. This villanous custom is too often practised, chiefly by the Bristol and Liverpool ships, and is a great detriment to the Slave Trade on the Windward coast.†—(p. 475, 476.)

Mons. Brüe, (vol. iv.) relating a dispute he had with the Damel, respecting his giving an English ship liberty to trade in his dominions, on which M. Brüe seized and confiscated the vessel, says, "Most of the Negroes on board, he found, were free fishermen of the coast, whom the king had decoyed to Potadàlly, under the pretence of employing their canoes to trans-

* Compare this with Mr. Howe's evidence.
† Compare this with the absolute denial of such practices, or of any term for them, by Opponents' witnesses.

port

<small>Depredatory Acts occasioned by the Slave Trade.</small> port his troops to attack Goree; but as soon as by this pretence he had assembled them, he sent them on board, and sold them as Slaves. There was not the smallest appearance that the Damel had even conceived so extravagant a project, says M. Brüe, but it was necessary to form some scheme to entrap these men, and sell them." Although the injustice of the king in trepanning and selling them was notorious, it mattered not; they were all sent to America, and sold as Slaves.— (p. 204.)

Labat mentions that a Captain of a French man of war, at the suggestion of a French trader, (the Captain's name was Montorsies, and the ship's, Lion, and Fond was the name of the trader) pillaged the Isle of Cazegat, one of the Bassagos Islands. They landed 200 men without the smallest resistance. The king of the island, named Duquermaney, was surrounded in his houses, and he chose to burn himself rather than fall into the European hands; the natives fled to the woods and mountains, so that, of about 3,000 inhabitants, they took only about a dozen. This unfortunate enterprise, says our author, made M. Fond greatly fear, lest he should lose all trade with these people : but he managed the matter so cleverly, " *il se donna tant de mouvemens, et fit jouer tant de ressorts,*" says Labat, that he made them believe he had no hand at all in the affair, and assured them it was a parcel of ruffians, a set of pirates and banditti, who had made this incursion, by which their king was lost, and their country laid waste.

Depredations—Effect of Slave Trade.

In old Calabar River are two towns, Old Town and New Town. A rivalship in trade produced a jealousy between the towns; so that, through fear of each other, for a considerable time no canoe would leave

leave their towns to go up the river for slaves. In 1767, seven ships lay off the point which separates the towns; six of the captains invited the people of both towns on board on a certain day, as if to reconcile them; at the same time agreed with the people of New Town to cut off the Old Town people who should remain on board the next morning. The Old Town people, persuaded of the sincerity of the captains' proposal, went on board in great numbers. Next morning, at eight o'clock, one of the ships fired a gun, as the signal for commencing hostilities. Some of the traders were secured on board, some were killed in resisting, and some got overboard and were fired upon. When the firing began, the New Town people, who were in ambush behind the Point, came forward and picked up the people of Old Town, who were swimming, and had escaped the firing. After the firing was over, the captains of five of the ships delivered their prisoners (persons of consequence) to the New Town canoes; two of whom were beheaded alongside the ships; the inferior prisoners were carried to the West Indies. One of the captains, who had secured three of the king's brothers, delivered one of them to the chief man of New Town, who was one of the two beheaded alongside; the other brothers he kept on board, promising, when the ship was slaved, to deliver them to the chief man of New Town. This ship was soon slaved, from this promise, and the number of prisoners made that day; but he refused to deliver the king's two brothers, and carried them to the West Indies, and sold them.

Natural Disposition of the Africans, and Capacity for Civilization.—Astley's Voyages, vol. i.

James Welsh's Voyage to Benin.—The people are very gentle, and loving.—(202.)

The

Astley's Voyages

The inhabitants of Whidah are more polite and civilized than most people in the world, not excepting the European. (vol. iii. p. 14.)

Marchais.—There are no people on earth, says that author, more tender of their offspring, or that shew more parental affection.—(p. 20.)

Nyendael.—Kingdom of Benin. The inhabitants are generally good-natured and civil, and may be brought to any thing by fair and soft means. If you make them presents, they will recompense them doubly. If you want any thing of them, and ask it, they seldom deny it, even though they had occasion for it themselves: but to treat them harshly, or to think to gain any thing of them by force, is to dispute with the moon.

Artus says, that the people of Benin are a sincere, inoffensive people, and do no injustice either to one another, or strangers.—(p. 95.)

Although some of them be surly and proud, yet in general they carry themselves very friendly towards strangers; being of a mild conversation, courteous, affable, and easy to be overcome with reason, yet inclined to drink, especially Spanish wine and brandy. In conversation, they discover great quickness of parts and understanding, delivering themselves with so much sense and humour, that the most knowing persons take delight in hearing them.—(p. 247.)

The Negroes at Whidah are so industrious, that no spot of land, except what is naturally barren, escapes planting, though even within the inclosures of their villages and houses.—(p. 8.)

The soil is so fruitful, that as soon as one harvest is over, the ground is sowed with some other grain; so that they have two or three crops in a year. (p. 8.)

Captain Stibbs, about 1724.—The Foleys are a cleanly, decent, industrious people, very affable.— (p. 199.)

Moore's

Moóre's Travels.—Their form of government goes on easily, because the people are of a quiet, good disposition, and so well instructed in what is juft and right, that a man who does ill is the abomination of all. Their humanity extends to all, but they are doubly kind to their own race; so that if one of them be made a Slave, all the Fûli will join to redeem him. And as they have plenty of food, they never suffer any of their own nation to want, but support the old, the blind, and the lame; and, as far as their ability goes, supply the wants of the Mandingoes, great numbers of whom they have maintained in famines. They rarely are angry; yet this mildness does not proceed from want of courage, for they are as brave a people as any in Africa. *Astley's Voyages.*

Winterbottom's Travels, about 1796, &c. &c.—The Foolas impart to leather a red colour, equal to that of morocco in beauty; and by fteeping it, they obtain a beautiful shining black. Another class of men are equally celebrated as blacksmiths; besides making every kind of necessary utensil, they inlay the handles, and chase the blades of swords, &c. with great neatness, and they make a variety of elegant fancy ornaments for the women, out of pieces of gold and silver dollars. A considerable degree of ingenuity in the arts with which they are acquainted must be allowed to all these nations, and is evident in the conftruction of their houses, and the formation of a variety of domeftic and agricultural utensils. With the rudest instruments, they form canoes from a single tree, capable of carrying eight or ten tons; their mats shew much neatness and ingenuity, &c. &c.—(p. 91, 92.)

They have various subftitutes for hemp and flax, of which they make fishing-lines and nets, equal in ftrength and durability to those of Europeans.—(p. 93.)

They

Astley's Voyages. They make earthen pots fit for every domestic use. (p. 94.)

I have been often gratified by observing the strength and tenderness of the attachment subsisting between mothers and sons.—(p. 152.)

It is my earnest wish to divest myself of partiality, and neither to "extenuate or set down aught in "malice." They (the Africans) are in general of mild external manners; but they possess a great share of pride, and are easily affected by an insult; they cannot hear even a harsh expression, or a raised tone of voice, without shewing that they feel it. As a proof that they are not deficient in natural affection, one of the severest insults which can be offered to an African, is to speak disrespectfully of his mother. (p. 211.) The respect which they pay to old people is very great.—(p. 211.)

The hospitality of the Africans has been noticed by almost every traveller.—(p. 213.)

I have ever met with a welcome and hospitable reception on arriving at their villages; mats have been brought out for myself and friends to repose on; and if it happened to be meal time, we have been at liberty to join them without ceremony, or to wait till something better could be provided. If we intended to spend the night there, a house has been set apart for us; and, on taking leave in the morning, a guide has generally offered to shew us on our way.—(p. 213.)

As soon as a stranger is observed, all the inhabitants quit their occupations, and hasten to shake him by the hand, repeating several times the word "Senno," welcome. Even the children who can barely lisp a welcome, when a little custom has diminished the dread attending a white face, are eager to discharge this duty of hospitality, and with a smile hold out their little hands, and seem delighted if he deigns to notice them.—(p. 214.)

Smith's

Smith's Guinea, about 1730.—These Negroes seem to be very induſtrious, for they all go clad with their own manufactures.—(p. 104.) *Astley's Voyages.*

The natives of Axim induſtriously employ themselves either in trade, fishing, or agriculture. (p. 115.)

Whydah.—Before the king of Dahomey conquered this place, the natives were so induſtrious, that no place which was thought fertile could escape being planted.—(p. 199.)

The discerning natives account it their greateſt unhappiness that they were ever visited by Europeans. They say that we Chriſtians introduced the traffic of Slaves, and that before our coming, they lived in peace. But say they, it is observable, that wherever Chriſtianity comes there come, with it a sword, a gun, powder and ball. (p. 266.)

Africans natural Qualities, and Capacity for Civilization—Commercial Intercourse practicable.—Astley's Voyages, vol. iii.

Bosman.—Whidah.—All who have seen it allow it to be one of the moſt delightful countries of the world.

The number and variety of tall, beautiful, shady trees; the verdant fields, every where cultivated, and only divided by those groves, or in some places by a small footpath; together with the innumerable little agreeable villages.

The farther you go from it (the ocean) the more beautiful and populous you find the country; so that it resembles the Elysian fields.

There is also a weekly market in the province of Aplogua, which is so resorted to, that there are usually five or six thousand merchants.—(p. 11.)

Ogilby.—Kingdom of Loango.—There are many handicrafts among them, as weavers, smiths, capmakers,

Astley's Voyages. makers, bead-makers, potters, carpenters, vintners, fishermen, canoe-makers, besides merchants and other traders. (p. 221.)

There are whole mountains of porphyry, jasper, and marble, of divers colours, which in Rome are called marbles of Numidia, Africa, and Ethiopia; certain pillars whereof may be seen in the palace of Pope Gregory. (p. 299.)

Natural Qualities and Disposition of Africans.

Capt. Wilson, of the Royal Navy (in Africa about 1783-4) fully believes Africans to be equal to Europeans in capacity. They have various manufactures, chiefly for home consumption. They make cotton cloths beautifully fine, under every want of machinery: also very curious ornaments of gold, and weapons and tools of iron, which their experience makes them prefer to those sent from hence, which are made for them.

The Africans are most grateful and affectionate: they treated him most kindly, when many miles up their country, and unprotected; and numbers shed tears on his departure.

Mr. Wadstrom (in Africa, about 1787-8.) thinks the Africans very honest and hospitable; was treated by them with all civility and kindness. Is clearly convinced that the Negroes surpass such Europeans as he has known, in affection. Has been surprised at their industry in manufacturing cotton, indigo, iron, soap, wood, pottery, leather, and other articles. They work gold so well, that witness never saw better wrought trinkets and ornaments in Europe. They manufacture cloth and leather with uncommon neatness. The latter they tan and work into saddles, sandals, and a variety of useful and ornamental articles. They forge iron
very

very dexterously on anvils of a remarkably hard and heavy wood, when they cannot get stone for the purpose.

The Negroes are particularly fkilful in manufacturing iron and gold. They are equal to any European goldsmith in fillagree, and even other articles, as buckles, except the chafes, tongues, and anchors.

The Rev. John Newton:—Made five voyages to Africa, the laft in 1754, as mafter of a slave ship. Lived ashore about a year and a half, chiefly at the island of Plantanes, at the mouth of the river Sherbro.

Always judged, that, with equal advantage, the natives capacities would be equal to ours. Has known many of real and decided capacity.

The beft people he met with were on the R. Gaboon, and at C. Lopas. These had then the leaft intercourse with Europe. Believes they had then no Slave Trade, and has heard them speak againft it. They traded in ivory and wax. One great man said, " if I was to be angry, and sell my " boy, how should I get my boy back when my " anger was gone?"

They are generally worse in their conduct in proportion to their acquaintance with us.

Capt. Sir George Young, Royal Navy; in Africa from 1768 to 1792.—Many Negroes he met with seemed to possess as ftrong natural sense as any set of people whatever; their temper appeared to be very good-natured and civil, unless where they suspected some injury; are, however, naturally vindictive, and revenge the injury done.

Henry Hew Dalrymple, Esq.; in Africa 1779.— As far as he could judge, in natural capacity, the Negroes are equal to any people whatever; and in

B b . temper

temper and disposition they appeared to be humane, hospitable, and well-disposed.

James Towne; about 1760, Carpenter of his Majesty's ship Syren.—The natives are hospitable and kind, and capable of learning quicker than white men. They differ as our own people in character; those on the coast learn to be roguish; inland, they are innocent. The intercourse with Europeans has improved them in roguery, to plunder and steal, and pick up one another to sell.

African Commercial Tendencies.

Mr. Wadstrom.—The Africans have an extraordinary genius for commerce and industry. The Slave Trade makes it dangerous for the Negroes to pass from one part of their country to another, and is the chief hindrance to the improvement of their cultivation, since they never venture into the fields, unless very well armed.

The Negroes are particularly skilful in manufacturing iron and gold; they are equal to any European goldsmith in fillagree, and even other articles, as buckles, except the chapes, tongues, and anchors.

Captain Sir George Young, Royal Navy.—He verily believes that the natives would cultivate the soil for natural productions, provided they had no other means of obtaining European commodities. He recollects some circumstances in proof of their industry. A number of people from the Bullam shore came over to Sierra Leone, and offered their services to work at a very low price; he accepted of a few (who worked very well) and might have had thousands of the same description. Further is of opinion, from observation, that Africa is capable of producing every thing of the East and West Indies, in equal perfection, with equal cultivation.

Is

Is of opinion, that, by shewing the natives of Africa how to cultivate the land, a greater quantity of shipping and seamen would be called for in the commerce, for the natural productions of that country, without any greater inconvenience, in point of health to the seamen, than in the present West Indian trade.

Astley's Voyages.

Anthony Pantaleo How, Esq.; in Africa about 1785.—Saw no European commodities in the interior parts; is sure no European spirits were to be had there. The inhabitants there remarkably industrious, also hospitable and obliging. A village of several hundred houses on the Lake of Appolonia, whence in the rainy season they supply the sea coast with vegetables, grain, palm wine, &c. Thinks they have but little capacity in regard to manufactures, but quick in learning languages.

Has no doubt but spices in general, and all other tropical productions, might be cultivated with success there. The soil and climate adapted to produce the sandal wood. Has seen indigo at Apollonia in its raw state, and also manufactured, but not manufacturing; also cotton growing in great abundance; but knows not that any or either of these two articles were exported.

Cinnamon plants at St. Thomas, at the sea side, about twenty feet high; from what he heard, grew inland to a higher size; those on the sea-side he considered only as shrubs. He saw a number of them, and, from the appearance of the bark brought down, concludes there must be a great quantity inland.

Henry Hew Dalrymple, Esq.; in Africa about 1779.—They manufacture cotton cloths, almost equal in the workmanship to those of Europe; they work in gold, silver, and iron remarkably neat, also in wood, and make saddles, bow-cases, scabbards, grisgris,

Golberry. grisgris, and other things of leather, with great neatness.

Richard Storey; in Africa, about 1766 to 1770.—He looks upon the natives of the Windward coast to be in general a hospitable, friendly people, always willing to sell what they have, and also to give the best provisions the country affords. The men in general are very active and industrious, and chiefly employed in fishing, and trade with the Europeans; the women chiefly in cultivating rice and other vegetables.

Has every reason to believe, that if there was nobody to purchase Slaves, they would turn themselves to cultivate their ground, and raise rice, &c. to purchase European goods. The quality of African rice is far superior to that of Carolina, bearing one-fourth more water.

Mr. James Kiernan; in Africa from 1775 to 1780: knows the Negroes manufacture cotton, leather, and metals, for they supply Senegal with cloathing, articles of leather, and ornaments of gold and silver; they die some of their cottons very finely, blues and scarlets; believes their consumption of cotton cloths is very considerable.

Africans' Natural Disposition.—*Golberey's Travels, about* 1786.

The Foulhas of the banks of the Senegal are intelligent and industrious; but, by their habitual commerce with the Moors of Zahara, they have become savage and cruel, and our convoys from Galam have more than once experienced their perfidy.

The Mandings are likewise dispersed over the western countries; they are well-informed, graceful, and active, and in their mercantile character, they are as clever as they are indefatigable.

The

The Jalofs are the finest Negroes of this part of Golberry.
Africa; they are tall, and well made; their features are regular, their physiognomy is open, and inspires confidence; they are honest, hospitable, generous, and faithful; their character is mild, they are inclined to good order and civilization, and possess an evident disposition for benevolent actions.

Vol. ii. page 40. At Senegal I was treated with a cordiality, frankness, and generosity, which will never be obliterated from my memory.

Page 93. Their character is in general, honest and sincere; hospitality is a natural virtue among them.

Page 141. Ali Sonko had governed the kingdom of Barra for seven years, with all the ability, wisdom, and prudence, of an enlightened European; his physiognomy was regular and agreeable, and there was seen in him that wisdom and experience which generally distinguish the Manding nation. His estimable character was replete with benevolence and energy; all his actions were regulated by wisdom, and every trait in this prince announced him to be a man of a superior kind.

Page 146. Mandings are very active, intelligent, and cunning, in commercial affairs; notwithstanding which, their general character is very hospitable, sociable, and benevolent; their women are also very lively, spirited, good, and agreeable.

Page 306. The Negroes have both taste and ingenuity.

Page 309. The women are always kind, attentive, and complaisant.

Page 313. The Negro race is perhaps the most prolific of all the human species that exist on our globe. Their infancy and youth are singularly happy; the mothers are passionately fond of their children.

Golberry. Page 314. It ought to be understood, that in the general situation of the Negroes, on their native soil, their life passes without labour, chagrin, or even care.

Page 315. The passing almost the whole of the human life in a nearly equal and permanent state of health, is owing to the moderation the Negroes in general observe in their habits, regimen, and pleasures.

Page 326. These Negroes, whom we call Savages, respect the ashes of their relations, friends, and chiefs.

Page 336. It cannot be denied that the Negroes are extremely clever.

Page 346. Among the Negroes are to be found virtuous and sensible men, who, as well as those of the best education and information in Europe, are susceptible of attachment, respect, delicate conduct, and a noble generosity.

Page 348. These examples of delicacy and friendship are not by any means rare in Africa.

Page 382. Hospitality is in Africa a general virtue, and misers are unknown in the country.

Page 412. All that I have said of the Negroes tends to prove that they are in general good men, naturally gentle and benevolent.

Page 413. The Moors are perfidious, cruel, capable of all crimes, and are addicted to every vice; but the Negroes have many naturally good qualities, and their general character does honour to human nature.

The picture I have given of the situation of the Blacks, and of the peaceable, careless, and simple life of these favourites of Nature, is by no means exaggerated.

State

State of Slaves on Shipboard.

They often disagree in the night about their sleeping-places; the men linked together often fight, when one wants perhaps to obey the calls of nature, and the other is unwilling to go with him.

They often refused to eat, especially beans, when they were corrected with a cat-o'-nine-tails. He has known their refusal to eat attributed to sullenness, when owing to sickness; particularly one man, who was corrected moderately for not eating, and was found dead next morning. They were made after meals to jump, on beating a drum; this is called dancing; when they refused, they were compelled by the cat.

It is very common for the Slaves to refuse sustenance; with such, gentle means are used; but if without success, the cat is generally applied.

An instance on board induced him to believe they were as affectionate as most other people. Bonny, one of the higher class, was brought on board; he seemed to take his situation to heart, and got ill, but, from indulgencies which none of the rest had, he partly recovered. When he was convalescent, a young woman was also brought on board, who proved to be his sister. At their first meeting, they stood in silence, and looked at each other, apparently with the greatest affection; they rushed into each others arms, embraced, separated themselves again, and again embraced: the witness perceived the tears to run down the female's cheeks.

They are made to jump in their irons; this is called dancing by Slave-dealers. While a surgeon in a Slave ship, has been often desired, in every ship, to flog such as would not jump: he had generally a cat in his hand among the women.

Africans Natural Dispositions, and Capacity for Civilization.— Parke's Travels.

Parke. Jillifree is much resorted to by Europeans, on account of the great quantities of bees wax which are brought hither for sale: the wax is collected in the woods by the Feloops, a wild and unsociable race of people; their country, which is of considerable extent, abounds in rice; and the natives supply the traders, both on the Gambia and Cassamansa rivers, with that article, and also with goats and poultry, on very reasonable terms.—(p. 4.)

The usual beast of burthen in all the Negro territories is the ass.—(p. 12.)

Their fierce and unrelenting disposition is, however, counterbalanced by many good qualities; they display the utmost gratitude and affection towards their benefactors; and the fidelity with which they preserve whatever is entrusted to them is remarkable. During the present war they have more than once taken up arms to defend our merchant vessels from French privateers; and English property, of considerable value, has frequently been left at Vintain, for a long time, entirely under the care of the Feloops, who have uniformly manifested on such occasions the strictest honesty and punctuality.—(p. 16.)

The government in all the Mandingo States, near the Gambia, is monarchical. The power of the sovereign is, however, by no means unlimited. In all affairs of importance, the king calls an assembly of the principal men, or elders, by whose councils he is directed.—(p. 19.)

In every considerale town there is a chief magistrate, called the Alcaid, whose office is hereditary, and whose business it is to preserve order, to levy duties on travellers, and to preside at all conferences

conferences in the exercise of local jurisdiction and the administration of justice. These courts are composed of the elders of the town (of free condition) and are termed Palavers; and their proceedings are conducted in the open air, with sufficient solemnity. Both sides of a question are freely canvassed, witnesses are publicly examined, and the decisions which follow generally meet with the approbation of the surrounding audience. (p. 19.)

Professional advocates, or expounders of the law, who are allowed to appear, and to plead for plaintiff or defendant, much in the same manner as in the law courts of Great Britain.—(p. 20.)

The Mandingoes, generally speaking, are of a mild, sociable, and obliging disposition.—(p. 21.)

The Negroes do not go to supper till late, and, in order to amuse themselves while our beef was preparing, a Mandingo was desired to relate some diverting stories; in listening to which, and smoking tobacco, we spent three hours. These stories bear some resemblance to those in the Arabian Night's Entertainments; but, in general, are of a more ludicrous cast.—(p. 31.)

It is worthy of remark, that an African will sooner forgive a blow, than a term of reproach applied to his ancestors: "Strike me, but do not curse my mother!" is a common expression among the Slaves.—(p. 47.)

We were amused by an itinerant singing-man, who told a number of diverting stories, and played some sweet airs. These are a sort of travelling bards and musicians, who sing extempore songs in praise of those who employ them.—(p. 48.)

The industry of the Foulahs, in the occupations of pasturage and agriculture, is every where remarkable.—(p. 61.)

In Bondou they are opulent in a high degree, and enjoy all the necessaries of life in the greatest profusion.

Parks. fusion. They display great skill in the management of their cattle, making them extremely gentle by kindness and familiarity.—(p. 61.)

"At two o'clock we came in sight of Jumbo, the Blacksmith's native town, from whence he had been absent more than four years. Soon after this his brother, who had by some means been apprized of his coming, came out to meet him, accompanied by a singing-man; he brought a horse for the Blacksmith, that he might enter his native town in a dignified manner; and he desired each of us to put a good charge of powder into our guns. The singing-man now led the way, followed by the two brothers; and we were presently joined by a number of people from the town, all of whom demonstrated great joy at seeing their old acquaintance the Blacksmith, by the moſt extravagant jumping and singing. On entering the town the singing man began an extempore song in praise of the Blacksmith, extolling his courage in having overcome so many difficulties, and concluding with a ſtrict injunction to his friends to dress him plenty of victuals.—(p. 81.)

"When we arrived at the Blacksmith's place of residence, we dismounted, and fired our muskets. The meeting between him and his relations was very tender; for these rude children of nature, free from reſtraint, display their emotions in the ſtrongeſt and moſt expressive manner. Amid these transports, the Blacksmith's aged mother was led forth leaning upon a ſtaff. *Every one made way for her*; and she ſtretched forth her hand to bid her son welcome. Being totally blind, she ſtroked his hands, arms, and face, with great care, and seemed highly delighted that her latter days were blessed by his return, and that her ears once more heard the music of his voice. From this interview, I was fully convinced, that whatever difference there is between the Negro and European, in the conformation of the nose, and the

colour

colour of the skin, there is none in the genuine sympathies and charaƈteriſtic feelings of our common nature."—(p. 81.)

"With these worthy people I spent the remainder of that and the whole of the ensuing day in feaſting and merriment."—(p. 83.)

"I had a moſt enchanting prospeƈt of the country. The number of towns and villages, and the extensive cultivation around them, surpassed every thing I had ever seen in Africa."—(p. 88.)

"Feb. 4th. We departed from Loomoo, and continued our route along the banks of the Krieks, which are every where well cultivated, and swarm with inhabitants."—(p. 89.)

"I lodged at the house of a Negro who praƈtised the art of making gunpowder. He shewed me a bag of nitre, very white, but the cryſtals were much smaller than common. They procure it in considerable quantities from the ponds, which are filled in the rainy season."—(p. 116.)

"The Moors supply them with sulphur from the Mediterranean; and the process is completed by pounding the different articles together in a wooden mortar."—(p. 117.)

"Their sabres, as well as their fire-arms and ammunition, they purchase from the Europeans, in exchange for the Negro Slaves, which they obtain in their predatory excursions."—(p. 150.)

"Cultivation is carried on here on a very extensive scale; and, as the natives themselves express it, hunger is never known."—(p. 187.)

"From the best inquiries I could make, I have reason to believe that Lego contains altogether about thirty thousand inhabitants."—"The view of this extensive city, the numerous canoes upon the river, the crowded population, and the cultivated state of the surrounding country, formed altogether a prospect of civilization and magnificence, which I little expected

Park. expected to find in the bosom of Africa."—(p. 195 & 196.)

"I was regarded with astonishment and fear, and was obliged to sit all day without victuals, in the shade of a tree, and the night threatened to be very uncomfortable, for the wind rose, and there was great appearance of a heavy rain; and the wild beasts are so very numerous in the neighbourhood, that I should have been under the necessity of climbing up the tree, and resting among the branches. About sun-set, however, as I was preparing to pass the night in this manner, and had turned my horse loose that he might graze at liberty, a woman, returning from the labours of the field, stopped to observe me, and perceiving that I was weary and dejected, inquired into my situation, which I briefly explained to her; whereupon, with looks of great compassion, she took up my saddle and bridle, and told me to follow her. Having conducted me into her hut, she lighted up a lamp, spread a mat on the floor, and told me I might remain there for the night. Fnding that I was very hungry, she said she would procure me something to eat; she accordingly went out, and returned in a short time with a very fine fish, which, having caused to be half broiled upon some embers, she gave me for supper. The rites of hospitality being thus performed towards a stranger in distress, my worthy benefactress (pointing to the mat, and telling me I might sleep there without apprehension), called to the female part of her family, who had stood gazing on me all the while in fixed astonishment, to resume their task of spinning cotton; in which they continued to employ themselves great part of the night. They lightened their labour by songs, one of which was composed extempore, for I was myself the subject of it; it was sung by one of the young women, the rest joining in a sort of chorus. The air was sweet and plaintive, and the words, literally translated, were these:—' The winds roared, and the rains fell—The poor white man, faint and weary, came and sat under our tree—He has no mother to bring him milk, no wife to grind his corn. Chorus: " Let us pity the white man; no mother has he," &c. &c.—Trifling as this recital may appear to the reader, to a person in my situation the circumstance was affecting in the highest degree. I was oppressed by such unexpected kindness, and sleep fell from my eyes. In the morning I presented my compassionate landlady with two of the four brass buttons which remained on my waistcoat, the only recompence I could make her." (pp. 197-198.)

" About eight o'clock we passed a large town called Kabba, situated in the midst of a beautiful and highly cultivated country, bearing a greater resemblance to the centre of England, than to what I should have supposed had been the middle of Africa."—(p. 202)..

" We passed, in the course of the day, a great many villages, inhabited chiefly by fishermen; and in the evening, about five o'clock, arrived at Sansanding, a very large town, containing, as I was told, from eight to ten thousand inhabitants."—(p. 203.)

" We accordingly rode along between the town and the river, passing by a creek or harbour, in which I observed twenty large canoes, most of them fully loaded, and covered with mats, to prevent the rain from injuring the goods.

" He shewed me some gunpowder of his own manufacturing."—(p. 206.)

" About fifteen years ago, when the present king of Bambarra's father desolated Maniana, the dooty of Sai had two sons slain in battle, fighting in the king's cause..

cause. He had a third son living; and when the king demanded a further reinforcement of men, and this youth among the rest, the dooty refused to send him. This conduct so enraged the king, that when he returned from Maniana, about the beginning of the rainy season, and found the dooty protected by the inhabitants, he sat down before Sai, with his army, and surrounded the town with the trenches I had now seen. After a siege of two months, the towns-people became involved in all the horrors of famine; and whilst the king's army were feasting in their trenches, they saw with pleasure the miserable inhabitants of Sai devour the leaves and bark of the bentang tree that stood in the middle of the town. Finding, however, that the besieged would sooner perish than surrender, the king had recourse to treachery. He promised, that if they would open the gates, no person should be put to death, nor suffer any injury, but the dooty alone. The poor old man determined to sacrifice himself for the sake of his fellow-citizens, and immediately walked over to the king's army, where he was put to death. His son, in attempting to escape, was caught and massacred in the trenches; and the rest of the towns people were carried away captives, and sold as Slaves to the different Negro Traders."—(p. 227.)

" The Mandingoes in particular are a very gentle race; cheerful in their dispositions, inquisitive, credulous, simple, and fond of flattery."—(p. 261.)

" It is impossible for me to forget the disinterested charity, and tender solicitude, with which many of these poor heathens (from the sovereign of Sego, to the poor women who received me at different times into their cottages, when I was perishing of hunger) sympathized with me in my sufferings, relieved my distresses, and contributed to my safety."— (p. 262.)

" Accordingly,

"Accordingly, the maternal affection (neither suppressed by the restraints, nor diverted by the solicitudes of civilized life) is every where conspicuous among them, and creates a correspondent return of tenderness in the child. An illustration of this has been given in p. 47. "Strike me," said my attendant, "but do not curse my mother!" The same sentiment I found universally to prevail; and observed in all parts of Africa, that the greatest affront which could be offered to a Negro, was to reflect on her who gave him birth."—(p. 264.)

"One of the first lessons, in which the Mandingo women instruct their children, is the *practice of truth*. The reader will probably recollect the case of the unhappy mother, whose son was murdered by the Moorish banditti at Funingkedy, page 102. Her only consolation in her uttermost distress, was the reflection, that the poor boy, in the course of his blameless life, had *never told a lie.*"

"For, though the Negro women are very cheerful and frank in their behaviour, they are by no means given to intrigue: I believe that instances of conjugal infidelity are not common."—(p. 268.)

"With the love of music is naturally connected a taste for poetry; and, fortunately for the poets of Africa, they are in a great measure exempted from that neglect and indigence, which, in more polished countries, commonly attend the votaries of the Muses. They consist of two classes; the most numerous are the singing-men, called jilli kea, mentioned in a former part of my narrative. One or more of these may be found in every town. They sing extempore songs in honour of their chief men, or any other persons who are willing to give "solid pudding for empty praise." But a nobler part of their office is to recite the historical events of their country; hence, in war, they accompany the soldiers to the field, in order, by reciting the great actions of their

their ancestors, to awaken in them a spirit of glorious emulation. The other class are devotees of the Mahometan faith, who travel about the country singing devout hymns, and performing religious ceremonies, to conciliate the favour of the Almighty, either in averting calamity, or insuring success to any enterprise. Both descriptions of these itinerant bards are much employed, and respected by the people, and very liberal contributions are made for them."— (p. 278.)

" The Negroes in general, and the Mandingoes in particular, are considered by the whites on the coast as an indolent and inactive people; I think, without reason. Few people work harder, when occasion requires, than the Mandingoes; but, not having many opportunities of turning to advantage the superfluous produce of their labour, they are content with cultivating as much ground only as is necessary for their own support.—(pp. 280, 281.)

" The labours of the field give them pretty full employment during the rains; and in the dry season, the people who live in the vicinity of large rivers employ themselves chiefly in fishing." " Others of the natives employ themselves in hunting." " They are very dextrous marksmen, and will hit a lizard on a tree, or any other small object, at an amazing distance." " While the men are employed in these pursuits, the women are very diligent in manufacturing cotton cloth." " The thread is not fine, but well twisted, and makes a very durable cloth. A woman, with common diligence, will spin from six to nine garments of this cloth in one year." " The loom is made exactly upon the same principle as that of Europe, but so small and narrow, that the web is seldom more than four inches broad." " The women die this cloth of a rich and lasting blue colour, with a fine purple gloss, and equal, in my opinion, to the best Indian or European blue. This cloth is cut

cut into various pieces, and sewed into garments with needles of the natives own making."

" As the arts of weaving, dying, sewing, &c. may easily be acquired, those who exercise them are not considered in Africa as following any particular profession; for almost every Slave can weave, and every boy can sew. The only artists which are distinctly acknowledged as such by the Negroes, and who value themselves on exercising appropriate and peculiar trades, are the manufacturers of leather and iron." " They are to be found in almost every town." " They tan and dress leather with very great expedition." " They are at great pains to render the hide as soft and pliant as possible." " The hides of bullocks are converted chiefly into sandals, and therefore require less care in dressing than the skins of sheep and goats, which are used for covering quivers and saphies, and in making sheaths for swords and knives, belts, pockets, and a variety of ornaments."—(pp 281, 282.)

" The manufacturers of iron are not so numerous as of leather; but they appear to have studied their business with equal diligence." " In the inland parts, the natives smelt this useful metal in such quantities, as not only to supply themselves from it with all necessary weapons and instruments, but even to make it an article of commerce with some of the neighbouring states."—(p. 283.)

" Most of the African blacksmiths are acquainted also with the method of smelting gold." " They likewise draw the gold into wire, and form it into a variety of ornaments, some of which are executed with a great deal of taste and ingenuity." " I might add, though it is scarce worthy observation, that in Bambarra and Kaarta, the natives make very beautiful baskets, hats, and other articles, both for use and ornament, from rushes, which they stain of different colours; and they contrive also to cover their

their calabashes with interwoven cane, dyed in the same manner."—(p. 285.)

"It seems to be the universal wish of mankind to spend the evening of their days where they spent their infancy. The poor Negro feels this desire in its full force. To him, no water is sweet but what is drawn from his own well; and no tree has so cool and pleasant a shade as the tabba tree of his native village. When war compels him to abandon the delightful spot in which he first drew his breath, and seek for safety in some other kingdom, his time is spent in talking about the country of his ancestors; and no sooner is peace restored than he turns his back upon the land of strangers, rebuilds with haste his fallen walls, and exults to see the smoke ascend from his native village."—(p. 292.)

"It was not possible for me to behold the wonderful fertility of the soil, the vast herds of cattle, proper both for labour and food, and a variety of other circumstances favourable to colonization and agriculture; and reflect withal, on the means which presented themselves of a vast inland navigation, without lamenting that a country, so abundantly gifted and favoured by nature, should remain in its present savage and neglected state. Much more did I lament that a people, of manners and dispositions so gentle and benevolent, should either be left as they now are, immersed in the gross and uncomfortable blindness of Pagan superstition, or permitted to become converts to a system of bigotry and fanaticism."—(p. 312.)

"During a wearisome peregrination of more than five hundred British miles, exposed to the burning rays of a tropical sun, these poor Slaves, amidst their own infinitely greater sufferings, would commiserate mine; and frequently, of their own accord, bring water to quench my thirst, and at night collect

branches

branches and leaves to prepare me a bed in the wilderness."—(p. 356.) *Park.*

Effects of Slave Trade on Administration of Justice. By the Sieur Brüe, Director General of the French Senegal Company, about 1700.—*Astley's Voyages, vol. ii. & iii.*

"Crimes here are seldom punished with death, unless it be treason and murder. For other faults, the usual penalty is banishment, to which end the king generally sells them to the company, and disposes of their effects at his pleasure. In civil cases, the debtor, if unable, is sold with his family and effects, for the payment of the creditor, and the king has his thirds."—(p. 59.) *Astley's Voyages.*

Barbot says, that the Negro kings are so absolute, that upon any slight pretence, they order their subjects to be sold for Slaves, without regard to rank or profession. Thus a Marbut was sold to him at Goree by the Alkade of Rio Fresco, by special order of the Damel, for some misdemeanors. This priest was above two months aboard the ship before he would speak one word."—(*Travels of Barbot*, p. 257.)

"The smallest crimes whatever are punished with banishment.—(p. 315.)

Criminal causes are tried by a public Palaver, or Assembly of the head men of the country, and Slavery is the usual punishment; a circumstance which holds out a strong temptation to prefer false accusations, particularly as the African mode of trial furnishes convenient means of promoting purposes of avarice and oppression.—(*Winterbottom's Account, &c. &c.*)

<small>Astley's Voyages.</small>   Marchais.—In case of the debtor's insolvency, the king allows the creditor to sell him, his wives, and even his children, for the sum due. Here is also another extraordinary law; if the creditor, before witnesses, three times asks his debt of a person, whom he cannot arrest or sue on account of his dignity or power, and the debtor refuses to pay him, the creditor has a right to seize the first Slave he meets, let him belong to whom he will.

There is but one sort of punishment for offences here, the offender, and all his generation, being made Slaves.

In their proceedings they take no care whether the party be guilty, or deserves to be punished.

<small>Gulberry.</small>   It is a striking circumstance, that in Africa, before the Slave Trade was introduced, the punishments for offences generally consisted of mulcts or fines, as is evident from the testimony of Artus, Barbot, Ogilby, Bosman, Loyer, Nyendael, and others, and that nobody was mulcted beyond his ability, except by an accumulation of crimes. Murder and sorcery were punished capitally in some of the countries of Africa, but in others, murder and every species of offence had no other punishment than a fine. If people could not pay these fines, they were disposed of in two ways. Some of them were sent into a temporary banishment in Africa; others were sold into home slavery. Debtors also, who refused to pay their debts, or became insolvent, were sold for the benefit of their creditors, in case their relations would not redeem them, and worked for these at their respective homes. But since this trade has been used, says Moore, all *punishments* are changed into *slavery*: there being *an advantage* in such condemnation, they *strain* for crimes

very hard, in order to get the *benefit of selling the criminal*. Not only murder, theft, and adultery, are punished by selling the criminal for a Slave, but *every trifling* crime is punished in the same manner."*

Moore gives us a history of some of these crimes. " There was a man, says he, brought to me in Tommany, to be sold, for having stolen a tobacco-pipe. I sent for the alcade, and with much ado persuaded the party aggrieved to accept of a composition, and leave the man free. In Cantore, a man seeing a tyger eating a deer, which he had killed and hung up near his house, fired at the tyger, and the bullet killed a man. The king not only condemned him, but also *his mother, three brothers*, and *three sisters*, to be sold. These eight persons were brought down to me at Yamyamacunda. It made my heart ache, says Moore *(for this was in the infancy of the Trade)* to see them, and I did not buy them." But it appears in the sequel, that this kind action in Moore did not produce the desired end. " For they were sent, says he, further down the river, and sold to some *separate* traders at Joar, and the king *had the benefit of the goods* for which they were sold."

In estimating the revenues of king Forbana, he mentions † " the criminals that were sold, *a part of the profit of which* devolved *upon his majesty.*"

‡ " In Africa, says he, crimes are punished either by fines, slavery, or death. *Offences are rare*, but *accusations common*; because the chiefs frequently accuse for the purpose of *condemning*, that they may be able to procure Slaves."

* Page 42.
† Vol. ii. 237. English translation by Blagdon.
‡ Vol. ii. 340—1.

Golberry. "The crime of magic is that which the Negro kings and chiefs most frequently *cause* to be preferred against individuals of the lower class, *because this crime is punished by slavery*, and *consequently produces Slaves.*"

Evidences examined before the House of Commons.

House of Commons Evidence.
* Capt. Wilson, of the Royal Navy, says, it is universally acknowledged, and he believes it to be true, that free persons are sold for real or imputed crimes, for the benefit of their judges. Soon after his arrival at Goree, the king of Damel sent a free man to him for sale, and was to have the *price himself.* One of the king's guards, who came with the man, on being asked whether he was guilty of the crime imputed to him, replied, with great shrewdness—he did not conceive that was ever inquired into, or of any consequence.

† Dr. Trotter says, that of the whole cargo, he recollects only three criminals in the ship where he was. One of these had been sold for adultery, and the other for *witchcraft, whose whole family shared his fate.* The first said, he had been decoyed by a woman, who told her husband of the transaction, and he was sentenced to pay a Slave; but, being poor, he was sold himself. Such *stratagems* are *frequent.* The fourth mate of the ship Brookes was so decoyed, and obliged to pay a Slave, under the threat, that trade would be stopped if he did not. The other had quarrelled with one of the Cabosheers. The Cabosher, in revenge, accused him of witchcraft. In consequence of this accusation he was sold with his family. His mother, wife, and

---
* House of Commons Evidence, p. 4, 5.
† Ditto, p. 81-2.

two

two daughters, were sentenced with him. The women shewed the deepest affliction; the man a sullen melancholy; he refused his food, tore his throat open with his nails, and died.

* Lieutenant Simpson, of the Royal Marines, considered two crimes as almost made on purpose to procure Slaves. These were, adultery, and the removal of *Fetiches*, (or of *charms founded on a notion of witchcraft*. As to adultery, he was warned against connecting himself with any woman not pointed out to him, for that the kings *kept several, who were sent out to allure the unwary*; and that, if found to be connected with these, he would be seized, and made to pay the price of a man Slave. As to fetiches, consisting of pieces of wood, old pitchers, kettles, &c. laid in the path-ways, he was *warned to avoid displacing* them, for if he should, the natives, who were on the watch, would seize him, and, as before, exact the price of a man Slave. These baits were laid equally for the natives, as the Europeans; but the former were better acquainted with the law, and consequently more circumspect.

James Morley, 1760 and 1776.—On pretence of adultery, he remembers a woman sold. He learnt that this was only a pretence, from her own mouth, for she spake good English, and from the respect with which her husband, king Ephraim, treated her, when he came on board; whereas, in real cases of adultery, they are very desperate.

Sir George Young, 1767, 1768, 1771, 1772.— Has always heard, that the sovereign or chief of a district generally derives a certain profit from the sale of Slaves.

* House of Commons Evidence, p. 40.

Henry

<small>House of Commons Evidence.</small> Henry Hew Dalrymple, Esq. 1779.—All crimes, in the parts of Africa he was in, were punished with slavery.

James Towne, 1760, 1767.—He has repeatedly heard, both from the accused and accusers themselves, and he believes it common on the coast, to impute crimes falsely for the sake of having the accused person sold.

Mode of Warfare, &c.

<small>Parke.</small> The Moors purchase the fire-arms and ammunition from the Europeans in exchange for Negro Slaves, whom they obtain in their predatory excursions.—*Parke's Travels.*

"Some neighbouring and rebel Negroes plundered a large village belonging to Daisy (the king), and carried off a number of prisoners."—(p. 110.)

"They accordingly fell upon two of Daisy's (the king's) towns, and carried off the whole of the inhabitants."—(p. 169.)

"I passed, in the course of this day, the ruins of three towns; the inhabitants of which were all carried away by Daisy, king of Kaarta, on the same day that he took and plundered Yamina."—(p. 230.)

"Mansang separated the remainder of his army into small detachments, ordered them to over-run the country, and seize on the inhabitants before they had time to escape.

"Most of the poor inhabitants of the different towns and villages, being surprized in the night, fell an easy prey.

"Daisy had sent a number of people to plant corn, &c. &c. to supply his army; all these fell into the hands of Sambo Sego; they were afterwards sent in caravans to be sold to the French, on the Senegal."—(p. 109.)

African

African Population.

Winterbottom's Travels in Africa.—The towns on the seacoaft are in general small, and seldom consift of more than forty or fifty houses; but as we advance inland, they become more populous.—(p. 81.) Winterbottom.

The villages near the sea coaft not only consift of fewer houses than those more inland, but they also shew less neatness and ingenuity in their conftruction.—(p. 83.)

Teembo, the capital of the Foola kingdom, is computed to contain about 8,000 inhabitants; Laby, the second in size, has about 5,000; and several of those which I have visited in the Soosoo and Mandingo countries, contain from 1 to 2 or 3,000 inhabitants.—(p. 87.)

Domeftic Slaves State in Africa.—Travels of Moore, a Factor of African Company.

They seldom sell their family Slaves, except for great crimes.—(vol. iii. p. 242) Astley's Voyages.

Some of them have a good many house Slaves, in which they place a great pride; and these Slaves live so well and easy, that it is hard to know them from their Owners, being often better cloathed; especially the females, who have sometimes coral, amber, and silver necklaces and ornaments to the value of £. 20. or £. 30. sterling.

The author never heard of but one that ever sold a family Slave, except for such crimes as they would have been sold for if they had been free. If one of the family Slaves (where there are many) commits a crime, and the Mafter sells him for it without the consent of the reft, they will all run away, and be protected in the next kingdom.—(p. 267)

Winter-

Winter- Winterbottom's Travels.—Their domestics are in general treated by them with great humanity, and it is not uncommon to see the heir-apparent of a head man sitting down to eat with the meanest of his father's people, and in no wise distinguished from them by his dress.—(p. 127.)

Captain Wilson, 1783.—The Slaves employed by the Africans live with their Masters, and are so treated as scarcely to be distinguishable from them.

Isaac Parker, 1764.—Dick Ebro' had many Slaves of his own, whom he employed in cutting wood and fishing, &c. but he treated them always very well.

James Morley, 1760 and 1776.—They treat their Slaves with the greatest kindness, more so than our servants and Slaves in the West Indies.

Henry Hew Dalrymple, Esq. 1779.—Slaves are treated so well, eating and working with their Masters, that they are not distinguishable from free men.

James Kiernan.—Persons of property there have a great number of persons under the denomination of Slaves, whom they treat as Europeans would people of their own family.

Parke. "The Mandingo Master can neither deprive his domestic Slave of life, nor sell him to a stranger, without first calling a palaver on his conduct; or, in other words, bringing him to a public trial." (p. 23)

"He told me, that he had always behaved towards me as if I had been his father and master." (p. 68.)

"He sometimes eats out of the same bowl with his camel driver, and reposes himself, during the heat of the day, upon the same bed."—(p. 155.)

" In

"In all the laborious occupations above described, and his Slaves work together, without the Master superiority."
distinction of ority of the Master over the domestic
"The auth elsewhere observed, extends only to reasonable correction; for the Master cannot sell his domestic without having first brought him to a public trial before the chief men of the place."—(p. 286.)

Bristol Slave Trade formerly.—William of Malmsbury, book ii. ch. 20.—Life of St. Wolstan, Bishop of Worcester.

Directly opposite the Irish coast there is a seaport town called Bristol, the inhabitants of which, as well as others of the English, frequently sail into Ireland on trading speculations. St. Wolstan put an end to a very ancient custom of theirs, in which they had become so hardened, that neither the love of God, nor that of the king (William the Conqueror) had been able to abolish it. For they sold into Ireland, at a profit, people whom they had bought up throughout all England, and they exposed to sale maidens in a state of pregnancy, with whom they made a sort of mock marriages. There you might see with grief, fastened together by ropes, whole rows of wretched beings of both sexes, of elegant forms and in the very bloom of youth, a sight sufficient to excite pity even in Barbarians, daily offered for sale to the first purchaser. Accursed deed! infamous disgrace! that men, acting in a manner which brutal instinct alone would have forbidden, should sell into slavery their relations, nay, even their own offspring; yet, St. Wolstan destroyed at length this inveterate and hereditary custom. The historian goes on to state, that from the effect of religious instruction, the people of Bristol not only renounced this vicious practice themselves,

themselves, but afforded an example of reform to the rest of England; harsh methods however were resorted to where persuasion was in vain; for one of the inhabitants of Bristol who resisted the good bishop's reform with peculiar obstinacy, was expelled from the city, and had his eyes put out.

In 1171, on the invasion and conquest of Ireland by Henry II. it was the unanimous judgment of a great ecclesiastical council, called at Armagh, that the event was to be regarded as a providential visitation for their guilt in making Slaves of the English, whether obtained from merchants, robbers, or pirates; and this opinion was regarded as the more probable, because England herself, the natives of which, by a vice common to that nation, had been used to sell their children and nearest relatives, even when not under the pressure of famine or other necessity, had formerly expiated a similar crime by a similar punishment (alluding to the Norman Conquest.) To the honour of the Irish, a resolution was then passed, that throughout the kingdom the English Slaves should be immediately emancipated. I trust their Hibernian descendants, in our day, will shew themselves actuated by a like humane spirit, and that the English will no longer continue subject to that foul stain with which, even in these early days, she was contaminated.

The city of Bristol is once more exempt from the disgrace of being concerned in the traffic of human beings.

FINIS.

Printed by Luke Hansard & Sons,
near Lincoln's-Inn Fields.

Druck:
Customized Business Services GmbH
im Auftrag der KNV-Gruppe
Ferdinand-Jühlke-Str. 7
99095 Erfurt